Climate Change in Grasslands, Shrublands, and Deserts of the Interior American West:

A Review and Needs Assessment

United States Department of Agriculture / Forest Service
Rocky Mountain Research Station

General Technical Report RMRS-GTR-285

August 2012

Abstract

Recent research and species distribution modeling predict large changes in the distributions of species and vegetation types in the western interior of the United States in response to climate change. This volume reviews existing climate models that predict species and vegetation changes in the western United States, and it synthesizes knowledge about climate change impacts on the native fauna and flora of grasslands, shrublands and deserts of the interior American West. Species' responses will depend not only on their physiological tolerances but also on their phenology, establishment properties, biotic interactions, and capacity to evolve and migrate. The volume is divided into eight chapters that cover the topics of carbon mitigation and adaptation. Current and likely responses of species and habitats to climate change are examined in relation to taxonomic group and ecoregion and with regard to other disturbances. The volume ends with a review of management decision support needs and tools for assessing vulnerability of natural resources and conserving and restoring ecosystems that are or may be impacted by climate change.

Keywords: climate change, grasslands, shrublands, deserts, assessment

Acknowledgments

We are grateful to Julie McIntyre and Karen Wetherill for helpful discussions on pollinators. We thank David Hawksworth, Melinda Larson, Jennifer Jacobs, and Megan Friggens for their help in reviewing and formatting content. We are grateful to Karen Bagne, Megan Friggens, and California Game and Fish Department for reviews of the manuscript, and Kal Louks and MacKenzie Romero for facilitating financial arrangements. Funding was provided by USDA Forest Service Research and Development, Washington Office, and Rocky Mountain Research Station.

Cover photos: **Upper left and lower photos, © Larry Jones. Upper right and lower right, USDA Forest Service.**

Climate Change in Grasslands, Shrublands, and Deserts of the Interior American West:

A Review and Needs Assessment

Deborah M. Finch, Editor
United States Department of Agriculture
Forest Service
Rocky Mountain Research Station

General Technical Report RMRS-GTR-285
August 2012

Contents

Chapter 1

Modeling and Predicting Vegetation Response of Western USA Grasslands, Shrublands, and Deserts to Climate Change

Megan M. Friggens[1], Marcus V. Warwell[2], Jeanne C. Chambers[3], and Stanley G. Kitchen[4]

[1] U.S. Forest Service, Rocky Mountain Research Station; Grassland, Shrubland, and Desert Ecosystems Program; Forestry Sciences Laboratory, Albuquerque, New Mexico

[2] U.S. Forest Service, Rocky Mountain Research Station; Forest and Woodland Ecosystems Program; Forestry Sciences Laboratory, Moscow, Idaho

[3] U.S. Forest Service, Rocky Mountain Research Station; Grassland, Shrubland, and Desert Ecosystems Program; Great Basin Ecology Laboratory, Reno, Nevada

[4] U.S. Forest Service, Rocky Mountain Research Station; Grassland, Shrubland, and Desert Ecosystems Program; Shrub Sciences Laboratory, Provo, Utah

Executive Summary

Experimental research and species distribution modeling predict large changes in the distributions of species and vegetation types in the Interior West due to climate change. Species' responses will depend not only on their physiological tolerances but also on their phenology, establishment properties, biotic interactions, and capacity to evolve and migrate. Because individual species respond to climate variation and change independently and differently, plant assemblages with no modern analogs can be expected in areas where novel climate conditions develop. The capacity to accurately predict how species distributions and plant assemblages will change under future warming is essential for developing effective strategies for maintaining and restoring sustainable ecosystems.

The rate of predicted change in climate is unprecedented relative to the three centuries prior to industrialization. A conservative forecast for western North America (using 21 global climate models for the A1B scenario) is a linear change in mean temperatures and precipitation ranging from +2.1 °C to +5.7 °C and -3% to +14%, respectively, over the rest of the century. A number of recent studies that have used bioclimatic and related models predict drastic changes in vegetation types and native and invasive flora at regional scales in response to the change in climate. By the end of the century, 55% of future landscapes in the West likely will have climates that are incompatible with the vegetation types that now occur on those landscapes. Specifically:

- Suitable habitat for Rocky Mountain subalpine conifer forests and Rocky Mountain and Great Basin alpine tundra declines substantially (>97%) or disappears.

- Projected habitat suitable for Great Basin pinyon and juniper woodlands moves northward and upslope.

- Semi-desert grassland habitat expands northward and occupies an area nearly four times that of the present.

- Habitat suitable for Great Basin shrub/grassland decreases by 40% and becomes fragmented.

- Great Basin montane scrub habitat experiences moderate decline (69% decrease) and displacement through time.
- Climate changes appear to be most favorable for Mohave Desert, Sonoran Desert, and Chihuahuan Desert scrub vegetation types, which are all projected to expand.

Species' specific analyses predict:

- Sagebrush (*Artemisia tridentata*), Joshua tree (*Yucca brevifolia*), saguaro (*Carnegiea gigantea*), and creosote bush (*Larrea tridentata*) shift northwards.
- Species with small distributions, such as smooth Arizona cypress (*Cupressus arizonica* ssp. *glabra*) and the endangered perennial MacFarlane's four-o'clock (*Mirabilis macfarlanei*), experience complete climate disequilibrium early in the century.
- Invasive species, such as buffelgrass (*Pennisetum ciliare*), Lehmann lovegrass (*Eragrostis lehmanniana*), spotted knapweed (*Centaurea bieberrsteinii*), and leafy spurge (*Euphorbia esula*), expand under future climate regimes.
- The invasive annual grass cheatgrass (*Bromus tectorum*) shifts northward with increased risk in Idaho, Montana, and Wyoming but reduced risk in southern Nevada and Utah and an overall loss of 13% of suitable habitat.

Currently, the three primary approaches for projecting the ecological effects of climate change are experimental and observational studies, mechanistic modeling, and bioclimatic modeling. A framework for integrating these approaches could improve our ability to forecast changes in vegetation types and species. Such a framework could include long-term experiments (for specific species, locations, and climate change scenarios) designed to support more comprehensive mechanistic models and to provide for testing bioclimatic models, and could be used to both identify and address the following critical research needs:

- Obtain the necessary species-specific data regarding important climate variables, biotic interactions, genetic variation, and adaptive capacity to improve predictive capacity.
- Determine the interacting effects of climate and other global change processes such as extreme events, increasing CO_2, nitrogen deposition, pests, and disease on species distributions and community composition to improve predictions and develop adaptation strategies.
- Evaluate the interacting effects of socioeconomic and biophysical factors on land use and land cover change and, consequently, on species distribution and community composition to improve predictions and develop adaptation strategies.
- Increase our knowledge of the effects of species diversity and functional groups on ecosystem processes as they relate to climate and other global change factors to improve predictions and develop adaptation strategies.
- Continue to advance modeling efforts that couple bioclimate analyses with models that are able to estimate feedback, competitive interactions, and disturbance effects.
- Continue to explore other modeling approaches, such as combining historic distribution data with contemporary distributions, to identify species-specific climate limitations that can then be used to parameterize models.

Introduction

Experimental research and species distribution modeling predict that large changes in the distributions of species and vegetation types will occur due to climate change.

Species responses will depend not only on their physiological tolerances but also on their phenology, establishment properties, biotic interactions (Brown and others 1997), and ability to evolve and migrate (Davis and Shaw 2001). The capacity of species and, thus, their distributions to respond to a warming environment also will be affected by changing disturbance regimes and other global change factors (Turner 2010). Because individual species respond to climate variation and change independently and differently, plant assemblages with no modern analogs can be expected (Williams and Jackson 2007). New plant assemblages might also arise in areas where novel climatic conditions develop (Williams and Jackson 2007). Support for predictions of novel climate regimes and corresponding plant assemblages is found in studies examining relationships among paleo-climate and plant community reconstructions. As Williams and Jackson (2007) pointed out: (1) many past ecological communities are compositionally unlike modern communities; (2) the formation and dissolution of past "no-analog" communities appear to be climatically driven and linked to climates without modern analogs; (3) many future climate regimes will probably lack modern analogs; and (4) novel communities and surprises should be expected in the future. Novel climate conditions coupled with vegetation communities that lack modern analogs pose significant challenges for resource managers. Accurate predictions of how species distributions will change under future warming are essential for developing effective strategies for maintaining and restoring sustainable ecosystems (Harris and others 2006).

Several factors make predicting how species distributions and vegetation communities will change difficult. Global Circulation Models (GCMs) exhibit significant variation in forecasts of future temperature and especially precipitation (Christensen and others 2007). This variation is often amplified for topographically variable areas such as the Interior West (Rehfeldt 2006; Saenz-Romero and others 2010). In addition, information on species' relationships to climate variables is often lacking and must be inferred from data on current species distributions. And other factors such as competitive interactions with other species and disturbance regimes often obfuscate interpretation of species climate profiles in projected future climate space.

In grassland, shrubland, and desert ecosystems, our understanding of likely changes in climate is limited. Also, we lack information on the climate profiles of the vast majority of species. Here, we provide (1) current forecasts for changes in climate over the remainder of the century and (2) available predictions for changes in regional vegetation types and individual species distributions. We then discuss the types of approaches that can be used to increase our predictive capacity and the research needs for these ecosystems.

How Is Climate Predicted to Change?

Global climate is predicted to continue to undergo substantial change through the current century. The rate of predicted change is unprecedented relative to the three centuries prior to industrialization (North and others 2006). The effect of greenhouse gas emissions on future temperatures is considered using a set of emission scenarios. These scenarios predict future CO_2 concentrations given human activities. The most optimistic scenario (B1) involves rapid reductions in emissions as societies turn toward a global vision of sustainable land use. More commonly used in modeling efforts, however, are scenarios that assume a continued increase in human population growth and consumption of fossil fuel. In particular, scenarios that predict a moderately high CO_2 output with continued focus on economic growth (A2) or a more optimistic scenario that includes an emphasis on multiple energy sources (A1B) are used in the models discussed here. Western North American is projected (using 21 global models for the A1B scenario) to experience a linear change in mean temperatures and precipitation ranging from +2.1 °C to +5.7 °C and -3% to +14%, respectively, over the rest of the century (Christensen and others 2007). Recent models indicate that actual CO_2 concentrations are likely to be higher than those used in the A1B scenario resulting in temperatures at the warmer end of those ranges (Tom and Harte 2006; Füssel 2009).

Within the region, patterns of temperature and precipitation change are expected to vary in magnitude and direction and in seasonal timing across the landscape. Figures 1-1 through 1-3 illustrate this variation for projected change in summer temperatures (degree days >5 °C), winter temperatures (mean temperature in the coldest month), and aridity (dryness index) across the interior western United States using three GCMs under the assumptions of the A2 emissions scenario, (see Rehfeldt and others 2009). In general, summer temperatures and aridity are projected to increase the most in the southwestern United States and at lower elevations throughout the Interior West (figs. 1-1 and 1-3). Predicted patterns of occurrence vary broadly across the region by GCM. Winter temperatures are projected to increase by 2 °C to 9 °C (fig. 1-2). Changing balance of temperature and precipitation is projected to result in earlier spring snow run off (Stewart and others 2004), declines in snow pack in the northern and central Rocky Mountains (Plummer and others 2006) and in the Great Basin (Mote and others 2005), and increased frequency, duration, and spatial extent of drought events (Seager and others 2007; Sheffield and Wood 2008). Climate change effects are also likely to change disturbance processes, leading to increases in insect and disease outbreaks (see Chapter 7) and extended fire seasons with more frequent and intense fires (see Chapter 6).

Modeling Vegetation Response to Climate Change

Three main types of approach exist for projecting the ecological effects of climate change, and each of these differs in type of information provided and the zone of inference.

- **Experimental and observations** studies include climate manipulation experiments (e.g., Harte and Shaw 1995; Suttle and others 2007), observations across climate gradients (e.g., Peñualus and others 2007), and observations over time (e.g., Alward and others 1999). These studies generate detailed data and provide valuable information on the complex interactions between species- and system-level responses. Results are often specific to the study system and are primarily relevant at local to regional scales.

- **Mechanistic modeling** has been used to scale local processes to regional scales (Araújo and others 2005; Berger and others 2008; Jeltsch and others 2008). Mechanistic modeling is a bottom-up approach that uses measurements or expert opinion about species' life histories, physiology, and competitive interactions to predict distribution under changing climate conditions. The results of this approach differ depending on the emphasis of the model and are limited by whether the physiological constraints used to parameterize them hold at regional scales.

- **Bioclimatic envelope modeling** (BEM) uses the relationships among regional distributions of species and physical variables (e.g., climate) to constrain the potential distribution of species or groups of species (Pearson and Dawson 2003). BEM is a top-down approach that relies on biogeography to project distribution changes (Hijmans and Graham 2006), but that does not directly consider species attributes. BEMs have rarely been experimentally validated or tested (but see Chew and others 2004; Farber and Kadmon 2003). This general approach has been vastly improved

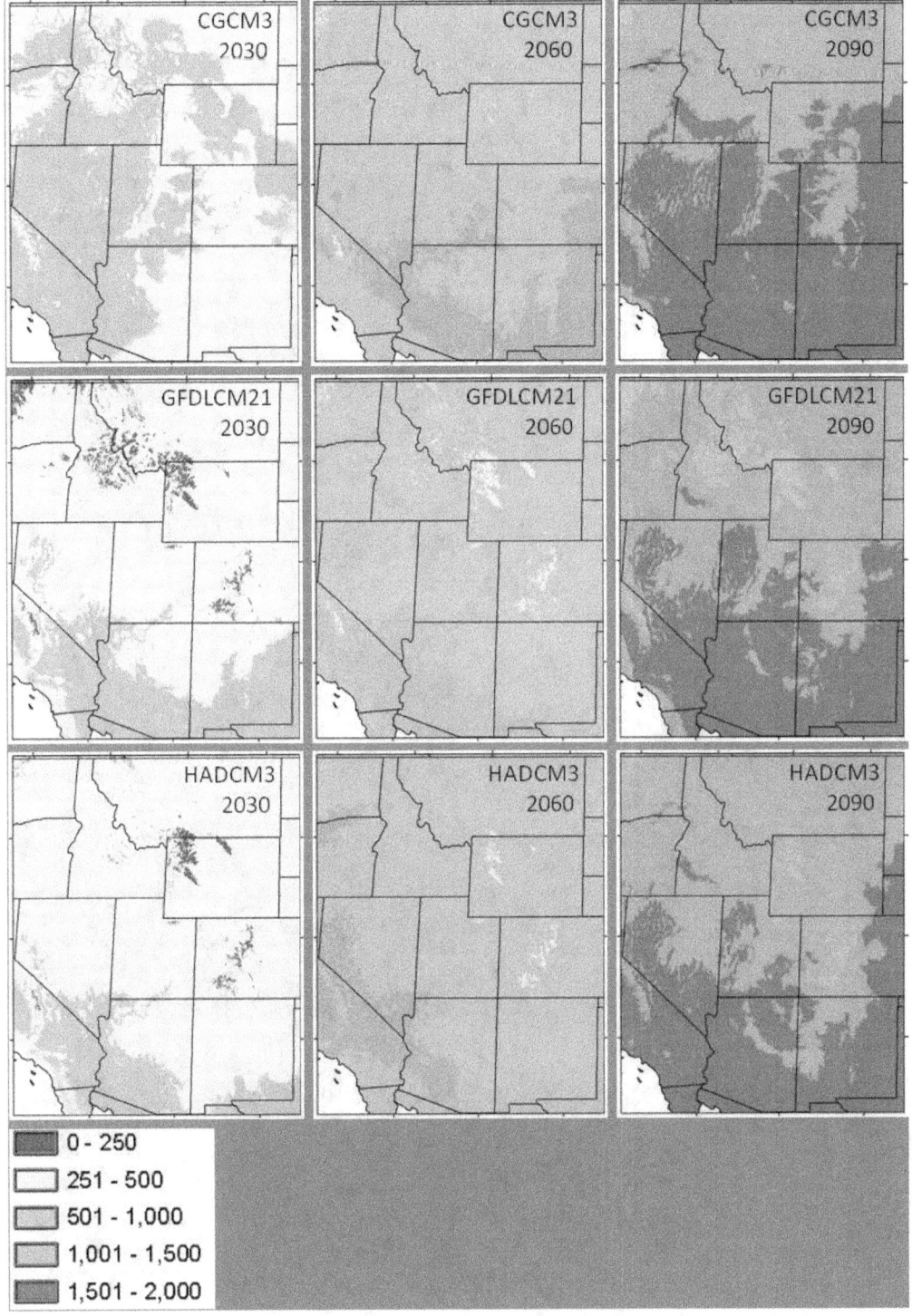

Figure 1-1. Mapped predictions of increase in the yearly accumulation of daily temperature sums over 5 °C for decades 2030, 2060, and 2090 relative to the contemporary climate (1961-1990) for the A2 scenario using Canadian Center for Climate Modeling (CGCM3), Geophysical Fluid Dynamics Laboratory (GFDLCM21) and Hadley Center/World Data Center (HADCM3) (see Rehfeldt and others 2009).

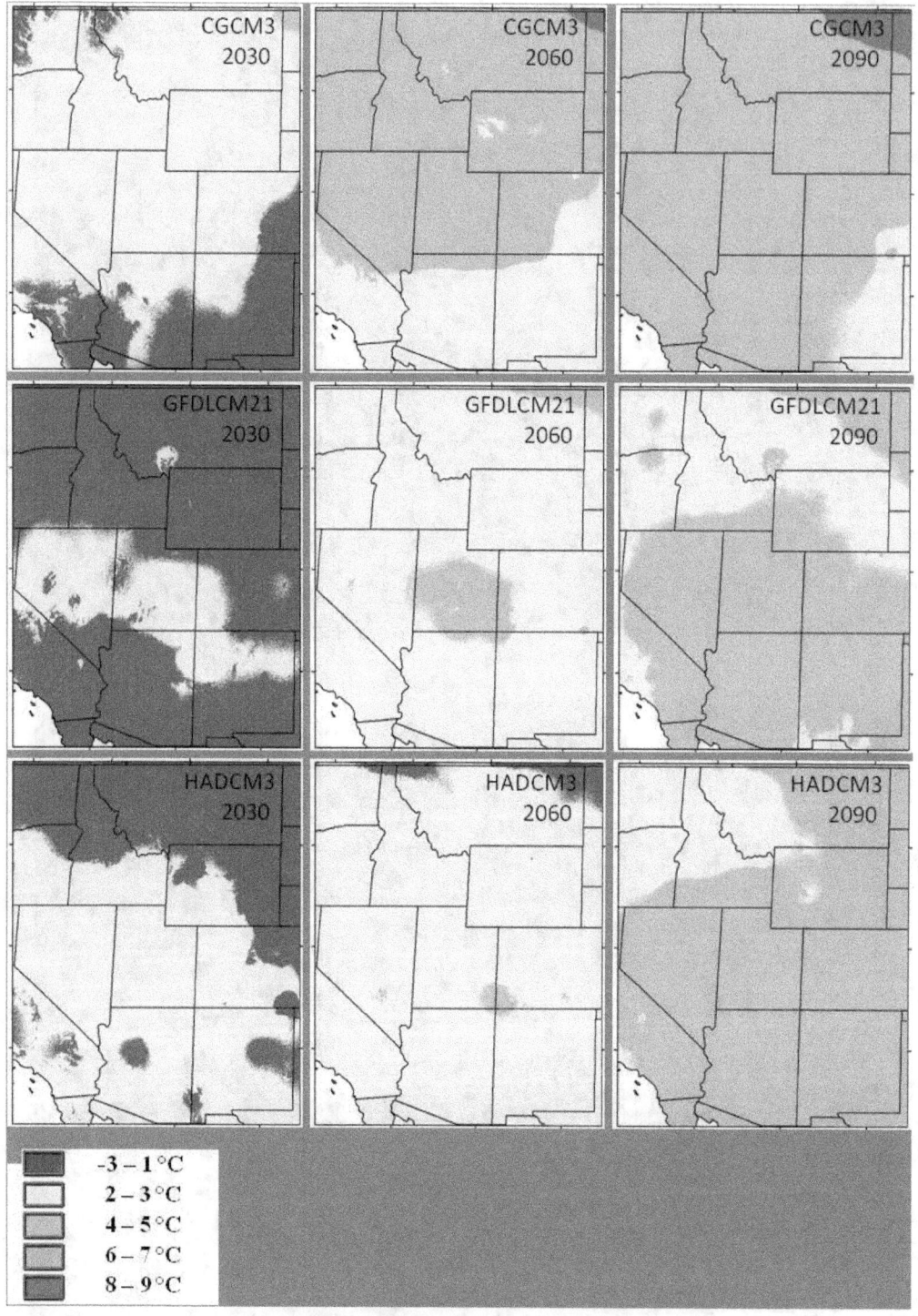

Figure 1-2. Mapped predictions of increase in mean temperature of the coldest month for decades 2030, 2060, and 2090 relative to the contemporary climate (1961-1990) for the A2 scenario using Canadian Center for Climate Modeling (CGCM3), Geophysical Fluid Dynamics Laboratory (GFDLCM21) and Hadley Center/World Data Center (HADCM3) GCMs (see Rehfeldt and others 2009).

USDA Forest Service RMRS-GTR-285. 2012.

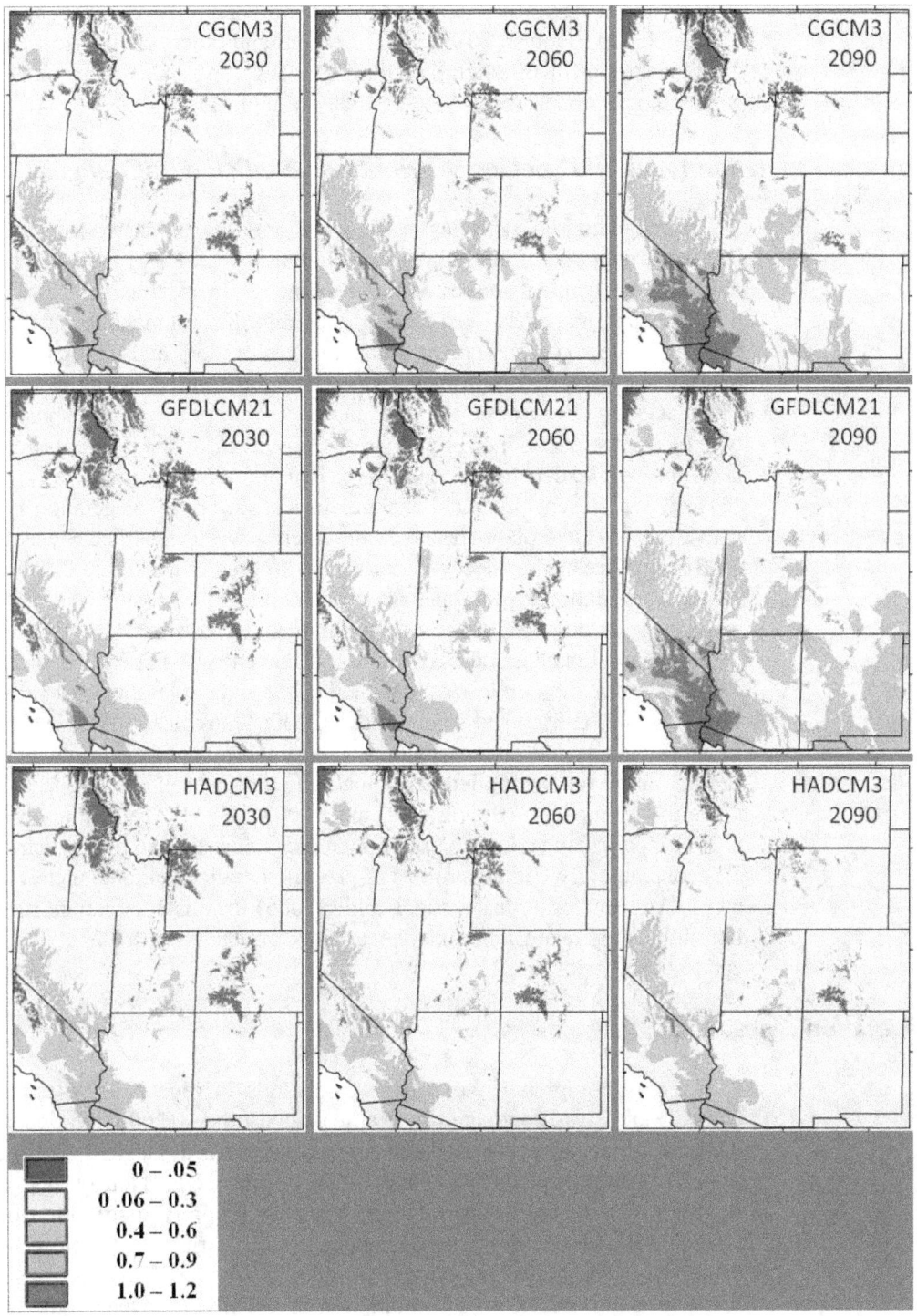

■	0 – .05
□	0 .06 – 0.3
□	0.4 – 0.6
□	0.7 – 0.9
■	1.0 – 1.2

Figure 1-3. Mapped predictions of increase in annual dryness index for decades 2030, 2060, and 2090 relative to the contemporary climate (1961-1990) for the A2 scenario using Canadian Center for Climate Modeling (CGCM3), Geophysical Fluid Dynamics Laboratory (GFDLCM21) and Hadley Center/World Data Center (HADCM3) GCMs (see Rehfeldt and others 2009).

upon by newer bioclimate modeling techniques (see Rehfeldt and others 2006; Rehfeldt and Jaquish 2010; Saenz-Romero and others 2010). However, lack of detailed species distribution data limits the development of these more sophisticated bioclimate models for use in the Rocky Mountains.

How are Vegetation Types and Species Distributions Predicted to Change?

Understanding how species distributions and vegetation types will change due to increased temperature and altered precipitation regimes is essential for developing effective management and restoration approaches. In order to make efficient and effective decisions, managers must be able to identify the best management trajectory under future climate changes. Habitat protection, restoration, and facilitated adaptation are options that vary widely in their implementation, approach, and ultimate objectives. The feasibility of one approach over another will vary depending upon the degree and type of change experienced by an area. Consequently, many successful management decisions will be dependent on efforts to define future conditions.

Here, we present predicted changes in distribution of vegetation types and both native and invasive plant species in the interior western United States that are based on BEM and related analyses. Our capacity to predict the future distributions of species and vegetation types depends on our ability to accurately model future climate and relate species occurrence to environmental characteristics. BEMs describe the fundamental climate associated with the occurrence of a species and can incorporate detailed information on loss of suitable habitat and succession over time (Guisan and Thuiller 2005; Guisan and Zimmermann 2000; Franklin 1995). BEMs can be used to forecast a single species distribution based upon a set of environmental variables or can be more broadly applied to evaluate the distribution of a group of species (e.g., niche-theory models) (Botkin and others 2007). BEMs are commonly coupled with GCM output using various emission scenarios to predict the future distribution of species contemporary climate profiles or predicted realized climate niches based on their current distribution (Guisan and Thuiller 2005). In this application, resulting projections inherently retain substantial uncertainty associated with output from GCMs using emission scenarios.

Vegetation Types

The most comprehensive analysis of changes in vegetation types for the western United States was conducted by Rehfeldt and others (2006). In general, their predictions are consistent with those for more localized analyses of vegetation types (Kupfer and others 2004) and individual species (e.g., Neilson and others 2005). Rehfeldt and others (2006) modeled the contemporary distribution of Brown and others' (1998) biotic communities using climate variables and projected future distributions using the IS92a scenario (also known as the "business as usual" emission scenario) summarized for a combination of GCMs produced by the Hadley Center and Canadian Center for Climate Modeling and Analysis (table 1-1 and fig. 1-4). Rehfeldt and others (2006) estimated that by the end of the century, 55% of future landscapes in the West will have climates that are incompatible with the vegetation communities that now occur on those landscapes. In addition, 85% of the affected area is estimated to have a climate that does not match the climate profile of any contemporary western biotic communities. Figure 1-4 shows projections of the climate profile of Brown and others' (1998) biotic communities and responses under climate change during this century. The contemporary climate profile of the closest matching

Table 1-1. Mean and range of three climate variables for nine biomes (Brown and others 1998) of the Interior West.

Biome	Data points	Degree-days >5 °C		Coldest month mean temperature (°C)		Annual moisture index[a]	
		Mean	Range	Mean	Range	Mean	Range
Sonoran Desert	4,338	5849	2439–6379	11.2	2.2–12.8	0.47	0.18–1.00
Mojave Desert	5,963	4491	3041–6220	6.3	-6.5–9.4	0.43	0.20–0.68
Great Basin Desertscrub	29,047	2227	571–3088	-3.7	-10.8–11.9	0.19	0.11–0.29
Great Basin Shrub-Grassland	36,348	2030	1187–2933	-3.6	-81 – -0.4	0.14	0.07–0.25
Great Plains	16,153	2321	1498–3427	-2.8	-8.7–3.2	0.13	0.09–0.17
Pinyon-Juniper Woodlands	82,248	2189	322–3138	-2.1	-11.5–2.8	0.14	0.08–0.24
Rocky Mountain Montane Forest	52,735	1444	988–3425	-5.0	-8.1–3.2	0.07	0.04–0.09
Rocky Mountain Subalpine Forest	41,646	812	542–2149	-8.5	-11.4 – -3.4	0.02	0.01–0.03
Alpine Tundra	8,344	413	237–1711	-10.6	-13.2 – -3.4	0.02	0.01–0.03

[a] (degree-days >5 °C)$^{0.5}$ / mean annual precipitation.

biotic community is used. It is worthwhile to note several general trends (calculated as percent change between current and year 2060 projections):

- Suitable habitat for Rocky Mountain subalpine conifer forests that account for approximately 1% of current cover disappears almost completely (99.7%) by 2090. Suitable climate for Rocky Mountain and Great Basin alpine tundra disappears completely by 2060.

- Habitat with climate suitable for Rocky Mountain conifer forest shifts upslope, displacing habitat currently occupied by subalpine coniferous forests, and shows corresponding losses at low elevations. Localized extinctions are expected, especially in the south.

- Habitat suitable for Great Basin conifer woodlands is projected to move north and upslope with principal gains in Colorado and southwest Wyoming and losses in the Southwest. An equivalent spatial shift for this vegetation type would constitute a continuation of migratory trends documented from the late Pleistocene to the present (Betancourt 1987).

- The climate conducive for Plains grasslands is reduced slightly with losses occurring primarily in Colorado and New Mexico. Semi-desert grassland habitat expands northward from the Southwest into the Great Basin, Colorado Plateau, and southern Great Plains and occupies an area nearly four times that of the present. Habitat suitable for Great Basin shrub grassland decreases by 40% and becomes highly fragmented.

- In addition to semi-desert grasslands, projected climate changes through 2060 appear to be most favorable for Mohave Desert (85% increase), Sonoran Desert (79% increase), and Chihuahuan Desert (167% increase) scrub vegetation types. Between 2060 and 2090, Mojave and Sonoran Desert vegetation communities will continue to expand while Chihuahuan Desert vegetation will contract. In general, habitat suitable for the Sonoran Desert scrub type expands northward as the Mojave Desert scrub type migrates to the Great Basin and Snake and Columbia River Plains.

- Habitat favorable to Great Basin Desert scrub is projected to expand in the short term and then becomes fragmented as it contracts later in the century. Great Basin montane scrub habitat will experience moderate decline and displacement by Mojave Desert species through time (69% decrease) (fig. 1-4). Fragmentation of these and other habitats can exacerbate other negative effects of climate change and influence realized shifts and persistence of habitats and species.

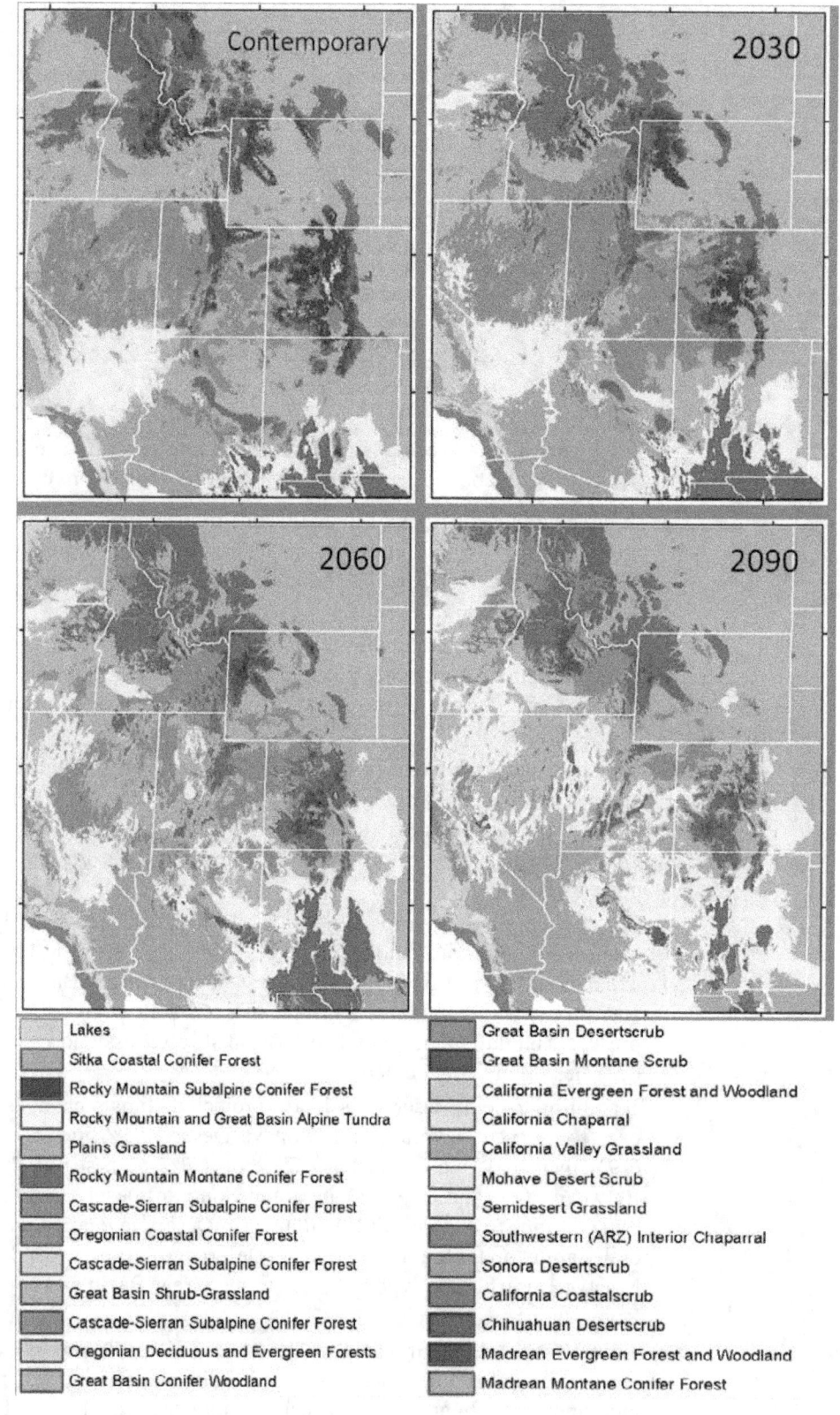

Figure 1-4. Modeled realized climatic niche (upper left) and their predicted future distributions for Brown and others (1998) biotic communities in the interior western United States (Rehfeldt and others 2006). Lake positions were omitted from future projections.

The legend for the figure includes:

Lakes
Sitka Coastal Conifer Forest
Rocky Mountain Subalpine Conifer Forest
Rocky Mountain and Great Basin Alpine Tundra
Plains Grassland
Rocky Mountain Montane Conifer Forest
Cascade-Sierran Subalpine Conifer Forest
Oregonian Coastal Conifer Forest
Cascade-Sierran Subalpine Conifer Forest
Great Basin Shrub-Grassland
Cascade-Sierran Subalpine Conifer Forest
Oregonian Deciduous and Evergreen Forests
Great Basin Conifer Woodland

Great Basin Desertscrub
Great Basin Montane Scrub
California Evergreen Forest and Woodland
California Chaparral
California Valley Grassland
Mohave Desert Scrub
Semidesert Grassland
Southwestern (ARZ) Interior Chaparral
Sonora Desertscrub
California Coastalscrub
Chihuahuan Desertscrub
Madrean Evergreen Forest and Woodland
Madrean Montane Conifer Forest

Native Species

Analyses specific to species in the Interior West are limited but provide insights into the effects of climate change on several of the region's keystone species. Following are some examples of these analyses:

- Crookston (see http://forest.moscowfsl.wsu.edu/climate/) used methodology described by Refeldt and others (2009) to create a species climate profile (contemporary realized climate niche) projected in six future climates (three GCMs and two scenarios) for several western species. Among these, one seed juniper (*Juniperus monosperma*) (fig. 1-5), Utah juniper (*Juniperus osteosperma*) (fig. 1-6), two needle pinyon pine (*Pinus edulis*) (fig. 1-7), and single leaf pinyon pine (*Pinus monophylla*) (fig. 1-8) are presented. These predictions generally agree with those of Rehfeldt and others (2006) for Great Basin conifer woodlands and indicate a continuation of migratory trends documented from the late Pleistocene to the present (Betancourt 1987).

- Neilson and others (2005) used a coupled bioclimate model to predict a decline in sagebrush habitat in the Great Basin due to the synergistic effects of temperature increases and fire and disease, and to displacement by species moving north from the Mojave Desert in response to the northward shift in frost lines.

- Bradley (2010) used risk analysis to assess the interactive impacts of land use conversion (woodland expansion), land use (roads, agriculture, etc.), and cheatgrass (*Bromus tectorum*) invasion on sagebrush (*Artemisia* spp.) habitat in Nevada. Changes to the climatic habitat of *Artemisia* spp. were estimated using an ensemble of 10 atmospheric-ocean GCMs and 2 BEMs. Sagebrush vegetation types in southern Nevada were at the greatest risk of losing suitable habitat due to climate change. Disturbance risk was greatest in the northern section of the state. Overall, Bradley (2010) supported the conclusion that climate change poses a substantial risk to sagebrush ecosystems in the Great Basin.

- Shafer and others (2001) used bioclimate modeling to predict that sagebrush (*Artemisia tridentata*) will shift northward and exhibit substantial range contraction due to increased summer moisture stress. They also predicted northward expansions of Joshua tree (*Yucca brevifolia*), saguaro (*Carnegiea gigantea*), and creosote bush (*Larrea tridentata*). Creosote bush is expected to expand northward into areas currently occupied by big sagebrush, matching Neilson and others' (2005) prediction.

- Warwell and others (2008) used bioclimate modeling to conclude that the contemporary populations of species with small distributions such as smooth Arizona cypress (*Cupressus arizonica* ssp. *glabra*) and the endangered perennial MacFarlane's four-o'clock (*Mirabilis macfarlanei*) are likely to be subjected to complete climate disequilibrium earlier in the century than more broadly distributed species.

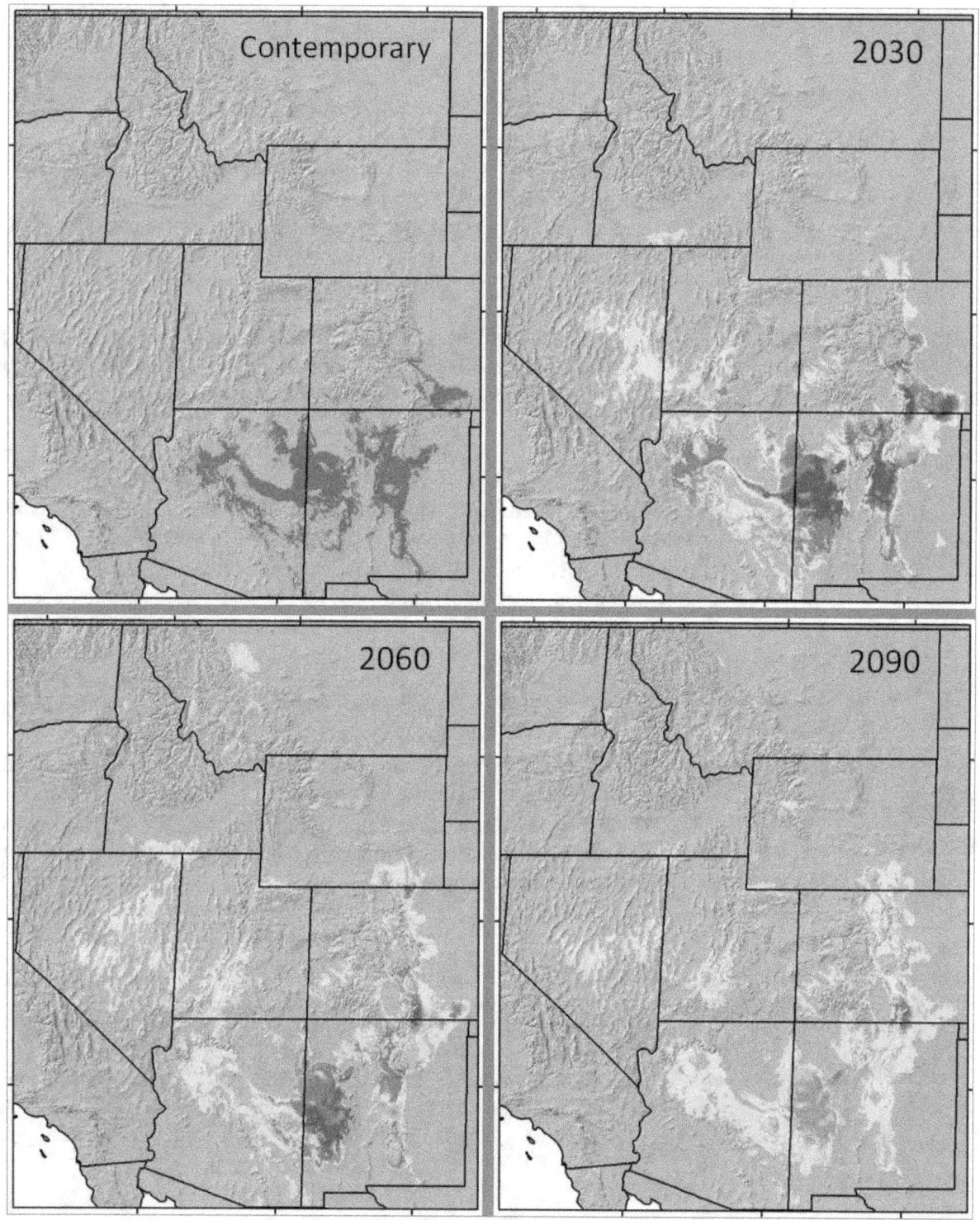

Figure 1-5. Mapped realized climate niche of one seed juniper (*Juniperus monosperma*; green) for contemporary climate (1961-1990) and future climates for decades 2030, 2060, and 2090. Colors coding in future projections indicate occurrence of agreement among 3 GCMs and 2 scenarios. Dark red = complete agreement for all 6 combinations; red = agreement for 5 combinations; dark orange = 4; orange = 3; yellow = 2; and tan = 1 (see Rehfeldt and others 2009).

USDA Forest Service RMRS-GTR-285. 2012.

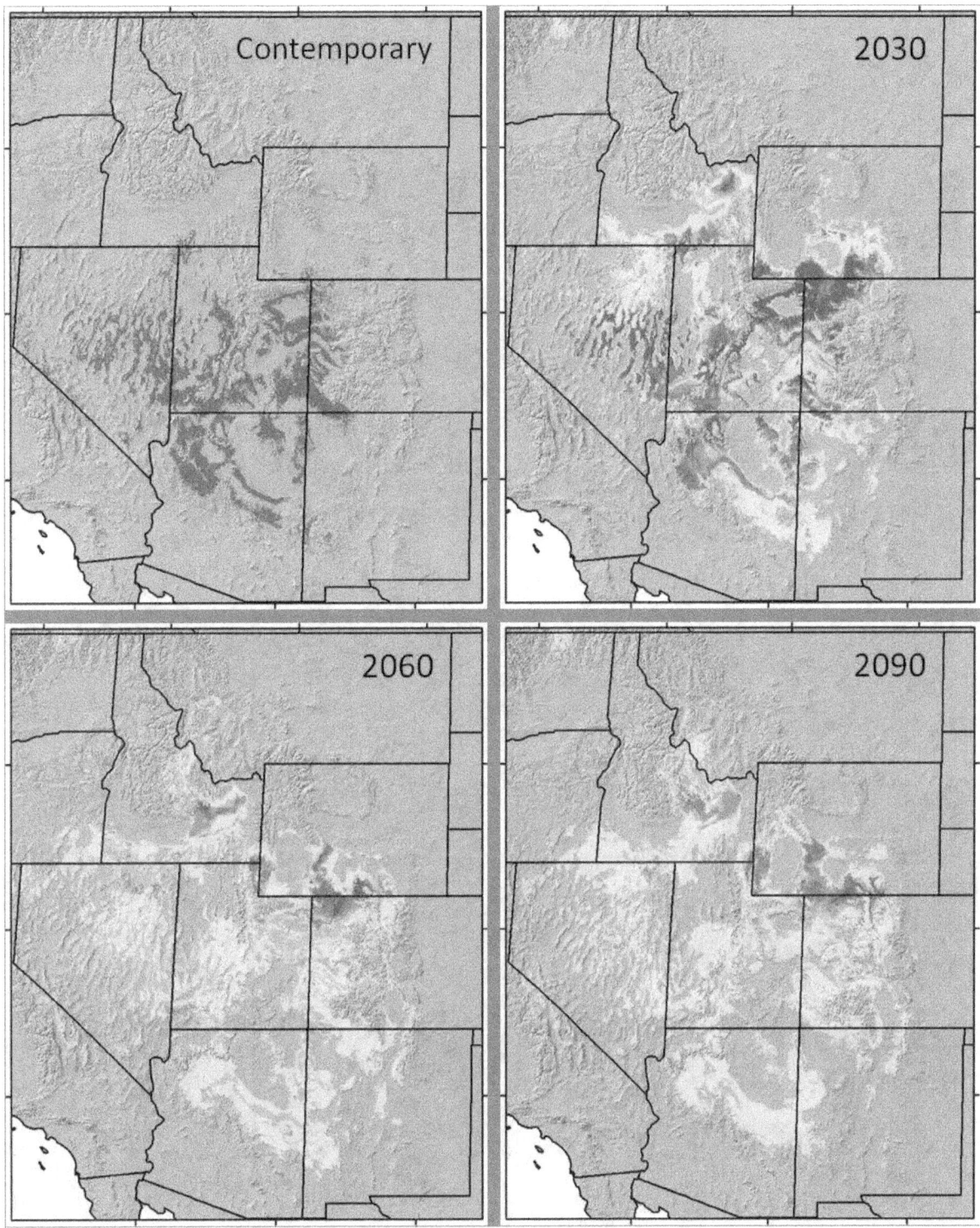

Figure 1-6. Mapped realized climate niche of Utah juniper (*Juniperus osteosperma*; green) for contemporary climate (1961-1990) and future climates for decades 2030, 2060, and 2090. Colors coding in future projections indicate occurrence of agreement among 3 GCMs and 2 scenarios. Dark red = complete agreement for all 6 combinations; red = agreement for 5 combinations; dark orange = 4; orange = 3; yellow = 2; and tan = 1 (see Rehfeldt and others 2009).

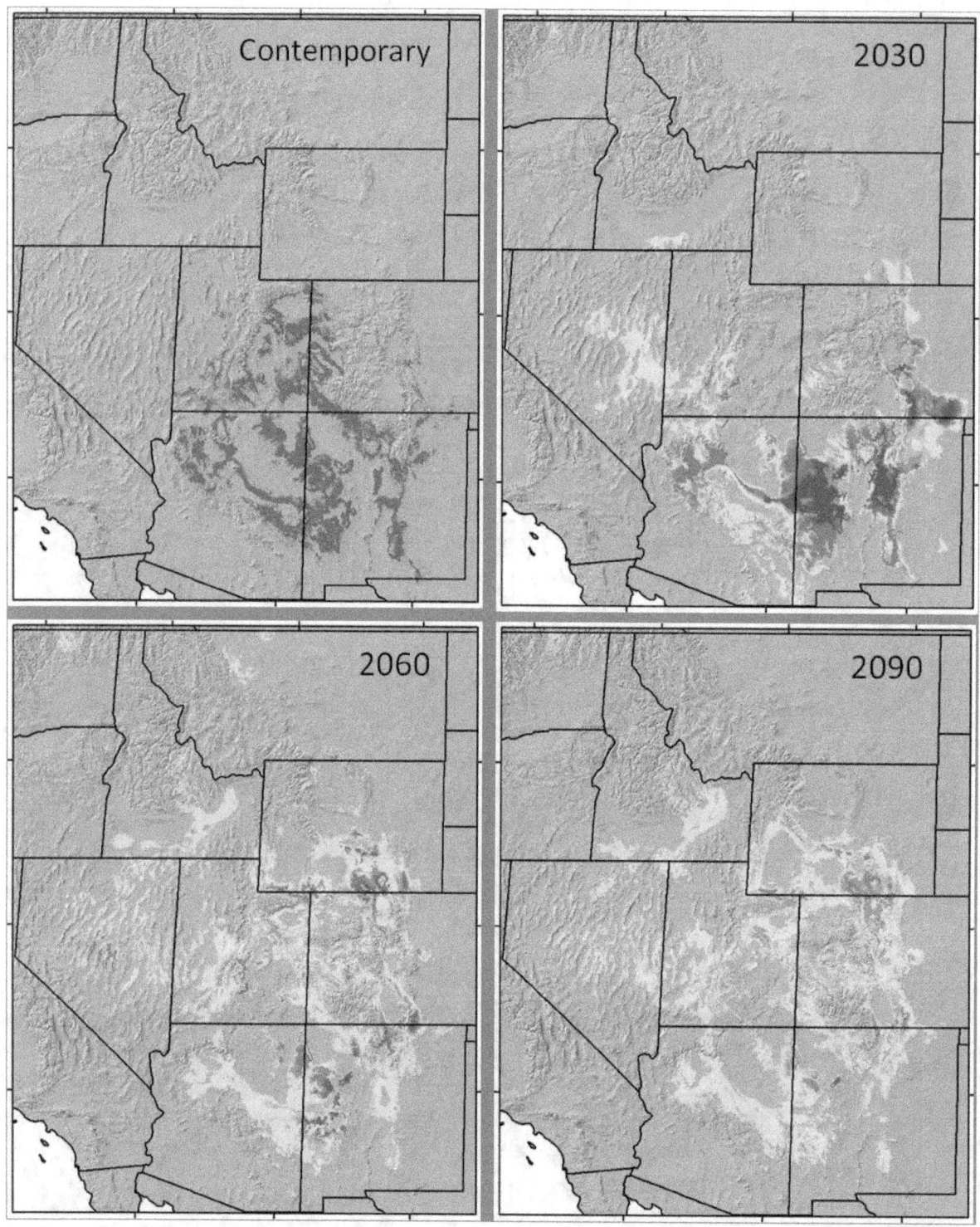

Figure 1-7. Mapped realized climate niche of two needle pinyon pine (*Pinus edulis*; green) for contemporary climate (1961-1990) and future climates for decades 2030, 2060, and 2090. Colors coding in future projections indicate occurrence of agreement among 3 GCMs and 2 scenarios. Dark red = complete agreement for all 6 combinations; red = agreement for 5 combinations; dark orange = 4; orange = 3; yellow = 2; and tan = 1 (see Rehfeldt and others 2009).

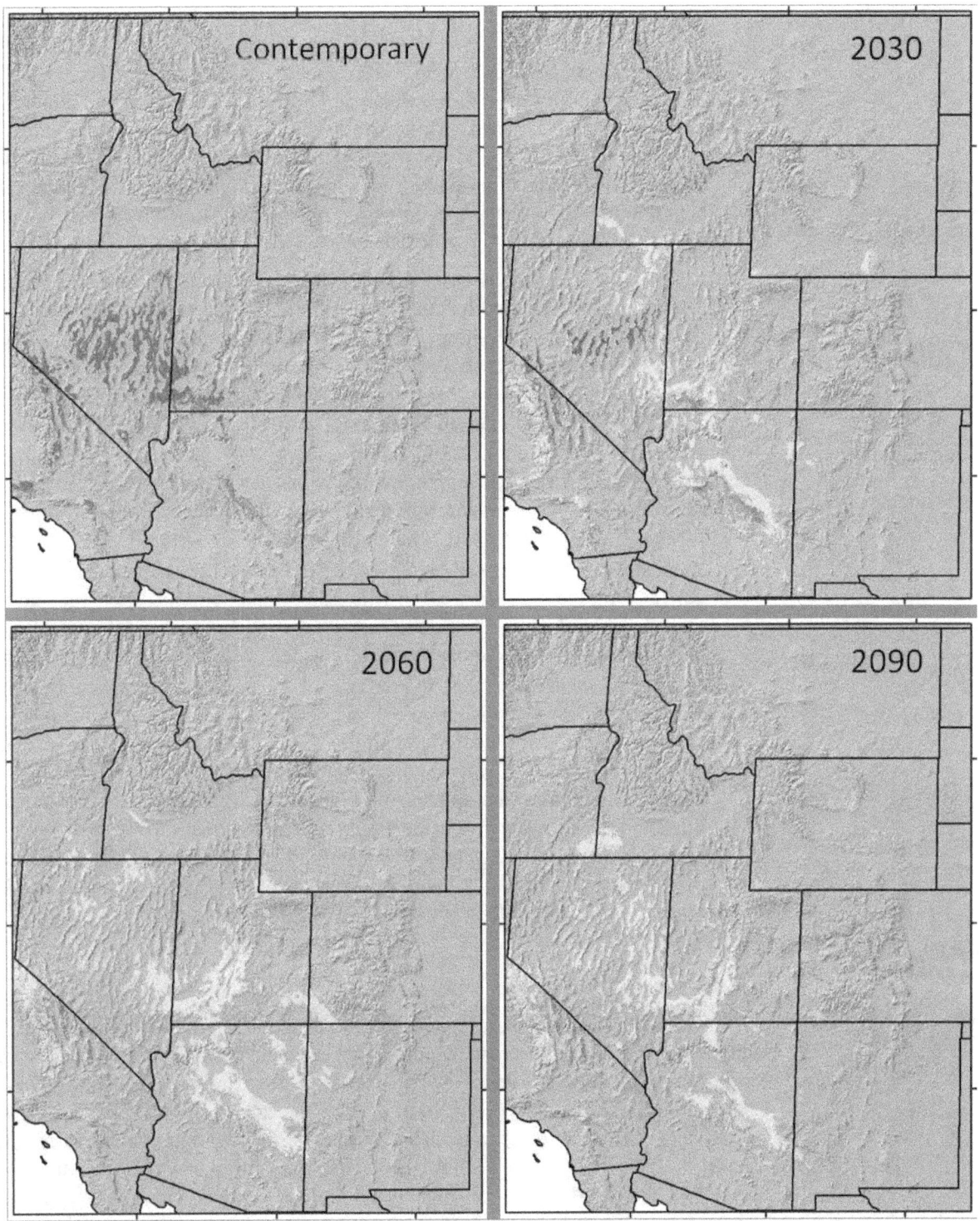

Figure 1-8. Mapped realized climate niche of one seed juniper (*Pinus monophylla*; green) for contemporary climate (1961-1990) and future climates for decades 2030, 2060, and 2090. Colors coding in future projections indicate occurrence of agreement among 3 GCMs and 2 scenarios. Dark red = complete agreement for all 6 combinations; red = agreement for 5 combinations; dark orange = 4; orange = 3; yellow = 2; and tan = 1 (see Rehfeldt and others 2009).

Invasive Species

There is increasing evidence that invasive species also are being affected by climate change (Dukes and Mooney 1999; Walther and others 2009; Bradley and others 2010). However, forecasting changes in invasive species distributions poses some unique challenges because these species may not be in equilibrium with their newly invaded habitat. Analyses specific to invasive species are limited for the Rocky Mountain region and focus on only a few species. Bradley and others (2009) used bioclimate models to identify the risk of spread of four invasive species in the western Unites States:

- Spotted knapweed (*Centaurea biebersteinii*) is expected to expand into new areas of California and Nevada. Its current distribution in the coastal states (California, Oregon, and Washington) showed little change (loss of suitability) under future scenarios, but climate change may result in a transition to higher elevations in interior states (e.g., Montana, Wyoming, Colorado, and Utah).

- Tamarisk (*Tamarix* spp.) distributions were not well constrained by environmental characteristics, and the authors found no evidence for temperature constraints. Not surprisingly, the risk of tamarisk spread, which occurs within riparian areas and elevated water tables across most of the western United States, was not shown to be influenced by the direct effects of climate change.

- In contrast, leafy spurge (*Euphorbia esula*) is expected to expand throughout the majority of northern states west of Mississippi and some of the rangelands west of the Rocky Mountains. However, leafy spurge is likely to retreat from Colorado, Nebraska, Oregon, and Idaho as result of warmer temperatures.

- Cheatgrass (*Bromus tectorum*) is constrained by multiple precipitation variables and winter maximum temperature. Climate change is expected to shift potentially susceptible habitats northward, creating an increased risk in Idaho, Montana, and Wyoming but reduced risk in southern Nevada and Utah. Currently infested areas of central Utah and southern and central Nevada did not appear to remain suitable to this species, which may indicate a future range contraction. As much as 13% of the current invaded lands may not be suitable for this species under global warming and replacement by other invasive species is probable (e.g., red brome [*Bromus rubens*]). This pattern may be repeated with other invasive species.

Research Needs

Developing a framework for integrating the different approaches could significantly improve our ability to forecast changes in vegetation types and species. Such a framework might include long-term experiments (e.g., for explicit species, locations, and climate change scenarios) designed to explore the local complexities of species and ecosystem responses to climate change that support more comprehensive mechanistic models and provide for testing BEMs. The integration of experimental work and modeling could further our understanding of the ecological consequences of climate change, improve our projections for the future, and provide information necessary to maintain ecosystem services through development of effective conservation and restoration strategies in the context of climate change. Frameworks for predicting vegetation response to climate change that include research experiments, mechanistic modeling, and species distribution modeling can be used to identify and address critical information gaps, including the following:

- Obtain the necessary species-specific data regarding important climate variables, biotic interactions, genetic variation, and adaptive capacity to improve model predictions. To date, the primary emphasis has been placed on tree species. For deserts, grasslands, and shrublands, an increased emphasis needs to be placed on determining the relationships among climate variables and establishment and growth and reproduction of grasses, forbs, and shrubs. And in these arid to semi-arid systems, climate variables other than temperature and precipitation, such as snowpack duration and water-balance deficit, may better reflect the resources that are available for plant growth (Stephenson 1990, 1998).

- Determine the interacting effects of climate and other global change processes such as extreme events, increasing CO_2, nitrogen deposition, pests, and disease on species distributions and community composition to improve model predictions of the synergistic effects of these processes (Campbell and others 2000). Long-term research and regional monitoring may be necessary to distinguish the effects of climate from other change agents and identify the indirect effects of climate on species interactions (Pearson and Dawson 2003).

- Evaluate the interacting effects of socioeconomic and biophysical factors on land use and land cover change and, consequently, on species distribution and community composition (Hansen and others 2001).

- Increase our knowledge of the effects of species diversity and functional groups on ecosystem processes as they relate to climate and other global change factor.

- Continue to advance modeling efforts that couple bioclimate analyses with models that are able to estimate feedback, competitive interactions, and disturbance effects (e.g., Huntley and others 2010; Franklin 2010). Risk models can incorporate empirical, experimental, or observational information into a geospatial (GIS) framework to create spatially explicit predictions of threats and change (Bradley and others 2010).

- Continue to explore other modeling approaches, such as combining historic distribution data with contemporary distributions, to identify species specific climate limitations that may then be used to parameterize models (e.g., Arundel 2005).

Literature Cited

Alward, R. D., J. K. Detling and M. G. Milchunas. 1999. Grassland vegetation changes and nocturnal global warming. Science 283: 229.

Araújo, M. B., R. G. Pearson, W. Thuiller and M. Erhard. 2005. Validation of species-climate impact models under climate change. Global Change Biology 11: 1504-1513.

Arundel, S. T. 2005. Using spatial models to establish climatic limiters of plant species' distributions. Ecological Modelling 182: 159-181.

Berger, U., C. Piou, K. Schiffers and V. Grimm. 2008. Competition among plants: concepts, individual-based modeling approaches, and a proposal for a future research strategy. Perspectives in Plant Ecology Evolution and Systematics 9: 121-135.

Betancourt, J. L. 1987. Paleoecology of pinyon-juniper woodlands: summary. In: Everett, R. L., compiler. Proceedings: Pinyon-Juniper Conference. Gen. Tech. Rep. INT-215. Ogden, UT: U.S. Department of Agriculture, Forest Service, Intermountain Research Station: 164-185.

Botkin, D. B., H. Saxe, M. B. Araujo, R. Betts and others. 2007. Forecasting the effects of global warming on biodiversity. Bioscience 57: 227-236.

Bradley, B. A. 2009. Regional analysis of the impacts of climate change on cheatgrass invasion shows potential risk and opportunity. Global Change Biology 15: 196-208.

Bradley, B. A. 2010. Assessing ecosystem threats from global and regional change: hierarchical modeling of risk to sagebrush ecosystems from climate change, land use and invasive species in Nevada, USA. Ecography 33: 198-208.

Bradley, B. A., D. M. Blumenthal, D. S. Wilcove and L. H. Ziska. 2010. Predicting plant invasions in an era of global change. Trends in Ecology and Evolution 25: 310-318.

Brown, D. E., F. Reichenbacher and S. E. Franson. 1998. A classification of North American biotic communities. University of Utah Press, Salt Lake City. 141 p.

Brown, J. H., T. J. Valone and C. G. Curtin. 1997. Reorganization of an arid ecosystem in response to recent climate change. Proceedings of the National Academy of Science 94: 9729-9733.

Campbell, B. D. 2000. A synthesis of recent global change research on pasture and rangeland production: reduced uncertainties and their management implications. Agriculture, Ecosystems and Environment 82: 39-55.

Chew, J. D., C. Stalling and K. Moeller. 2004. Integrating knowledge for simulating vegetation change at landscape scales. Western Journal of Applied Forestry 19: 102-108.

Christensen, J. H., B. Hewitson, A. Busuioc, A. Chen and others. 2007. Regional climate projections. In: Solomon, S., D. Qin, M. Manning, Z. Chen, M. Marquis, K. B. Averyt, M. Tignor and H. L. Miller, eds. Climate Change 2007: The Physical Science Basis. Contribution of Working Group I to the Fourth Assessment Report of the Intergovernmental Panel on Climate Change. New York: Cambridge University Press.

Davis, M. B. and R. G. Shaw. 2001. Range shifts and adaptive responses to quaternary climate change. Science 292: 673-679.

Dukes, J. S. 2002. Comparison of the effect of elevated CO_2 on an invasive species (*Centaurea solstitialis*) in monoculture and community settings. Plant Ecology 160: 225-234.

Dukes, J. S. and H. A. Mooney. 1999. Does global change increase the success of biological invaders? Trends in Ecology and Evolution 14: 135-139.

Farber, O. and R. Kadmon. 2003. Assessment of alternative approaches for bioclimatic modeling with special emphasis on the Mahalanobis distance. Ecological Modeling 160: 115-130.

Franklin, J. 1995. Predictive vegetation mapping: geographic modelling of biospatial patterns in relation to environmental gradients. Progress in Physical Geography 19: 474-499.

Franklin, J. 2010. Moving beyond static species distribution models in support of conservation biogeography. Diversity and Distributions 16: 321-330.

Guisan, A. and W. Thuiller. 2005. Predicting species distribution: offering more than simple habitat models. Ecology Letters 8: 993-1009.

Guisan, A. and N. E. Zimmermann. 2000. Predictive habitat distribution models in ecology. Ecological Modelling 135: 147-186.

Hansen, A. J., R. P. Neilson, V. H. Dale, C. H. Flather and others. 2001. Global change in forest: responses of species, communities and biomes. BioScience 51: 765-779.

Harris, J. A., R. J. Hobbs, E. Higgs and J. Aronson. 2006. Ecological restoration and global climate change. Restoration Ecology 14:170-176.

Harte, J. and R. Shaw. 1995. Shifting dominance within a montane vegetation community—results of a climate-warming experiment. Science 267: 876-880.

Hijmans, R. J. and C. H. Graham. 2006. The ability of climate envelope models to predict the effect of climate change on species distributions. Global Change Biology 12: 2272-2281.

Huntley, B., P. Barnard, R. Altwegg, L. Chambers and others. 2010. Beyond bioclimatic envelopes: dynamic species' range and abundance modeling in the context of climatic change. Ecography 33: 621-626.

Intergovernmental Panel on Climate Change [IPCC]. 2007. Climate Change 2007: Impacts, adaptation and vulnerability. In: Parry, M. L., O. F. Canziani, J. P. Palutikof, P. J. van der Linden and C. E. Hanson, eds. Contribution of Working Group II to the Fourth Assessment Report of the Intergovernmental Panel on Climate Change. Cambridge, United Kingdom: Cambridge University Press. 976 p.

Jeltsch, F., K. A. Moloney, F. M. Schurr, M. Kochy and M. Schwager. 2008. The state of plant population modeling in light of environmental change. Perspectives in Plant Ecology Evolution and Systematics 9: 171-189.

Kupfer, J. A., J. Balmat and J. L. Smith. 2004. Shift in the potential distribution of shy island plant communities in response to climate change. In: Gottfried, G. J., B. S. Gebow, L. G. Eskew, C. B. Edminster, eds. Proceedings: Connecting mountain islands and desert seas: biodiversity and management of the Madrean Archipelago II. RMRS-P-36. Fort Collins, CO: U.S. Department of Agriculture, Forest Service, Rocky Mountain Research Station: 485-590.

Nielson, R. P., J. M. Lenihan, D. Bachelet and R. J. Drapek. 2005. Climate change implications for sagebrush ecosystems. Transactions of the 70th North American Wildlife and Natural Resources Conference, March 16-19, 2005. Arlington, VA: Wildlife Management Institution Publications Department: 145-159.

North, G. R., F. Biondi, P. Bloomfield, J. R. Christy and others. 2006. Surface temperature reconstructions for the last 2,000 years. The National Academies Press. Washington, DC. 160 p.

Pearson, R. G. and T. P. Dawson. 2003. Predicting the impacts of climate change on the distribution of species: are bioclimate envelope models useful? Global Ecology and Biogeography 12: 361-371.

Peñuelas, J., P. Prieto, C. Beier, C. Cesaraccio and others. 2007. Response of plant species richness and primary productivity in shrublands along a north–south gradient in Europe to seven years of experimental warming and drought: reductions in primary productivity in the heat and drought year of 2003. Global Change Biology 13: 25632581.

Plummer, D. A., D. Caya, A. Frigon, H. Côté and others. 2006. Climate and climate change over North America as simulated by the Canadian Regional Climate Model. Journal of Climate 19: 3112-3132.

Randall, D. A., R. A. Wood, S. Bony, R. Colman and others. 2007. Climate models and their evaluation. In: Solomon, S., D. Qin, M. Manning, Z. Chen, M. Marquis, K. B. Averyt, M. Tignor and H. L. Miller, eds. Climate Change 2007: The Physical Science Basis. Contribution of Working Group I to the Fourth Assessment Report of the Intergovernmental Panel on Climate Change. New York: Cambridge University Press.

Rehfeldt, G. E. 2006. A spline model of climate for the western United States. Gen. Tech. Rep. RMRS-GTR-165. Fort Collins: U.S. Department of Agriculture, Forest Service, Rocky Mountain Research Station. 21 p.

Rehfeldt, G. E., N. L. Crookston, M. Warwell and J. S. Evans. 2006. Empirical analyses of plant-climate relationships for the western United States. Journal of Plant Science 167: 1123-1150.

Rehfeldt, G. E., D. E. Ferguson and N. L. Crookston. 2009. Aspen, climate and sudden decline in western USA. Forest Ecology and Management 258: 2353-2364.

Rehfeldt, G. E. and B. C. Jaquish. 2010. Ecological impacts and management strategies for western larch in the face of climate-change. Mitigation and Adaptation Strategies for Global Change 15(3): 283-306.

Sáenz-Romero, C., G. E. Rehfeldt, N. L. Crookston, P. Duval and others. 2010. Spline models of contemporary, 2030, 2060, and 2090 climates for Mexico and their use in understanding climate-change impacts on the vegetation. Climatic Change 102: 595-623.

Seager, R., M. F. Ting, I. Held, Y. Kushnir and others. 2007. Model projections of an imminent transition to a more arid climate in southwestern North America. Science 316: 1181-1184.

Shafer, S. L., P. J. Bartlein and R. S. Thompson. 2001. Potential changes in the distribution of western North America tree and shrub taxa under future climate scenarios. Ecosystems 4: 200-215.

Sheffield, J. and E. F. Wood. 2008. Projected changes in drought occurrence under future global warming from multi-model, multi-scenario, IPCC AR4 simulations. Climate Dynamics 31: 79-105.

Stewart, I. T., D. R. Cayan and M. D. Dettinger. 2004. Changes in snowmelt runoff timing in western North America under a 'business as usual' climate change scenario. Climatic Change 62: 217-232.

Suttle, K. B., M. A. Thomsen and M. E. Power. 2007. Species interactions reverse grassland responses to changing climate. Science 315: 640-642.

Torn, M. S. and J. Harte. 2006. Missing feedbacks, asymmetric uncertainties, and the underestimation of future warming. Geophysical Research Letters 33, L10703.

Turner, M. G. 2010. Disturbance and landscape dynamics in a changing world. Ecology 91(10): 2833-2849.

Walther, G. R., A. Roques, P. E. Hulme, M. T. Sykes and others. 2009. Alien species in a warmer world: risks and opportunities. Trends in Ecology and Evolution 24: 686-693.

Warwell, M. V., G. E. Rehfeldt and N. L. Crookston. 2010. Modeling species realized climatic niche space and predicting their response to global warming for several western forest species with small geographic distributions. In: Pye, J. M., H. M. Rauscher, Y. Sands, D. C. Lee and J. S. Beatty, eds. Advances in threat assessment and their application to forest and rangeland management-Volume 1. Gen. Tech. Rep. PNW-GTR-802. Portland, OR: U.S. Department of Agriculture, Forest Service, Pacific Northwest and Southern Research Stations: 36-59.

Williams, J. J. and S. T. Jackson. 2007. Novel climates, no-analog communities, and ecological surprises. Paleoecology 5(9): 475-482.

Chapter 2

Restoring and Managing Cold Desert Shrublands for Climate Change Mitigation

Susan E. Meyer[1]

[1] U.S. Forest Service, Rocky Mountain Research Station; Grassland, Shrublands, and Desert Ecosystems Program; Shrub Sciences Laboratory, Provo, Utah

Executive Summary

The equation for slowing global warming includes decreasing carbon emissions into the atmosphere as well as increasing carbon sequestration in the biosphere. Many proposed schemes for increasing carbon sequestration, such as afforestation of non-forested lands, involve tradeoffs with other resource values, including water availability. An alternative idea is to restore native plant communities to a condition that maximizes carbon storage without the need for continued resource inputs. Cold desert shrublands are a particularly good choice for management for increased carbon sequestration for the following reasons:

- Because of deep rooting systems, high root:shoot ratios, and relatively high standing biomass and soil organic carbon reserves, intact cold desert shrublands can store impressive amounts of carbon, more than one-third as much as the average biome on a per-area basis, in spite of dramatically lower productivity.

- The low productivity of cold deserts makes them relatively unimportant from an agricultural economics perspective. In a world where carbon sequestration itself is destined to become a commodity, shrubland management for increased carbon storage could potentially become a source of revenue that would offset the investments necessary to achieve restoration and management goals.

- A large fraction of cold desert shrubland in the Interior West is in severely degraded condition, with immense acreages dominated by weedy annual grasses that turn these systems into net carbon sources rather than sinks. While this is unfortunate in the short term, it means immense potential for increasing carbon sequestration through restoration of these degraded systems.

Accomplishing the task of returning degraded cold desert shrublands to their status as net carbon sinks will not be easy. The success of large-scale restoration through direct seeding is hampered by low and unpredictable amounts of precipitation, and this problem will only be exacerbated as climate continues to warm. The relatively low success rate for cold desert shrubland seedings highlights the need for innovative shrubland restoration research. Ongoing research by Rocky Mountain Research Station (RMRS) scientists in the Grassland, Desert, and Shrubland Ecosystems (GSD) Program that addresses these issues includes:

- Developing novel biocontrol strategies for both weedy annual grasses and secondary dicot weeds.

- Developing the knowledge and technology to increase supplies of seeds of diverse native species, including nontraditional early seral species that may be better able to cope with current and future disturbance regimes.
- Developing improved technology for site preparation and seeding.
- Developing knowledge and technology needed to restore microbiotic soil crusts.
- Developing knowledge of genetic variation in traits important to climatic adaptation in key species such as big sagebrush to better match seed source to current and future site conditions.
- Increasing understanding of successional processes in desert shrublands, grasslands, and woodlands in the context of global climate change and disturbance regime.

Introduction

Deserts and semideserts occupy approximately 22% of the Earth's land surface (Janzen 2004), yet because of their low productivity, they are generally assumed to be relatively minor players in the global carbon cycle. Schemes to mitigate global climate change have rarely considered that improving carbon sequestration in deserts could make a significant contribution at a global scale. Many ideas for increasing carbon sequestration, such as tree plantations in marginally suitable environments, involve tradeoffs with other resource values such as water use and quality (Jackson and others 2005). In contrast, improving carbon sequestration in deserts by restoring degraded shrublands to a more functional state would address a broad suite of resource values, including improved air and water quality, wildland fire abatement, enhanced wildlife habitat, biodiversity conservation, and aesthetic and recreational values.

Because cold deserts store much of their carbon belowground and that carbon is stored in deeper soil layers, these deserts are likely to store more carbon per unit area than warm deserts with monsoonal moisture regimes. In addition, the desert shrublands of the interior West might be more appropriately classified as semideserts, as they generally have much higher standing biomass than the true deserts, for example, the Sahara Desert of North Africa, which is virtually plantless over large areas except in drainages ("wadis"). This combination of high belowground allocation and relatively high biomass production appears to make cold deserts exceptionally good candidates for carbon sequestration.

The question addressed here is whether restoration on a broad scale in the interior West could make a significant contribution to climate change mitigation. The premise is that restoration of degraded cold desert shrublands could result in sequestration of significant amounts of carbon and could also reduce the negative climatic effects of excessive windblown dust. The consumptive uses of these ecosystems (e.g., livestock grazing), which could potentially interfere with management for carbon sequestration, could be said to be relatively unimportant economically, at least in the Interior West. If the carbon credit market that is taking shape internationally becomes fully functional, well-managed cold deserts may be able to provide more revenue as carbon sinks than as grazing lands. In addition, management for carbon sequestration can also be viewed as management for maximum return in terms of many other ecosystem services and amenity resources.

Carbon Storage in Deserts

Examination of carbon (C) storage patterns in major biomes on a global scale reveals that deserts (including semideserts) are responsible for the storage of a substantial proportion of the terrestrial C pool. Stored carbon may be present as standing biomass or as soil organic carbon (SOC), which is generally considered to be the more stable and persistent form. It dominates the terrestrial carbon pool at about 80% of total stored C (table 2-1; Janzen 2004). The relative contribution of C as standing biomass versus SOC in deserts is even more strongly biased, with over 95% of the stored C as SOC. Standing biomass C in deserts is estimated to account for only 1.7% of global total, whereas desert SOC is estimated to account for 9.5%. Overall, deserts, which occupy about 22% of the total land area, account for about 8% of terrestrial C stocks (Janzen 2004), indicating deserts are generally about a third as effective as the average biome at storing C on a per area basis. Given the intrinsically unproductive nature of deserts, these figures at first seem surprisingly high. It is hard to see how systems that support such low standing biomass can generate so much SOC. But the same factor that generally limits biomass production in deserts, namely lack of water during much of the year, particularly when temperatures are warm, also limits the rate of microbial respiration in soil, leading to accumulation and persistence of SOC (Jobbagy and Jackson 2000).

The vertical distribution of C in deserts also helps explain how they can be effective carbon sinks (fig. 2-1). When compared with other temperate region biomes, standing biomass, particularly in cold deserts, is dominated by the belowground portion, with root:shoot ratios averaging between four and five (Jackson and others 1996; fig. 2-2). The maximum rooting depth is deeper for cold deserts than for any other biome examined (Canadell and others 1996), and less than 55% of root biomass is found in the upper 30 cm of soil (Jackson and others 1996). This contrasts with perennial grasslands, which have similar standing biomass and relatively high root:shoot ratios, but with >80% of the root biomass in the surface 30 cm. This pattern of deep and extensive rooting in cold deserts is probably related to the need to capture winter precipitation stored at depth during the ensuing growing season, which is usually quite dry. The pattern is not seen in warm deserts, where summer monsoonal moisture patterns dominate and root:shoot ratios average less than one (Jackson and others 1996).

Table 2-1. Estimated terrestrial global carbon stocks by biome (Janzen 2004) and estimated mean carbon stock per unit area for each biome.

Biome	Area (10⁹ ha)	Global carbon stocks (Pg)			Carbon stock/area
		Plants	Soil	Total	
Temperate Forests	1.04	59	100	159	152.9
Boreal Forests	1.37	88	471	559	111.6
Temperate Grasslands/Shrublands	1.25	9	295	304	89.3
Deserts and Semideserts[1]	3.04	8	191	199	58.2
Tundra	0.95	6	121	127	17.9
Croplands	1.60	3	128	131	81.9
Tropical Forests	1.76	212	216	428	243.2
Tropical Savannahs/Grasslands	2.25	66	264	330	108.1
Wetlands	0.35	15	225	240	68.6
Total (not including ice cover)	13.61	466	2011	2477	182
% of total in deserts/semideserts	22.3%	1.7%	9.5%	8.0%	

[1]Area and carbon stock per area estimates in Janzen (2004) for the desert/semidesert biome have been adjusted by removal of areas of ice cover.

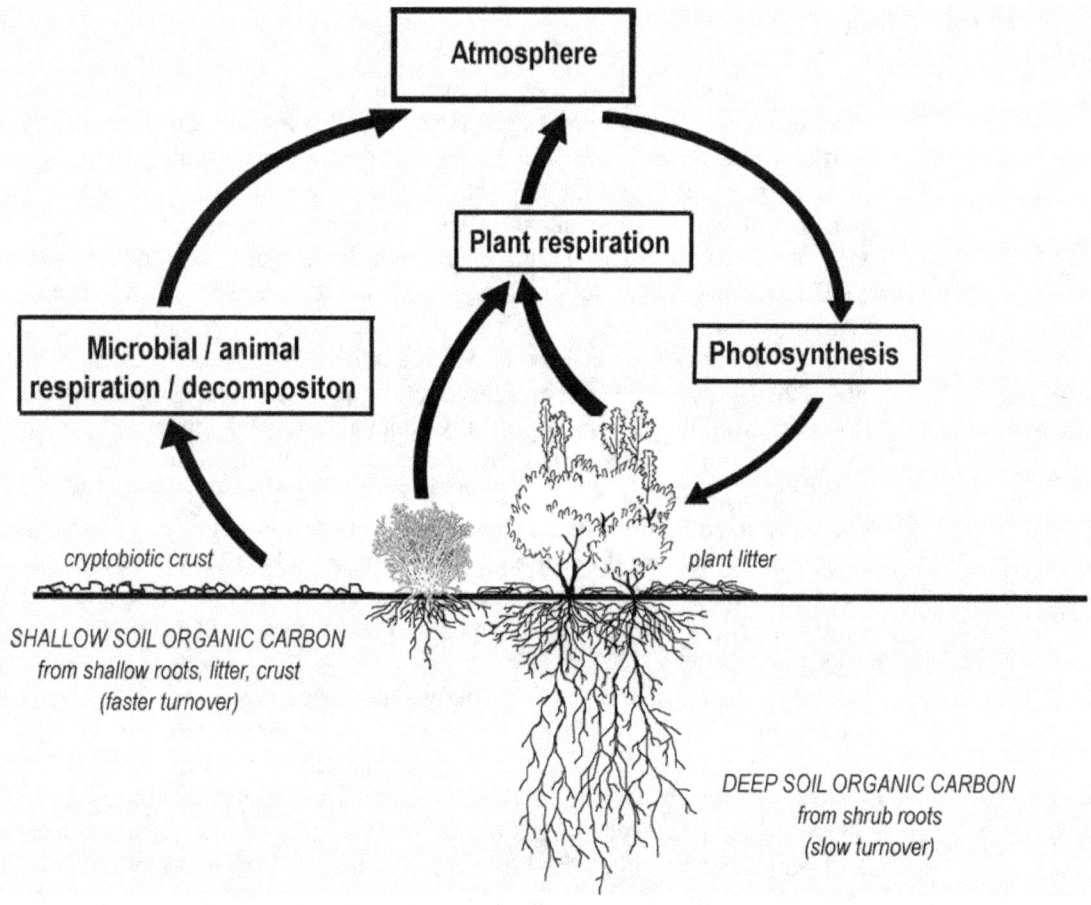

Figure 2-1. The carbon cycle in a cold desert ecosystem, showing fluxes to the atmosphere (plant respiration and animal/microbial respiration/decomposition), uptake from the atmosphere by plants (primarily shrubs and grasses; photosynthesis), standing plant biomass, and shallow and deep soil organic carbon (SOC). If C uptake exceeds C flux to the atmosphere, C sequestration to a net C sink takes place, whereas if flux to the atmosphere exceeds uptake, the system functions as a net carbon source. Deep SOC, the most stable form of stored C, dominates C storage in deserts and semideserts.

In deserts and shrublands in general, SOC and standing belowground biomass follow similar distribution patterns, that is, with more SOC in deeper soil layers relative to the surface layer than is found in either grassland or forest vegetation (Jobbagy and Jackson 2000). The estimated proportion of total SOC found from 1 to 3 m in depth is higher for deserts (0.86) than for any other temperate ecosystem. In general, SOC has a deeper distribution in soil than roots, and this is especially true in ecosystems with lower precipitation. The most likely explanation for this is that SOC turnover at depth is very slow. Dominance of more slowly degrading forms of carbon, lower nutrient concentrations, and more resistant root tissues at depth contribute to SOC persistence (Jobbagy and Jackson 2000).

The ability of cold desert soils to retain SOC could be reduced by the effects of ongoing climate change. Aanderud and others (2010) showed in an 11-year rain manipulation study that near-surface (0 to 30 cm) SOC stocks in a sagebrush steppe (*Artemisia tridentata*) community were significantly reduced when precipitation was shifted from a winter pattern to a spring-summer pattern. They credited this loss to increased microbial activity in wet surface soil at warm temperatures. Shifts from winter to spring-summer rainfall patterns are predicted for many parts of the Interior West as climate continues to warm (Zhang and others 2007). Rainfall timing impacts on

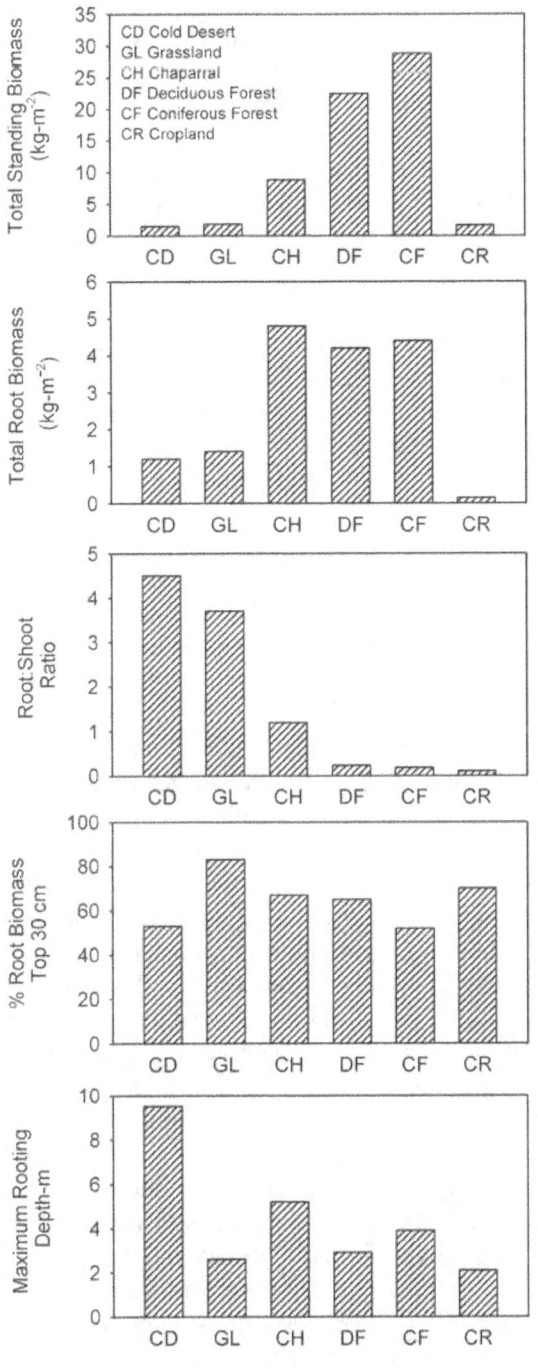

Figure 2-2. Quantity and distribution of biomass carbon in cold desert biomes contrasted with other temperate zone biomes (grassland, chaparral, deciduous forest, coniferous forest, and cropland): (A) total standing biomass, (B) total root biomass, (C) root:shoot ratio, (D) % root biomass in the top 30 cm, and E) maximum rooting depth (adapted from Jackson and others 1996).

deep SOC would be expected to be lower, however, because deep SOC is more buffered from seasonal temperature changes. This would tend to mitigate the effects of increased warm-season precipitation on soil C storage.

C cycling on U.S. rangelands has been the subject of several recent studies and reviews (e.g., Bird and others 2002; Hunt and others 2004; Schuman and others 2002; Svejcar and others 2008; Follett and Reed 2010; Brown and others 2010). Synthesis of information on carbon storage on rangelands is complicated by the fact that many different vegetation types occurring under many different climatic regimes fall under the rubric of rangelands. Hunt and others (2004), working in Wyoming, found that mixed grass prairie vegetation was carbon-neutral, whereas sagebrush steppe vegetation was acting as a carbon sink. Schuman and others (2002) focused on the potential to increase carbon sequestration in rangelands through improved management, particularly grazing management—their emphasis was primarily on grasslands. Svejcar and others (2008) reported the results of an interesting six-year study on net ecosystem C exchange at eight rangeland sites across a range of habitats. They found that both sagebrush steppe (cold desert shrubland) sites and three of four perennial grassland sites generally acted as C sinks during the course of the study, whereas the two warm desert sites acted as C sources. Whether a site acted as a source or a sink varied across years and was closely tied to precipitation patterns. Drought years limited productivity and tended to make even the most productive sites temporary C sources because even though C loss was also lowered by dry conditions, much reduced productivity shifted the C balance to net loss over the short term. The potential for increased C sequestration on rangelands, especially cold desert shrublands, is high, but the dynamics of the C cycle in rangelands are complex and temporally variable.

Shrubland Degradation and Carbon Storage

Historically, intact desert ecosystems were most likely in a steady state relationship with regard to carbon budgets, acting in the long term neither as sources nor sinks. But two sets of factors have been operating to disturb this steady state, and these factors generally operate in opposing directions. First, woody "encroachment" of former desert and other temperate grasslands is often thought to have shifted the carbon balance in these ecosystems to make them net carbon sinks. Whether conversion from perennial grassland to woody vegetation results in a net increase in C sequestration is the subject of considerable debate, however. Jackson and others (2002) found that whether woody encroachment of perennial grasslands resulted in an increase or decrease in SOC depended on precipitation. There was substantial loss of SOC with woody encroachment in more mesic environments, a loss sufficient to more than counterbalance the increase in standing biomass C resulting from the conversion to dominance by woody species. At the dry end of the spectrum, on the other hand, conversion from perennial desert grassland to shrubland resulted in increases in both standing biomass C and SOC. Most land managers regard woody encroachment as a form of degradation, but its causes are complex and, in many cases, not completely understood. Climate change may be driving woody encroachment in some ecosystems, for example, in the northern Chihuahuan Desert, where creosote bush (*Larrea tridentata*) and tarbush (*Flourensia cernua*) are actively invading desert grasslands (Van Auken 2000). Changes in historic fire regimes, poor grazing management, and other factors may contribute to woody encroachment in other semiarid ecosystems, for example, the invasion of juniper (*Juniperus* spp.) species into sagebrush steppe in the Interior West.

The second process that has had a major impact on carbon storage in the deserts of western North America is the displacement of desert shrubs by invasive annual grasses through increased frequency of fire following destruction of the perennial herbaceous understory through improper grazing management. The conversion to annual grassland results in a transformation from slow to rapid C cycling, the cessation of C deposition in deeper soil layers, and the direct and rapid transfer of aboveground biomass C to atmospheric C associated both with the initial loss through fire of standing shrub biomass C and with subsequent increased fire frequency. This phenomenon has not received the attention of carbon brokers that has been given to woody encroachment, but it potentially has more impact on carbon budgets as it is very likely in the process of converting large portions of the Great Basin and surrounding areas into carbon sources. This possibility was apparently first noted by Bradley and others (Bradley and Mustard 2005; Bradley and others 2006). Using sophisticated remote sensing technologies, the authors conservatively estimated that as of 2006, the area of former salt desert and shrub steppe vegetation in the Great Basin alone that has been converted through repeated burning to cheatgrass monocultures was on the order of 20,000 km². In addition, cheatgrass is not the only invasive annual grass that is having major impacts in western North America. Medusahead wildrye (*Taeniatherum caput-medusae*) and North Africa grass (*Ventenata dubia*) are major invaders in the Interior Northwest, while red brome (*Bromus rubens*) has become a driver of frequent large-scale fires in the Mojave Desert. Many of these fires are occurring in fire-intolerant shrub communities, for example, blackbrush (*Coleogyne ramosissima*) shrublands, that had very low pre-invasion probabilities of burning (Brooks and others 2004).

Bradley and others (2006) also carried out an on-the-ground assessment of carbon stocks in cold desert shrublands versus cheatgrass monocultures. They measured aboveground carbon stocks and SOC in the near-surface soil horizon in burned and unburned salt desert shrubland (one site) and Wyoming big sagebrush steppe (two sites). They demonstrated a 3- to 30-fold decrease in standing aboveground carbon stocks as a consequence of type conversion to cheatgrass (figs. 2-3 and 2-4).

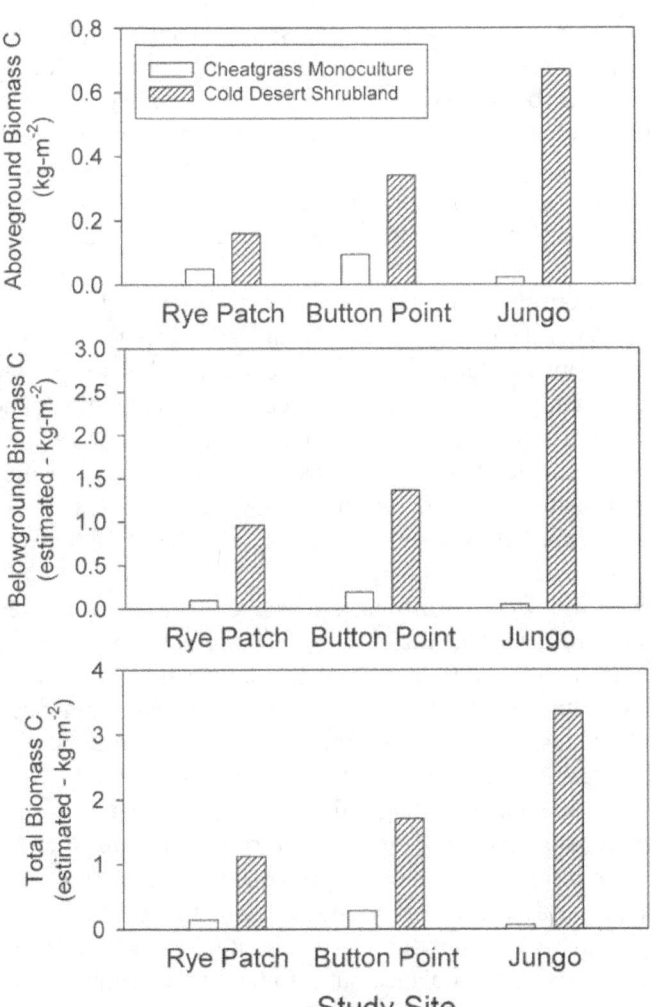

Figure 2-3. Standing biomass carbon in intact cold desert shrubland communities versus adjacent areas that have been converted to cheatgrass (*Bromus tectorum*) monocultures at Rye Patch, Nevada (salt desert shrubland), Button Point, Nevada (sagebrush steppe), and Jingo, Nevada (sagebrush steppe). Aboveground biomass data from Bradley and others (2006); belowground and total biomass estimated from independent root:shoot ratio data.

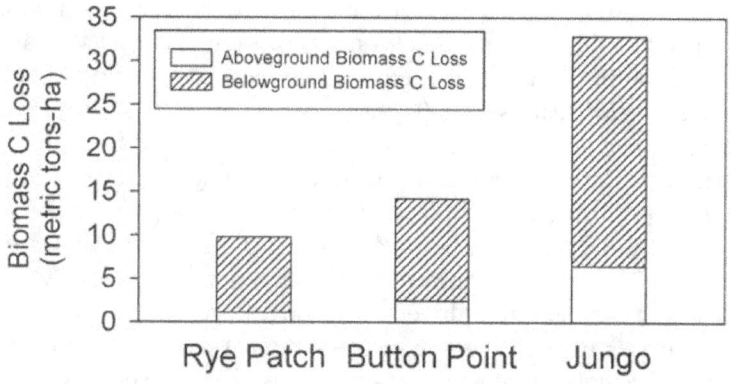

Figure 2-4. Estimated loss of biomass carbon resulting from conversion from cold desert shrubland to cheatgrass (*Bromus tectorum*) monoculture at three Nevada sites (adapted from Bradley and others 2006).

While Bradley and others' (2006) study did not include any assessment or estimate of root biomass C, root:shoot ratio information for the dominant species obtained from other studies can provide at least a rough estimate of root biomass C in these communities. A root:shoot ratio estimate of two was used for cheatgrass in the calculations that follow. This estimate is undoubtedly high; in greenhouse and field studies, root:shoot ratios greater than one for this species are rarely encountered, but a conservative estimate was chosen to avoid exaggeration of pre and post-burn differences (Meyer unpublished data). The estimate of six for the root:shoot ratio of *Atriplex* shrubs is based on estimates by Brewster (1968), while the estimate of four for the root:shoot ratio of *Artemisia* is similar to the estimates for cold desert shrublands in Jackson and others (1996). By revising the carbon stock data of Bradley and others (2006) to include these rough estimates, it can be demonstrated that the loss of belowground biomass carbon has the potential to contribute greatly to the effect of burning on carbon storage in these shrublands (fig. 2-2). Using these estimates, the biomass carbon stocks in the salt desert shrubland were reduced eight-fold through burning and conversion to annual grasslands, while those of sagebrush steppe were reduced from at least 6-fold to over 50-fold.

It is true that belowground C from shrub roots is still present for some undetermined length of time post-conversion, after the large pulse of CO_2 emission from the combustion of the aboveground shrub biomass. But ultimately, this carbon will be released to the atmosphere, and without actively growing shrubs to replenish this belowground stock, the effect will be conversion of this formerly carbon-efficient system into a long-term source of atmospheric C. Estimates of biomass C loss from the study of Bradley and others (2006) ranged from 1.1 to 6.5 metric tons per ha for aboveground biomass C, 8.6 to 26.4 metric tons per ha for belowground biomass C, and 9.8 to 32.8 metric tons per ha for total biomass C.

Bradley and others (2006) combined their estimates of the areal extent of conversion to cheatgrass monoculture in the Great Basin with their estimates of reduction in aboveground biomass C stocks as a consequence of this conversion to calculate total biomass C released to the atmosphere (table 2-2). They estimated that about 8 teragrams of C have been released to the atmosphere through shrubland conversion to annual grassland in the Great Basin as of 2006, and the potential for continuing type conversion and carbon release is immense. Adding estimated long-term belowground biomass carbon stock reduction resulted in an estimate of 29 to 60 teragrams of C that will ultimately be released to the atmosphere as a consequence of type conversion from shrubland to annual grassland that has already occurred in the Great Basin.

Invasive annual grass monocultures are not only very poor at carbon sequestration in terms of standing biomass relative to shrublands but also tend to concentrate their SOC near the surface and facilitate rapid turnover of both soil C and nitrogen (Norton

Table 2-2. Estimated biomass carbon loss as a consequence of conversion from cold desert shrubland to cheatgrass (*Bromus tectorum*) monocultures in the Great Basin as of 2006 (adapted from Bradley and others 2006).

	Salt desert shrubland	Sagebrush steppe	Total
Aboveground biomass C loss (tons/km²)	110	250-650	360-670
Estimated total biomass C loss (tons/km²)	1000	1500-3200	2500-4200
Estimated area burned (km²)	2000	18,000	20,000
Estimated aboveground biomass C loss (teragrams)	0.2	4.5-11.7	4.7-11.9
Estimated total biomass C loss (teragrams)	2	27-58	29-60

and others 2004). This is perhaps one reason why it has been difficult to demonstrate direct losses of SOC following annual grass invasion or conversion to annual grass dysclimax (Gill and Burke 1999, Ogle and others 2004, Bradley and others 2006). Most of these studies have examined only the near-surface soil where SOC under annual grasslands is concentrated. The technology for the study of deep SOC remains cumbersome, so that information on this fraction of the C pool is not readily obtained.

Shrubland Degradation and Windblown Dust

Another consequence of anthropogenic disturbance on a landscape scale in arid and semiarid regions is a large increase in the load of windblown dust. This increased dust load results in negative health effects for the human population and also has the potential to exacerbate climate change by causing mountain snow cover to melt more quickly in the spring, reducing yield from the mountain watersheds that are the main source of water for human use. Restoring and managing cold desert shrublands for carbon storage also has the potential to reduce these negative effects of windblown dust by stabilizing the soil surface.

To examine the magnitude of the windblown dust effect, Neff and others (2008) analyzed rates of sediment accumulation in mountain lakes in southwestern Colorado over the last 5000 years. Results showed that the rate of sediment accumulation peaked very sharply in the second half of the Nineteenth Century, a time frame that corresponds with a massive increase in the scope and intensity of livestock grazing in the arid and semiarid regions to the west. The authors further demonstrated using mineralogical analysis that these sediments were not of local origin, but instead represented deposits of windblown dust from the valleys to the west of the watershed.

Livestock grazing and other human activities that disturb the surface soils of deserts generate dust by removing herbaceous plant cover and, often more importantly, through destruction of the cryptobiotic soil crust that stabilizes the surface in many desert regions (Neff and others 2005). These effects are further exacerbated by annual grass invasion and associated frequent fire. Annual grass cover provides some protection against wind erosion relative to bare ground but it prevents cryptobiotic crust recovery, resulting in increased dust generation, especially when these areas burn. The Milford Flat fire of 2007 was the largest wildfire in Utah's history (Miller and others 2011). An enduring legacy of this fire has been massive dust storms that have swept windborne dust into the urban areas of northern Utah and onto mountain watersheds. In addition to direct impacts on air quality and human health, this windborne dust exacerbates the effects of climate change through its effect on snow melt rates.

Snow cover has the highest albedo (light reflecting ability) of any natural land surface, and this ability to reflect light also reduces heat loading and melting rate (Flanner and others 2009). When particulate matter, such as dust or carbonaceous pollutants, is deposited along with snow, it lowers the albedo of the remaining snow cover as the snow melts because the dark particles are concentrated near the surface of the snow. While it is true that particulate matter in the air lowers insolation and heat load on snow at the surface, this "dimming" effect is more than compensated by the reduction in snow albedo from these particles once they are deposited ("darkening effect"). This effect is especially pronounced in spring when large areas are snow covered and incident solar radiation is high. Flanner and others (2009) found that progressively earlier snow melt dates observed in Europe over the last few decades are almost as much due to this snow darkening effect of pollutants from fossil fuel combustion as to long-term increases in spring temperature caused by global warming. Moreover, the positive feedback from earlier snow melt caused by darkening created warmer spring temperatures independently of the effects of global warming, thus compounding the problem.

Though not as potent a darkening agent as carbonaceous pollutants, windborne dust can also significantly increase snow melt rates (Painter and others 2007). Spring dust storms in the desert region to the west of the mountain study area in southwestern Colorado resulted in several dust-on-snow deposition events per year, with more events in a drought year (2006, eight events) than in an average moisture year (2005, four events). These dust-on-snow deposition events resulted in snow cover durations that were decreased by 18 to 35 days. Shortened snow cover duration has measurable ecological impacts at the local scale in alpine and subalpine areas (Steltzer and others 2009). More importantly, it also has the potential to significantly reduce water yields from mountain watersheds. Given that most of the agricultural and culinary water supplies in the Interior West are closely tied to mountain snowfall, and that the thickness and duration of the snow pack and its rate of melting have a strong impact on the ability to harvest this water supply, the fact that desert dust storms can shorten the duration of snow cover in mountainous areas downwind by a month or more should be of grave management concern (Painter and others 2007).

Managing Desert Shrublands for Climate Change Mitigation

Successful restoration of cold desert shrubland ecosystems on a large scale and subsequent management for ecosystem integrity could help to mitigate the adverse effects of climate change both through increased C sequestration and decreased effects of windblown dust. Climate change mitigation through desert shrubland management has the goal of maintaining or restoring adapted native shrubland vegetation that produces maximum carbon storage in the long term by exploiting all available niches, thereby maximizing productivity. It is likely that the vegetation that evolved in response to the selective forces in a particular environment will be best able to exploit its resources. This vegetation includes the woody shrub overstory, the herbaceous understory, and also the cryptobiotic crust community that occupies the interspaces. All these components are essential for long-term stability, including surface stability, and sustained carbon storage capacity.

An intact shrubland community is much more likely to be resilient in the face of continued climate change and other disturbances than "shrub plantations" analogous to the tree plantations being proposed and implemented for carbon sequestration. Emphasizing shrubs to the exclusion of other community components in a short-sighted effort to maximize carbon storage would probably result in vegetation that would require intensive management to be sustained. Annual grass weed invasion of the bare interspaces and consequent shrub loss through fire would be a constant threat. A more realistic goal, and one that is bound to be more effective in the long term, is to manage for intact shrubland communities that can rebound even from disturbances such as prolonged drought and fire without high risk of conversion to annual grass dysclimax. Both prevention of further degradation and restoration of degraded shrublands are part of this management scenario.

Cold desert shrublands in the Interior West currently exist in one of three states along a continuum of ecological condition:

(1) Some sites have relatively high-condition shrubland, with native understory and cryptobiotic crust still intact.

(2) Many more sites, perhaps most of the area still occupied by shrubs, are in some intermediate condition, with native perennial understory and/or cryptobiotic crust damaged or absent and with annual weed invasion in the understory. These sites are often at high risk of conversion to the third state.

(3) Loss of the shrub overstory through fire and post-burn dominance by annual grass weeds. Shrublands in these different states present different challenges and opportunities for management for carbon sequestration and windblown dust abatement.

The most important consideration for high-condition shrublands is prevention of degradation. This means keeping the cryptobiotic crust and the herbaceous understory in the best possible condition, which minimizes the probability of massive annual grass expansion after fire and maintains surface stability to minimize dust generation. Direct protection from invasion, for example, by controlling nearby weed infestations that could be propagule sources, is another way to maintain ecosystem integrity, as is providing priority protection in the event of wildfire. Even though occasional wildfire was a natural occurrence before settlement, especially in sagebrush steppe, protection from burning under current conditions is a top priority because of the threat of annual grass invasion.

Shrublands in intermediate condition often present more problems than opportunities in terms of improvement for climate change mitigation. Protection from further disturbance may result in little improvement in these shrublands. Loss of the seed bank of native understory species limits recruitment, and the cryptobiotic crust often cannot recover because of the heavy litter from annual grass invasion. In addition, a common occurrence, especially in sagebrush steppe, is shrub stand thickening or shrub canopy closure in response to loss of understory vegetation. The site at Jungo (Bradley and others 2006) seems to represent such a scenario. Sagebrush standing biomass was very high, and the understory was completely dominated by cheatgrass. Such a site could be described as "walking dead" in terms of the risk of conversion to annual grassland because a shrub-destroying fire is nearly inevitable. Natural shrub recovery after fire is often nil for dominant shrub species such as sagebrush and shadscale (*Atriplex confertifolia*), which cannot resprout after fire and rarely establish from seed in areas of high annual grass competition. Active management of shrublands with an understory dominated by cheatgrass will necessitate the development of effective tools to eliminate cheatgrass; reduce shrub cover, if necessary; establish understory species; and encourage cryptobiotic crust recovery, all with a minimum of surface disturbance. At present, such tools are largely unavailable.

Shrublands that have been converted to annual grass dysclimax communities have usually been given up for lost because of the futility of seeding into dense annual grass stands. But these annual grass dysclimax communities present the most hopeful scenario for increased carbon sequestration. If restoration of these communities is successful, substantial gains in carbon storage can be achieved. There should therefore be a strong emphasis on research aimed at increasing restoration success in areas that no longer support perennial vegetation. Many of the same tools needed to improve degraded shrublands will be needed to restore areas that no longer support shrubs, namely innovative methods for annual grass weed control and new approaches to improving seeding success in environments with low and variable precipitation. At present, many seedings in these environments fail, which may seem discouraging. But this points the way toward developing new approaches that, while they may be more expensive up front, could result in greatly improved seeding success and therefore a much better cost:benefit ratio for shrubland restoration in the long run. It is our challenge as researchers to develop these new approaches. With climate change mitigation as the goal rather than management of these shrublands for consumptive uses such as livestock grazing, scientists will be inspired to think outside the box and devise the methodology needed to make Interior West shrublands a significant C sink. This includes changing the paradigms for the timing of seedings to better take advantage of changed seasonal rainfall patterns. Even better, along with our partners in management, we will have the opportunity to simultaneously enhance the many other ecosystem services and amenity resources provided by these landscapes.

Research Needs and Activities

Scientists in the GSD Program at RMRS are actively involved in many areas of research that directly address the problems of desert shrubland restoration, and the potential exists for expansion into new areas of research that could yield a high return in useful knowledge for a relatively small investment of resources. Some examples of innovative research projects underway that will improve chances of restoration success are:

- Development of novel biocontrol strategies for eliminating the seed bank of cheatgrass and other invasive annual grasses through the use of augmentative mycoherbicidal approaches with naturally occurring fungal pathogens and endophytes.

- Development of classical biocontrol strategies with specialized herbivores from the native range for control of secondary dicot weeds, such as knapweeds and rush skeletonweed.

- Development of the knowledge and technology needed to produce seed supplies for diverse native species, including nontraditional early seral species such as annual and perennial forbs and shrubs that readily establish on disturbances.

- Increased understanding of the importance of seed microsites and development of new site preparation and seeding technology to increase probability of seeding success.

- Understanding of the biological importance of microbiotic soil crusts and development of technology for soil crust restoration.

- Knowledge of patterns of genetic variation in traits important to climatic adaptation in key species such as big sagebrush to better match seed source to current and future site conditions.

- Understanding of successional processes in desert shrublands, grasslands, and woodlands in order to separate the effects of climate change from the effects of disturbance regime and to potentially predict stable future plant communities to use as targets for restoration.

Some examples of new areas of research where rapid progress could be made if resources were made available are:

- Determination of limiting factors that restrict successful seedling emergence and establishment in restoration seedings in cold desert ecosystems, including soil crusting, absence of safe sites, pathogen attack, absence of beneficial symbionts, use of inappropriate seed sources, and uncontrolled competition from preexisting weeds, and devising strategies to overcome these limiting factors.

- Genetic characterization of a suite of native species potentially useful in cold desert shrubland restoration in terms of traits important in climatic adaptation in order to develop seed supplies specifically adapted to establish and persist in stable future plant communities on different site types.
- Development and field testing of seed sources for this suite of native species using a new set of criteria centered on ability to establish, compete, and persist on disturbed sites rather than on traditional agronomic criteria such as forage production and seed production.

Literature Cited

Aanderud, Z. T., J. H. Richards, T. Svejcar and J. J. James. 2010. A shift in seasonal rainfall reduces soil organic carbon storage in a cold desert. Ecosystems 13: 673-682.

Bird, S. B., J. E. Herrick, M. M. Wander and S. F. Wright. 2002. Spatial heterogeneity of aggregate stability and soil carbon in semi-arid rangeland. Environmental Pollution 116: 445-455.

Bradley, B. A., R. A. Houghton, J. F. Mustard and S. P. Hamburg. 2006. Invasive grass reduces aboveground carbon stocks in shrublands of the western US. Global Change Biology 12: 1815-1822.

Bradley, B. A. and J. F. Mustard. 2005. Identifying land cover variability distinct from land cover change: cheatgrass in the Great Basin. Remote Sensing of Environment 94: 204-213.

Brewster, Jr., S. R. 1968. A study of the effectiveness of precipitation in the salt desert shrub type. Thesis, Brigham Young University, Provo, Utah.

Brooks, M. L., C. M. D'Antonio, D. M. Richardson, J. B. Grace and others. 2004. Effects of invasive alien plants on fire regimes. BioScience 54: 677-688.

Brown, J., J. Angerer, S. W. Salley, R. Blaisdell and J. W. Stuth. 2010. Improving estimates of rangeland carbon sequestration potential in the U.S. Southwest. Rangeland Ecology and Management 63: 147-154.

Canadell J., R. B. Jackson, J. R. Ehleringer, H. A. Mooney, O. E. Sala and E. D. Schulze. 1996. Maximum rooting depth of vegetation types at the global scale. Oecologia 108: 583-595.

Flanner, M. G., C. S. Zender, P. G. Hess, N. M. Mahowald and others. 2009. Springtime warming and reduced snow cover from carbonaceous particles. Atmospheric Chemistry and Physics 9: 2481-2497.

Follett, R. F. and D. A. Reed. 2010. Soil carbon sequestration in grazing lands: social benefits and policy implications. Rangeland Ecology and Management 63: 4-15.

Gill, R. A. and I. C. Burke. 1999. Ecosystem consequences of plant life form changes at three sites in the semiarid United States. Oecologia 121: 551-563.

Hunt, E. A., R. D. Kelly, W. K. Smith, J. T. Fahnestock, J. M. Welker and W. A. Reiners. 2004. Estimation of carbon sequestration by combining remote sensing and net ecosystem exchange data for northern mixed-grass prairie and sagebrush–steppe ecosystems. Environmental Management Vol. 33, Supplement 1: pp. S432-S441.

Jackson, R. B., J. L. Banner, E. G. Jobbagy, W. T. Pockman and D. H. Wall. 2002. Ecosystem carbon loss with woody plant invasion of grasslands. Nature 418: 623-626.

Jackson, R. B., J. Canadell, J. R. Ehleringer, H. A. Mooney, O. E. Sala and E. D. Schulze. 1996. A global analysis of root distributions for terrestrial biomes. Oecologia 108: 389-411.

Jackson, R. B., E. G. Jobbagy, R. Avissar, S. W. Roy and others. 2005. Trading water for carbon with biological carbon sequestration. Science 310: 1944-1947.

Janzen, H. H. 2004. Carbon cycling in earth systems-a soil science perspective. Agriculture, Ecosystems and Environment 104: 399-417.

Jobbagy, E. G. and R. B. Jackson. 2000. The vertical distribution of soil organic carbon and its relation to climate and vegetation. Ecological Applications 10: 423-36.

Miller, M., R. Reynolds, M. Reheis, H. Goldstein and J. Yount. 2011. Wind erosion and post-fire rehabilitation strategies—lessons from the Milford Flat fire. Proceedings of the Sixteenth Wildland Shrub Symposium: Threats to Shrubland Ecosystem Integrity. May 18-20, 2010. Logan, Utah.

Neff, J. C., P. Ballentyne, G. L. Farmer, N. M. Mahowald and others. 2008. Increasing eolian dust deposition in the western United States linked to human activity. Nature Geoscience 1: 189-195.

Neff, J. C., R. L. Reynolds, J. Belnap and P. Lamothe. 2005. Multi-decadal impacts of grazing on soil physical and biogeochemical properties in southeast Utah. Ecological Applications 15: 87-95.

Norton, J. B., T. A. Monaco, J. M. Norton, D. A. Johnson and T. A. Jones. 2004. Soil morphology and organic matter dynamics under cheatgrass and sagebrush-steppe plant communities. Journal of Arid Environments 57: 445-466.

Ogle, S. M., D. Dojima and W. A. Reiners. 2004. Modeling the impact of exotic annual brome grasses on soil organic carbon storage in a northern mixed-grass prairie. Biological Invasions 6: 365-377.

Painter, T. H., A. P. Barrett, C. C. Landry, J. C. Neff and others. 2007. Impact of disturbed desert soils on duration of mountain snow cover. Geophysical Research Letters 34: L12502.

Schuman, G. E., H. H. Janzen and J. E. Herrick. 2002. Soil carbon dynamics and potential carbon sequestration by rangelands. Environmental Pollution 116: 391-396.

Steltzer, H., C. Landry, T. H. Painter, J. Anderson, and E. Ayres. 2009. Biological consequences of earlier snowmelt from desert dust deposition in alpine landscapes. Proceedings of the National Academy of Science 106: 11629-11634.

Svejcar, T., R. Angell, J. A. Bradford, W. Dugas and others. 2008. Carbon fluxes on North American rangelands. Rangeland Ecology and Management 61: 465-474.

Van Auken, O. W. 2000. Shrub invasions of North American semiarid grasslands. Annual Review of Ecology and Systematics 31: 197-215.

Zhang, X., F. W. Zwiers, G. C. Hegerl, F. H. Lambert and others. 2007. Detection of human influence on Twentieth-Century precipitation trends. Nature 448: 461-465.

Chapter 3

Climate Change and Arthropods: Pollinators, Herbivores, and Others

Sandra L. Brantley[1] and Paulette L. Ford[2]

[1] Museum of Southwestern Biology, University of New Mexico, Albuquerque, New Mexico

[2] U.S. Forest Service, Rocky Mountain Research Station; Grassland, Shrubland, and Desert Ecosystems Program; Forestry Sciences Laboratory, Albuquerque, New Mexico

Executive Summary

The Interior West is rich in arthropod diversity because of its varied topography, which provides a wide range of elevations and levels of isolation for these small animals (Parmenter and others 1995). Some taxa are known rather well, such as butterflies and tiger beetles, but we have little information on many groups, which are known only from a few locations although they are probably more widespread. Arthropods live at large to small scales (e.g., migrating butterflies crossing countries to habitat specialists on rock outcrops or sand dunes). They may be generalists or specialists, vagile or sedentary, and have immature life stages that are similar or different from the adult (Triplehorn and Johnson 2005).

Predicted climate changes for the interior of North America, particularly the western portion, include:

- drier summers,
- increased precipitation outside the summer season, and
- increased frequency of extreme events such as heat waves.

Arthropods are ectothermic, so the temperature increases associated with global warming directly affect their development time, usually by decreasing the time needed for immature stages to become adults. This allows not only more generations per year in a given habitat, but it also opens new habitat for colonization because minimum temperatures no longer exclude arthropods (Crozier 2003; Robinet and Roques 2010).

The ecological roles of arthropods are important, even critical, and should be included when monitoring and predicting effects of global warming. Although knowledge of many arthropod species is lacking (Cane and Tepedino 2001), some groups have been studied in many areas and for long periods, such as butterflies, grasshoppers, some bees, and some ants. While these groups do not represent all arthropods, data about them give us a place to start in understanding their responses to climate change.

Research needs for arthropods include:

- There is a lack of data for many species and scientists are urged to develop long-term monitoring efforts with as many taxa as possible. There is also a great need to identify species interactions as climate changes, whether between insects and host plants or among insects and their competitors and predators.
- Several studies have shown the value of museum collections and data from natural history surveys. There is increasing need and emphasis from funding sources on

grantees to publish specimen holdings online, including images, in order to build a more comprehensive understanding of species distributions.

- In the western United States, there is much state and Federal land that could be used for surveys and other interdisciplinary efforts. Opportunities are needed for collaborations among state and Federal agencies, universities, long-term ecological sites, state natural history surveys, and other natural heritage programs.

Introduction

The large number of arthropod (insects and their relatives) species in the world often means they are underrepresented in diversity assessments because of their "challenging taxonomy," meaning that they can be hard to identify and many species have yet to be described. The Interior West is rich in arthropod diversity because of its varied topography, which provides a wide range of elevations and levels of isolation for these small animals (Parmenter and others 1995). Some taxa are known rather well, such as butterflies and tiger beetles, but we have little information on many groups, which are known only from a few locations although they are probably more widespread.

The ecological roles of arthropods are important, even critical, and should be included when monitoring and predicting effects of global warming. Important ecological "services" provided by insects include:

- Pollination
- Herbivory
- Seed dispersal
- Soil aeration and mixing
- Plant/animal decomposition
- Predation/parasitism
- Food source for many vertebrate species

They live at large to small scales (e.g., migrating butterflies crossing countries to habitat specialists on rock outcrops or sand dunes). They may be generalists or specialists, vagile or sedentary, and have immature life stages that are similar or different from the adult (Triplehorn and Johnson 2005).

Arthropods are ectothermic, so the temperature increases associated with global warming directly affect their development time, usually by decreasing the time needed for immature stages to become adults. This allows not only more generations per year in a given habitat, but it opens new habitat for colonization because minimum temperatures no longer exclude arthropods (Crozier 2003; Robinet and Roques 2010).

Many of these species depend on plants as food for immature and adult stages; an expected problem is the different effects of climate change on plants and insects, resulting in mismatches in timing between insects and their host plants (e.g., budburst, flowering time, and seed production). Species living at high elevations may continue moving up until there is no place left to go, and specialists may lose habitat or other resources to climate change and other effects such as land use change.

Some of the current shifts in distributions give the impression that arthropods can accommodate temperature increases, but they cannot continue shifting indefinitely, especially if projected temperature increases become larger. In addition, it is important to remember that not all species will respond the same way to changes in temperature, precipitation, and/or shifts in vegetation. We present research from western North America when possible and expand to Europe, the Northern Hemisphere, or the globe when no more specific information is available.

Key Issues

Predicted climate changes for the interior of North America, particularly the western portion include:

- Drier summers
- Increased precipitation outside the summer season
- Increased frequency of extreme events, such as heat waves (Easterling and others 2000; Seager and others 2007; Diffenbaugh and Ashfaq 2010)

Over the Twentieth Century, average temperatures have increased about 0.6 °C, not only as higher maximum temperatures but also as higher minimum temperatures (Easterling and others 2000; Parmesan 2006) (i.e., there may be less difference between daily highs and lows). Seager and others (2007) suggested that one cause for these changes is a shift in atmospheric circulation cells toward the poles that is allowing sub-tropical dry zones to expand northward. Even if greenhouse gas levels do not increase above current levels, overall temperature increases will probably be 2 to 4 °C (Diffenbaugh and Ashfaq 2010).

Throughout the Midwest and the Southwest, the number of extreme precipitation events has increased over the Twentieth Century (Easterling and others 2000). Diffenbaugh and Ashfaq (2010) reported model results looking toward 2039, predicting increased winter precipitation but drying during the summer, so that soil moisture will decrease and evapotranspiration will increase. The authors also found that the Southwest is likely to experience summer heat waves every second or third year. Drought events from the El Nino Southern Oscillation system will also continue to occur and make the region drier still during those years (Seager and others 2007).

Within these broad-scale predictions, local conditions will vary, especially in arid regions where large daily temperature changes and variable precipitation virtually define the area (Noy-Meir 1973). Western North America contains numerous mountain ranges, which collect precipitation and nutrients such as nitrogen (N) and phosphorus (P) from air pollution. The complex topography can either retain these resources or transport them far from the source through watersheds (Seastedt and others 2004).

Increased winter precipitation in southeastern Arizona over 20+ years (Brown and others 1997) has resulted in species change in vegetation, insects and small mammal communities. Shrub establishment was improved so that they became a larger proportion of the vegetation cover, while grass species declined. Such a pattern had also been attributed to grazing effects or drought, but those factors were not involved at Brown and others' (1997) site. The number of arthropod species present at the site did not change significantly but species composition did. The seed harvester ants *Pogonomyrmex rugosus* and *P. desertorum*, originally dominant species, became locally extinct, while *Pheidole xerophila*, also seed collectors, did not change, showing the independent response of species, even within one subfamily (Myrmicinae).

Chapin and others (2001) examined possible impacts on biodiversity across world biomes from five drivers: climate change, land use change, N deposition, biotic exchange (e.g., invasive species), and increased atmospheric CO_2. The authors found that land use change produced impacts as large as or larger than climate change for most biomes (results summarized in Sala and others 2000). In many areas, land use change has already altered biodiversity extensively, so that climate change has not produced much additional change. As an example for deserts, Huenneke (2001) described the Chihuahuan Desert of southern New Mexico as an area further desertified by agricultural and grazing use. For grasslands, Sala (2001) noted that conversion to agriculture is the major impact and that climate change effects are expected to be moderate. Other human-caused factors of importance to grasslands are pollution from nearby cities and loss of water to cities and agriculture.

In desert systems, increased precipitation is usually thought of as beneficial, but if it arrives at the wrong time of year and as extreme events, as is predicted by Easterling and others (2000), the effects can be harmful, washing away soils, and ruining seed banks and insect eggs, and affecting water quality in rivers and lakes. In particular, specialist arthropods will be impacted because their host plants or substrates tend to be patchy in distribution in arid systems (Huenneke 2001).

Arthropods vary widely in their abilities to avoid or tolerate these kinds of changes. The distributions of many of the thousands of species are poorly understood, making it difficult to know how or if they will be affected by land use and changing climate. Because insects are ectothermic, temperature increases that most commonly character- ize climate change will undoubtedly affect them in various ways such as more rapid development through life stages, more generations per year, and an increase in favorable habitat that was formerly too cold.

There may also be contraction of species' ranges as some areas become too hot (Robinet and Roques 2010). If species are forced to move out of habitats that have be- come too hot, they are seen as "rescued" by having moved northward or up in elevation (Parmesan 2006). However, a given species may not be able to maintain populations in these new areas because of substrate or food needs and because there will already be other species established there. It is not clear that the shifting populations are undergoing genetic change over the short term to better fit them to the new habitats (Parmesan 2006). A likely negative impact will be a mismatch or asynchrony with host plants for lar- val growth or maintenance of adults during their reproduction periods (Parmesan 2007; Robinet and Roques 2010).

Following, we discuss current knowledge of representatives of pollinators, herbivores, omnivores, and detritivores (scavengers).

Pollinators: Butterflies

By far, the best known pollinators are butterflies because of their rather large size, relative ease of field identification, and attractiveness to the general public. They have become the representatives of all insects in climate change studies because datasets are available for them (Inouye 2007). However, butterflies do not necessarily respond as other insect taxa do (Hickling and others 2006), highlighting a need for monitoring stud- ies of other groups.

In the western United States, many studies have been done for the Pacific Coast (e.g., McLaughlin and others 2002; Crozier 2003; Preston and others 2008), but fewer have focused on the interior of the continent. In two mountain ranges in Nevada, Fleishman and MacNally (2003) studied species richness of butterflies from 1996 to 2002, test- ing how well a series of short sampling periods or "snapshots" would detect possible climate change effects. Their results showed that richness between the mountain ranges and even among sites within a range were greater than any changes across the six years. Species living successfully in arid climates already had life history strategies for habitat variability in abiotic and biotic resources (what the authors called "tough-tested"). In an earlier study modeling species changes in six mountain ranges (one in California, five in Nevada), Fleishman and others (2001) used a climate scenario that increased tem- peratures enough to move plant species up in elevation by 500 m. The butterflies were expected to move as much also, assuming their dispersal capabilities were good. Under a moderate temperature increase, the Great Basin area would probably not lose many but- terfly species, but each mountain range had its own patterns of species richness making it impossible to generalize outcomes to other areas.

Climate change patterns not only show an increase in maximum temperatures but in minimum temperatures as well, so that some areas experience fewer days of freezing or very cold weather. These minimum temperatures are increasing at a faster rate than the maximum temperatures (Easterling and others 2000; Parmesan 2006) and are important to monitor for their effects on arthropod distributions. Crozier (2003) tracked the northward movement of the sachem skipper (*Atalopedes campestris*) from its historical range in the southern and western United States and Mexico as it moved up the Pacific Coast to Eugene, Oregon, in 1967; Portland, Oregon, in 1985; Tri-Cities (Richland, Kennewick, and Pasco) area of Washington in 1993; and Yakima, Washington, in 1999. Her work showed that the skipper is limited by low temperature and can readily take advantage of increasing temperatures to move into new areas. The host plants for this species are grasses (Brock and Kaufman 2003), including crabgrass and Bermuda grass that are planted in cities and towns, so not only climate change but also conversion of land to urban settings favor the spread of this species. The author encouraged conservationists to not only save current habitat but also areas that may become suitable in the future.

A European butterfly dataset from the past 30 to 100 years found similar shifts (Parmesan and others 1999). For species whose entire range was known, the authors found 22 extended distributions to the north, 2 extended distributions to the south, and 11 remained stable. These changes reflect the 0.8 °C increase in temperature over the last century, suggesting that a further increase of 2 to 4 °C could leave some species with no further possible movement northward or upward in elevation. Poor dispersers would be particularly at risk because of the added factor of increasing habitat fragmentation, leaving them in shrinking "islands" of climatically suitable habitat.

Forister and others (2010) investigated the combined effects of climate change and habitat loss, the two most important drivers of species change (Sala and others 2000), on butterflies in the Sierra Nevada in California. The data covered 159 species over 35 years and an elevation gradient of 0 to 2775 m. The elevational gradient allowed the authors to determine whether climate or land use produced species changes. At lower elevations where human populations were higher, the greater impact on butterflies came from habitat loss. At intermediate and high elevations, climate change was the likely cause of species change. At middle elevations, species moved up, and at the highest elevations (alpine), habitat specialists declined as conditions warmed, but overall species and abundance increased because of the influx of intermediate elevation species. An unexpected result was the decline in ruderal species at low elevations. These widespread species are generally predicted to do well in the face of climate change. In this case, however, habitat destruction was severe enough to remove both larval host plants and nectar sources for adults, showing that even generalist species may also need conservation protection in some areas. The authors suggested that one reason generalists do well in Europe is that they have had centuries to adapt to land use change; what we see there today are the species that are successful in highly disturbed and managed habitats.

Generalist butterfly species were predicted to do well in Canada, based on models by White and Kerr (2007), for 102 species. The authors built a long-term dataset from museum records (some extending back to the Nineteenth Century) and added geographic features such as elevation and changes in land use, temperature, and precipitation. Temperature and elevation were the best predictors of butterfly species richness; precipitation was an important factor only in the driest areas, the prairies of south-central Canada. As is common in other studies, the authors found a decline in specialists due more to loss of forest habitat than climate change. High richness was found in two areas but for different reasons: in high elevations, habitat heterogeneity provided many suitable microhabitats; but in lower elevations, which are dominated by people, diversity was high because of land use change. The increased expansion of already widespread generalist species has led to what the authors called a "homogenization" of species across the southern part of the country. Though the diversity is high, it is being maintained by disturbance and agriculture.

From a pair of studies, we can compare two closely related butterflies, the Quino checkerspot (*Euphydryas editha quino*) and the Bay checkerspot (*Euphydryas editha bayensis*) in California. The Quino checkerspot is a well-studied endangered subspecies that is a habitat specialist in the shrublands of southern California. Preston and others (2008) modeled its possible population changes under temperature and precipitation changes. With a temperature increase of 0.6 °C and no change in precipitation, the butterfly would probably do well. Under temperature increases of 1.7 and 2.8 °C and precipitation changes of -50% or +150%, suitable habitat would be reduced by 98 to 100%. In this Mediterranean-type habitat, drought can be common, so the modeled reduction in precipitation would understandably produce habitat loss, but it is interesting to note that precipitation increases also virtually wiped out the habitat. In both cases, vegetation species and cover would presumably change so much that the butterfly could no longer be supported. Larval host plants are dwarf plantain, penstemon, and Indian paintbrush (Brock and Kaufman 2003). As a specialist, it is unlikely to move readily to grasslands or forests even if they are relatively close.

The Bay checkerspot butterfly (*Euphydryas editha bayensis*) is also a specialist on the same plants as the Quino checkerspot (Brock and Kaufman 2003) but lives in grasslands of the San Francisco Bay area of California. McLaughlin and others (2002) investigated the factors leading to the extinction of two populations (in 1991 and 1998) of this threatened subspecies. The most important factor was a change in the pattern of precipitation: increased variability after 1971, including more severe weather events. The larvae and their host plants were also affected, with a shortened period of overlap and a resulting increase in larval mortality. A second impact on the populations was the loss of metapopulations nearby to recolonize the area because of habitat fragmentation and urban growth.

Pollinators: Bees

Although bees are major pollinators of many wild and managed plants, they are less well-known than butterflies (Inouye 2007); many species are difficult to identify in the field. In North America, there are few data to document a decline in these pollinators because of high interannual variation in abundance, the effort and expense needed to adequately monitor and identify bee diversity, and our lack of knowledge about suitable habitat for many species (Cane and Tepedino 2001). Studies show varying amounts of response to climate or disturbance impacts; each local area has its own combination of factors that influence richness and abundance.

In 1997, the U.S. National Research Council published a report on the status of pollinators in North America in agricultural settings. Along with the honeybee (*Apis mellifera*), common introduced species that are extensively managed for crop production include several bumblebee species (*Bombus* spp.) and a leafcutter bee (*Megachile rotundata*). All are susceptible to parasites, pathogens, and pesticides, as are native species. In addition, these introduced generalist species frequently outcompete native species by reducing overall nectar availability in some areas. At present, the authors concluded that the effects of transgenic corn with incorporated *Bacillus thuringiensis* (Bt) poses a small threat to native bee species because Bt targets herbivorous caterpillars. However, a greater cause for concern is that crops with increased herbicide resistance allow farmers to treat their fields for weeds without damaging their crop species. Those weeds are nectar sources for many native bee species. If more cropland is developed with these resistant plants, a possible indirect result will be the loss of native pollinators on non-crop plants.

Little information about bees is available for western North America (Cane and Tepedino 2001), but two studies in the Rocky Mountains of Colorado illustrate shifts in the relationships between bumblebees and their host plants. Inouye (2007) has been monitoring bumblebees for several decades in the area surrounding Rocky Mountain Biological Laboratory in Crested Butte. At least one bumblebee species has moved upward some 457 m in elevation with a corresponding 1.4 °C increase in temperature during this time. Further temperature increases of 2 to 4 °C are predicted for the western United States over the next 30 years (Diffenbaugh and Ashfaq 2010), and it is not clear if bumblebees will be able to keep up with such change. Inouye (2007) noted that host plants may not be moving at the same rate as their pollinators (also in Parmesan 2007) because their needs also include soil moisture and substrate type.

In the second study in western Colorado, Thomson (2010) studied blooming and fruit set of a lily, *Erythronium grandiflorum*, which is pollinated by bumblebees. Some members of the lily population start blooming early as soon as snow melts, which may vary by a month from one year to the next. There were occasional frosts even after snowmelt, and even when early and mid-period blooming individuals survived frosts, they were often limited by the small number of pollinators available (they are ectothermic and limited by very cold temperatures). Later-blooming individuals had the advantage of a greater number of bumblebee colonies. Thomson reported that the lack of synchrony between lily and bumblebees has worsened in recent years. If winter precipitation patterns and extreme storm events increase as predicted (Easterling and others 2000), early blooming lilies will be severely limited by frosts and the lack of bumblebees.

In Carlinville, Illinois, Marlin and LaBerge (2001) compared bee data from surveys in the 1970s with records from Charles Robertson's surveys from 1884 to 1916. Of the 214 species that Robertson collected, Marlin and LaBerge found 140 (65%) in their surveys, as well as 14 species that Robertson did not collect. Since the 1880s, the area has lost and gained forest cover and has increased the amount of land converted from prairie to agriculture, yet the bee fauna was largely intact. The authors attributed this to a diversity of remnant habitats between agricultural fields. Winfree and others (2009) for bees, and Forister and others (2010) for butterflies, showed that insects managed relatively well below a threshold of extreme disturbance; the Illinois bee fauna in the 1970s had perhaps not experienced such severe disturbance. These studies show that in some cases, pollinators can cope with low to moderate levels of disturbance.

A more recent European study documented broader patterns and explanations for declines in bees. Biesmeijer and others (2006) took advantage of a good historical record of bee distributions in Britain and the Netherlands to compare changes in species richness in 10 km x 10 km map grid cells before and after 1980. For grid cells with enough data, bees in Britain declined in 52% of cells and increased in 10%, while in the Netherlands, bees declined in 67% of cells and increased in only 4%. The species with the largest declines were specialists on certain flowers or habitats, had only one generation per year, and did not migrate. The authors also found that plant species with specialist pollinators declined, wind-pollinated species increased, and self-pollinating species showed no change. In Britain, species increases were for those that were already widespread (as in White and Kerr [2007] for Canadian butterflies). In both countries, species became less evenly distributed, that is, fewer species made up a larger proportion of those present.

Winfree and others (2009) used datasets from the world in a meta-analysis of bees and human disturbance. Although their questions did not include climate change, their work showed the importance of land use change in altering bee communities. The biological aspects they looked at were managed versus wild species and solitary versus social species, grouping genera into *Apis*, *Bombus*, and other. Disturbance factors included habitat loss/fragmentation, pesticide use, fire, deforestation, and grazing. Habitat loss was the primary factor reducing bee species and abundance, but only when such loss was extreme. This was also the case with Sierra Nevada butterflies (Forister and others 2010) and their results agree with the predictions of Sala and others (2000). By dividing the bee data by genus and life history features, it became clear that disturbance impacts were varied (e.g., tree-nesting species would be negatively affected by deforestation, but the increase in open land might favor ground-nesting species). However, even with the combined power of multiple studies, it is not possible to extrapolate these results to all bees in all areas.

Pollinators: Flies

The true flies, Order Diptera, are a hyperdiverse group with over 21,000 species (86% endemic) in the Nearctic (Bio Systematic Database of World Diptera). They are usually thought of as disease vectors (mosquitoes), crop pests (leafminers), or livestock pests (stable flies), but they are important parasitoids of other arthropods and are pollinators as well. As pollinators, many species are generalists, but the syndrome called sapromyophily (flowers producing appearances or scents of decaying flesh as attractants) shows that plant-fly interactions have existed for long periods to produce such specializations (Kearns 2001). Flies are common at high elevations, pollinating a variety of arctic and alpine plants (Kearns 2001). Although they are often not the target of studies of plant-insect interactions in these habitats, large numbers of individuals may be collected but not prepared or identified because of time/budget constraints. Their identification can be difficult, but depositing specimens in museums can provide material for future research. Syrphidae, also known as flower flies or hoverflies, is a family of common and important pollinators (Triplehorn and Johnson 2005). In Britain and the Netherlands, Biesmeijer and others (2006) studied syrphid fly records before and after 1980 in 10 km x 10 km map grid cells as previously discussed for bees. In Britain, syrphid richness increased in 25% of cells but decreased in 33%, while in the Netherlands, richness increased in 34% of cells and decreased in 17%. The authors interpreted these changes as shifts in species' distributions in many cases. The study showed larger declines of specialists and those with only one generation per year. Compared with bees in the same study, the syrphid flies did not decline as much, perhaps in part because their larvae are more varied in food sources (some are predators, others are detritivores, and others are herbivores, while bee larvae feed only on pollen and nectar) (Triplehorn and Johnson 2005).

Herbivores

Two important groups of insects that feed on foliage are grasshoppers (Orthoptera) and moths and butterflies (Lepidoptera). Grasshoppers feed on foliage in all life stages, while lepidopterans feed on foliage in the larval or caterpillar stage. As adults, moths and butterflies are often important pollinators; (butterflies are discussed in the "Pollinators" section). There is little information on responses of moth pollinators to climate change. In Missouri, Forkner and others (2008) studied 15 families of moths whose caterpillars feed on oak leaves. Among these species were those with one generation per year or several, seasonal feeders or those feeding most of the year, and those that were mobile or that fed in leaf rolls or mines. The study questions involved variability in population density as a way of predicting which life history patterns might be more vulnerable to climate change. Those with the highest variability were spring feeders that were not mobile, suggesting that they may be most vulnerable to a mismatch in timing between caterpillar development and oak budburst. Species that fed over a longer period and that could move within or between trees would be able to compensate for plant/insect timing mismatches.

Melanoplus sanguinipes, the lesser migratory grasshopper, is found over all of the United States (except for Florida and western California) and into southern Canada (Capinera and Sechrist 1982), and because it can be an outbreak species on agricultural crops, it has been monitored well in some areas. Olfert and Weiss (2006) used records from Saskatchewan from 1931 to the present to model its possible response to climate warming. The most favorable habitats for the grasshopper were mixed grassland and moist mixed grassland. Under conditions of a 2 °C temperature increase, the species became a possible outbreak pest in 17.3% of Canada. With a 4 °C increase, the species colonized new habitats such as the Boreal Plains and Boreal Shield, and Canada's susceptibility to outbreaks increased to 28.2%. With a 6 °C increase, the species would be able to live in most of Canada. In all scenarios, *M. sanguinipes* had the potential to become a major pest in cereal crops.

Nufio and others (2009) made use of a collection of grasshopper data at the Colorado Museum of Natural History by comparing Gordon Alexander's collections from 1958 to 1960 with the present. Alexander surveyed grasshoppers at different elevations in the Rocky Mountains near Boulder, Colorado. Preliminary results from the present-day comparison showed that species are hatching and reaching adulthood 15 to 30 days earlier than in Alexander's time. Work will continue through 2012 (see www.ghopclimate.colorado.edu).

Omnivores: Ants

On a global scale, ants are thermophiles, with highest diversity in the tropics. In North and South America, their richness, both past and present, is well explained by temperature (Dunn and others 2009), but under current climate conditions, fewer species were found than expected in North America. Dunn and others (2009) suggested that current richness represents a loss due to past climate change as far back as the Eocene, after which North America began to cool more than South America. Some North American fossil species represent taxa that are now found only to the south in more tropical habitats. It is likely that increased temperatures will allow not only current species to move north but also allow species that were formerly in North America to return.

In western North America, Kaspari and others (2000) studied ants in numerous habitats: desert shrubland, grassland, coniferous forest, and tundra. They accounted for 70% of ant abundance through positive correlations with temperature, plant productivity, and seasonality. From this, the expectation was that increased regional temperatures would favor the activity and spread of ant species, but the authors suggested that the ants have also benefited from cold winter temperatures through lower metabolic costs. A shorter winter season would increase the amount of time available for foraging but there might not be increased plant productivity, in which case the ants would not recover their energy investment through seed harvesting or predation on herbivorous insects.

Detritivores and Predators

Very little work has been published on the effects of climate change on arthropods that have little impact on human activities. However, in Britain, Hickling and others (2006) compared occurrence records from 1960 to 1975 with those from 1985 to 2000 for many taxa. Species that were included were those found only in southern or lower elevations in Britain in the earlier years to see if they moved northward in the later years. On average, species shifted northward 31 to 60 km or upward 25 km. These shifts were significant for grasshoppers, butterflies, long-horned beetles, ground beetles, soldier beetles, metallic wood-boring beetles, millipedes, isopods, spiders, and dragonflies. Shifts were not significant for lacewings or harvestmen. These taxa cover a range of ecological roles, including predators, detritivores, and herbivores, with implications for local changes in ecosystem processes. Species responded independently; there was no overall pattern within a taxon or trophic group. The species considered here were moving at sometimes different rates than better-monitored species, such as butterflies. We should not assume that information on only a few taxa will be a good substitute for all arthropods.

Synthesis

A number of general patterns emerge from the information presented:

- Land use change (habitat loss/fragmentation) is as important as climate change as a driver for altering insect populations and communities. In some areas, species richness has already been affected by habitat loss, so climate change may not produce much more of an impact.
- Many insects have already expanded northward or upward in elevation in response to the 0.6 °C temperature increase of the last century. An additional increase of 2 to 4 °C as predicted may mean a permanent loss of habitat for some species.
- Many insect species are resilient to low to moderate amounts of disturbance. These changes favor some species and disfavor others.
- The mismatch between insects and their host plants is increasing for some species. Species most at risk are host specialists, active early in the growing season, poor dispersers, and/or have only one generation per year. Generalist species are likely to become even more widespread. There is a lack of information on interactions as a result of species shifting into new areas.
- There are not enough long-term datasets on most insect species. The predictions from models need to be validated with more field data—model results can vary widely. Insect species respond independently to environmental changes, so studying only a few species will not predict what the rest will do. Monitoring must involve interdisciplinary efforts to integrate data on species, climate, and other environmental factors.

Research Needs

- Almost all of the researchers cited in this chapter have noted the lack of data for many species and urged current workers to develop long-term monitoring efforts with as many taxa as possible. There is also a great need to look at species interactions as climate changes, whether between insects and host plants or insects and their competitors and predators.
- Several studies have shown the value of museum collections and data from natural history surveys. There is increasing emphasis from funding sources on grantees to publish specimen holdings online, including images, to build a more comprehensive understanding of species distributions.
- In the western United States, there is much state and Federal land that could be used for surveys and other interdisciplinary efforts. We can create opportunities for collaborations among state and Federal agencies, universities, long-term ecological sites, state natural history surveys, and other natural heritage programs.

Literature Cited

Biesmeijer, J. C., S. P. M. Roberts, M. Reemer, R. Ohlemüller and others. 2006. Parallel declines in pollinators and insect-pollinated plants in Britain and the Netherlands. Science 313: 351-354.

BioSystematic Database of World Diptera. Available: www.sel.barc.usda.gov/Diptera.

Brock, J. P. and K. Kaufman. 2003. Butterflies of North America. New York: Houghton Mifflin.

Brown, J. H., T. J. Valone and C. G. Curtin. 1997. Reorganization of an arid ecosystem in response to recent climate change. Proceedings of the National Academy of Sciences of the United States 94: 9729-9733.

Cane, J. H. and V. J. Tepedino. 2001. Causes and extent of declines among native North American invertebrate pollinators: detection, evidence, and consequences. Conservation Ecology. Available: www.consecol.org/vol5/iss1/art1.

Capinera, J. L. and T. S. Sechrist. 1982. Grasshoppers (Acrididae) of Colorado. Colorado State University Experiment Station, Fort Collins, Bulletin no. 584S: 1-161.

Chapin, F. S., O. E. Sala and E. Huber-Sannwald. 2001. Global biodiversity in a changing environment: Scenarios for the 21st Century. New York: Springer-Verlag.

Crozier, L. 2003. Winter warming facilitates range expansion: cold tolerance of the butterfly *Atalopedes campestris*. Oecologia 135: 648-656.

Diffenbaugh, N. S. and M. Ashfaq. 2010. Intensification of hot extremes in the United States. Geophysical Research Letters 37: L15701, doi:10.1029/2010GL043888.

Dunn, R. R., D. Agosti, A. N. Andersen, X. Arnan and others. 2009. Climatic drivers of hemispheric asymmetry in global patterns of ant species richness. Ecology Letters 12: 324-333.

Easterling, D. R., G. A. Meehl, C. Parmesan, S. A. Changnon, T. R. Karl and L. O. Mearns. 2000. Climate extremes: observations, modeling, and impacts. Science 289: 2068-2074.

Fleishman, E., G. T. Austin and D. D. Murphy. 2001. Biogeography of Great Basin butterflies: revisiting patterns, paradigms, and climate change scenarios. Biological Journal of the Linnean Society 74: 501-515.

Fleishman, E. and R. MacNally. 2003. Distinguishing between signal and noise in faunal responses to environmental change. Global Ecology and Biogeography 12: 395-402.

Forister, M. L., A. C. McCall, N. J. Sanders, J. A. Fordyce and others. 2010. Compounded effects of climate change and habitat alteration shift patterns of butterfly diversity. Proceedings of the National Academy of Sciences 107: 2088-2092.

Forkner, R. E., R. J. Marquis, J. T. Lill and J. Le Corff. 2008. Timing is everything? Phenological synchrony and population variability in leaf-chewing herbivores of *Quercus*. Ecological Entomology 33: 276-285.

Hickling, R., D. B. Roy, J. K. Hill, R. Fox and C. D. Thomas. 2006. The distributions of a wide range of taxonomic groups are expanding polewards. Global Change Biology 12: 450-455.

Huenneke, L. F. 2001. Deserts. Pages 201-222. In: Chapin, F. S., O. E. Sala and E. Huber-Sannwald, eds. Global Biodiversity in a Changing Environment: Scenarios for the 21st Century. New York: Springer-Verlag.

Inouye, D. 2007. Impacts of global warming on pollinators. Wings 30: 24-27.

Kaspari, M., L. Alonso and S. O'Donnell. 2000. Three energy variables predict ant abundance at a geographical scale. Proceedings of the Royal Society B: Biological Sciences 267: 485-489.

Kearns, C. A. 2001. North American dipteran pollinators: assessing their value and conservation status. Conservation Ecology. Available: www.consecol.org/vol5/iss1/art5.

Marlin, J. C. and W. E. LaBerge. 2001. The native bee fauna of Carlinville, Illinois, revisited after 75 years: a case for persistence. Conservation Ecology. Available: www.consecol.org/vol5/iss1/art9.

McLaughlin, J. F., J. H. Hellmann, C. L. Boggs and P. R. Ehrlich. 2002. Climate change hastens population extinctions. Proceedings of the National Academy of Sciences 99: 6070-6074.

National Research Council [NRC]. 2007. Status of Pollinators in North America. Washington, DC: National Academies Press.

Noy-Meir, I. 1973. Desert ecosystems: environment and producers. Annual Review of Ecology and Systematics 4: 25-51.

Nufio, C. R., K. J. Lloyd, M. D. Bowers and R. Guralnick. 2009. Gordon Alexander, grasshoppers, and climate change. American Entomologist 55: 10-13.

Olfert, O. and R. M. Weiss. 2006. Bioclimatic model of *Melanoplus sanguinipes* (Fabricius) (Orthoptera: Acrididae) populations in Canada and the potential impacts of climate change. Journal of Orthoptera Research 15: 65-77.

Parmenter, R. R., S. L. Brantley, J. H. Brown, C. S. Crawford, D. C. Lightfoot and T. L. Yates. 1995. Diversity of animal communities on southwestern rangelands: Species patterns, habitat relationship and land management. Pages 50-71. In: West, N. E., ed. Biodiversity of rangelands: natural resources and environmental issues. Logan: Utah State University.

Parmesan, C. 2006. Ecological and evolutionary responses to recent climate change. Annual Review of Ecology and Systematics 37: 637-669.

Parmesan, C. 2007. Influences of species, latitudes and methodologies on estimates of phenological response to global warming. Global Change Biology 13: 1860-1872.

Parmesan, C., N. Ryrholm, C. Stefanescu, J. K. Hill and others. 1999. Poleward shifts in geographical ranges of butterfly species associated with regional warming. Nature 399: 579-583.

Preston, K. L., J. T. Rotenberry, R. A. Redak and M. F. Allen. 2008. Habitat shifts of endangered species under altered climate conditions: importance of biotic interactions. Global Change Biology 14: 2501-2515.

Robinet, C. and A. Roques. 2010. Direct impacts of recent climate warming on insect populations. Integrative Zoology 5: 132-142.

Sala, O. E. 2001. Temperate grasslands. Pages 121-137. In: Chapin, F. S., III, O. E. Sala and E. Huber-Sannwald, eds. Global Biodiversity in a Changing Environment: Scenarios for the 21st Century. New York: Springer-Verlag.

Sala, O. E., F. S. Chapin, III, J. J. Armesto, E. Berlow and others. 2000. Global biodiversity scenarios for the year 2100. Science 287: 1770-1774.

Seager, R., M. Ting, I. Held, Y. Kushnir and others. 2007. Model projections of an imminent transition to a more arid climate in southwestern North America. Science 316: 1181-1184.

Seastedt, T. R., W. D. Bowman, T. N. Caine, D. McKnight, A. Townsend and M. W. Williams. 2004. The landscape continuum: a model for high-elevation ecosystems. BioScience 54: 11-121.

Thomson, J. D. 2010. Flowering phenology, fruiting success and progressing deteriorations of pollination in an early-flowering geophytes. Philosophical Transactions of the Royal Society 365(1555): 3187-3199.

Triplehorn, C. A. and N. F. Johnson. 2005. Borror and DeLong's Introduction to the Study of Insects. Belmont, CA: Thomson Brooks/Cole.

White, P. J. T. and J. T. Kerr. 2007. Human impacts on environment-diversity relationships: evidence for biotic homogenization from butterfly species richness patterns. Global Ecology and Biogeography 16: 290-299.

Winfree, R., R. Aguilar, D. P. Vásquez, G. LeBuhn and M. A. Aizen. 2009. A meta-analysis of bees' response to anthropogenic disturbance. Ecology 90: 2068-2076.

Chapter 4

Plant Vulnerabilities and Genetic Adaptation

Bryce A. Richardson[1], Nancy L. Shaw[2], and Rosemary L. Pendleton[3]

[1] U.S. Forest Service, Rocky Mountain Research Station; Grassland, Shrubland, and Desert Ecosystems Program; Shrub Sciences Laboratory, Provo, Utah

[2] U.S. Forest Service, Rocky Mountain Research Station; Grassland, Shrubland, and Desert Ecosystems Program; Aquatic Sciences Laboratory, Boise, Idaho

[3] U.S. Forest Service, Rocky Mountain Research Station; Grassland, Shrubland, and Desert Ecosystems Program; Forestry Sciences Laboratory, Albuquerque, New Mexico

Executive Summary

The biogeography of plant species and population genetic structure within species is principally governed by climate. The association between climate change and plant distributions has been well documented since the last ice age, and recent studies have shown contemporary climate changes can create landscape-scale die-offs or movement of plant taxa. Terrestrial ecosystem conservation and restoration success hinges on understanding the vulnerabilities imposed by climate on plant taxa. Successful conservation and restoration under a changing climate will require:

- Recognizing whether climate is the root cause of changes in biotic communities.
- Determination of which species and populations are most vulnerable and at the highest risk to extirpation.
- Accurate prediction of future displacement and movement of plant communities.
- Fostering regeneration or assisting the movement of appropriately adapted plant materials.

Genetic and ecological research can provide critical components to meet these goals. GSD scientists are focusing on the following areas of research:

- Plant species-climate relationships: a means to understand how climate shapes distribution of species on the landscape. This research provides a means of predicting how species distributions could be affected by climate change.
- Adaptive genetic variation: research aimed at quantifying plant responses from different populations in a common environment. This research provides the necessary component to develop seed transfer guidelines for plant species.
- Genetic diversity and structure: use of molecular markers to identify areas of high or low diversity and how genetic variation is structured across the landscape. This research provides a means to identify physical or biological barriers to gene flow and at-risk populations with low genetic diversity.
- Ecological interactions: research aimed at identifying biological interactions critical to the success and persistence of native plants. Plant movement, either natural or human mediated, may require other organisms for pollination, seed dispersal, or seedling establishment.

Plant Species Distributions and Climate

Plant biogeography is principally governed by climate, exhibiting strong responses with both temperature and precipitation (Brown and Gibson 1983). The relationship between climate and plant species distributions has been demonstrated through several lines of research. First, contemporary predictions of plant species distributions have been shown to be highly accurate based on models using climate variables as predictors of species presence or absence (Iverson and Prasad 1998; Rehfeldt and others 2006; Friggens and others, Chapter 1 this volume). Second, past range shifts in plant distributions have been documented through patterns of genetic variation (e.g., Richardson and others 2002; Petit and others, 2003; Davis and others 2005; Richardson and Meyer 2012) and in records from packrat middens (e.g., Betancourt and others 1990; Thompson and Andersen 2000). These range shifts have been mainly attributable to climate change and associated glacial and interglacial oscillations during the Pleistocene and early Holocene. Third, studies monitoring vegetation have shown that range shifts are ongoing for a number of plant taxa and most are likely attributable to climate warming (Soja and others 2007; Beckage and others 2008; Kelly and Goulden 2008; Thomas 2010). Given this close association between climate and plant biogeography, the predicted rapid change in climate by human-made greenhouse gas emissions should be the impetus for developing the knowledge base regarding seed transfer guidelines and other activities that mitigate this change.

In western North America, climate has been implicated as a factor in recent vegetation die-offs. The drought of 2002-2003 has been associated with the widespread mortality of pinyon (*Pinus edulis*) and juniper (*Juniperus* spp.) in the southwestern United States. Breshears and others (2005) showed that this drought coincided with warmer temperatures not seen in previous droughts during the Twentieth Century. Similarly, Rehfeldt and others (2009) used weather station data to show that the changes in climate variables important in predicting aspen (*Populus tremuloides*) distribution were also associated with stands of aspen die-off caused by sudden aspen decline. As with the pinyon die-off, drought and higher-than-average temperatures in 2002-2003 have been implicated as causative factors in sudden aspen decline. Based on predictions from GCMs, the aspen die-off may represent the trigger for a range shift, wherein many of these dead or dying stands will not recover (Rehfeldt and others 2009).

While die-offs of landscape dominant plant species, such as aspen and pinyon, may represent a fundamental change in ecosystem processes, climate change could also threaten other regionally distributed or endemic plant taxa with extinction. The varied topography and soils of western North America create isolated, discontinuous patches of habitat for plant specialization. Endemics are commonly found on exposed substrates such as shale or gypsum, or are associated with cliffs or shaded slopes of isolated mountain ranges (Johnston 1977; Meyer 1986; Sivinski and others 1996). These disjunct distributions limit the colonization pathways of potential habitat in future climates, especially in plant species with limited seed dispersal capabilities. For example, environments of river canyons create one source of endemism. These microclimates with perennial water sources create hanging gardens, supporting numerous endemic plants (Welsh 1989). The persistence of these microhabitats is dependent on sustaining ground water. If droughts in these regions become more common, the hanging gardens could dry up. Another example is provided by the isolated nature of mountain ranges in the southwest. These regions support some of the highest levels of plant endemism in North America (Warshall 1995; Anonymous 2007). The Madrean Archipelago of southern Arizona, southwestern New Mexico, and adjoining states of Sonora and Chihuahua Mexico consists of some 40 isolated mountains known as "sky islands." The effects of climate change may be particularly pronounced in these isolated ranges as vegetation zones shift upward and high-elevation habitat is lost. Bioclimatic modeling of Mexican spruce (*Picea mexicana*), which is isolated in small subalpine habitats, predicts the disappearance of contemporary habitat by 2030. However, re-emergence of suitable habitat for this species occurs 500 km to the south, a distance impossible for natural dispersal (Ledig and others 2010). Mexican spruce and other endemics will likely need human-assisted dispersal to areas of suitable habitat. To limit the vulnerabilities to climate-caused extirpation of plant taxa, bioclimatic analyses are of value in identifying new locations of suitable habitat that may emerge under climate change.

Biotic Interactions and Climate Change

In addition to direct effects, global drivers of climate change may affect plant distribution, abundance, and fitness through biotic interactions (Tylianakis and others 2008). Ecological disturbances creating large-scale plant mortality, such as insect and disease outbreaks, could be symptomatic of underlying plant stress due to climate change (Dale and others 2001). Temperature and moisture have been demonstrated to be critical components in the interaction between plants and insects or diseases, and climate change-caused stress can predispose plants to insect and disease outbreaks. However, determining whether climate change affects the intensity, geographic distribution, or longevity of an insect or disease outbreak is a complex task (Garrett and others 2006). Studies must take into account historical records of climate and outbreaks, spatial patterns of climate variables, host distributions, and other factors that affect the host and the disturbance agent interactions. Despite this complexity, some studies have shown a correlation between disturbance agent outbreaks and temperature or precipitation variability outside of the historical norms. Berg and others (2006) associated spruce beetle outbreaks in Alaska and the Yukon Territory with high summer temperatures. Likewise, Woods and others (2005) implicated climate change in an epidemic outbreak of Dothistroma needle blight. Widespread mortality of pinyon pine, previously mentioned, was further linked to outbreaks of the pinyon ips bark beetle (*Ips confuses*; Breshears and others 2005). Drought-stressed trees were unable to produce sufficient resin to ward off beetle attacks. A fungus carried by the ips may also have been a factor (P.L. Ford, personal communication).

Disruption of mutualistic relationships, such as plant-pollinator interactions, may also occur due to climate change. Many flowering plant taxa require animal pollinators for reproduction (Brantley and Ford, Chapter 4 this volume). Corresponding declines in pollinators and insect-pollinated plants have been found in northern Europe, whereas wind-pollinated plants were unaffected (Biesmeijer and others 2006). Other studies have shown that climate change could disrupt plant-pollinator interactions by changing floral phenology (Memmott and others 2007). Rising CO_2 levels and increased summer temperatures have been linked to changes in flowering phenology (Cleland and others 2007; Springer and Ward 2007; Crimmins and others 2009). Decoupling of plant flowering and pollinator availability could result in reproductive failure for both plant and pollinator. For example, flowering in ocotillo (*Fouquieria splendens*) is currently timed to synchronize with the northern migration of hummingbirds (Waser 1979). A lack of high-quality nectar resources could lead to a decline in hummingbird populations. Thus, mitigating the impacts of climate change on flowering plants that are dependent on pollinators has additional complexity and will require increased knowledge. Movement of plants to suitable habitats without recognizing the importance of pollinators could lead to failure. Other biotic interactions may also be affected, including inter- and intra-specific competition, herbivory, dispersal agents, mycorrhizae and other fungal mutualistic relationships

(Tylianakis and others 2008). The effects of climate change on these interactions have received very little attention.

Climate Change and Altered Fire Regimes

Disturbance resulting from improper grazing practices, off-road vehicle use, and other anthropogenic disturbances have contributed to the widespread invasion of exotic annual grasses, primarily *Bromus* spp. in the Great Basin and, more recently, *Bromus* spp. and *Schismus* spp. in the Mojave and Sonoran Deserts (Esque and Schwalbe 2002; Ford and others, Chapter 6 this volume). Resulting changes in wildfire regimes (shorter fire intervals and longer fire seasons) and increasing temperatures have combined to accelerate the further spread of annual and perennial exotics, deplete native seed banks, simplify community structure and species associations, and reduce landscape patchiness (Brooks and Pyke 2001; Esque and Schwalbe 2002). Ecosystem resilience declines with disruption of critical functions such as snow or water catchment, nutrient cycling, and loss of microbiotic crusts and mycorrhizae. As a consequence, the future of entire communities and their component species are at risk due to the direct impacts of wildfire and invasives, climate change, habitat fragmentation, and resulting bottlenecks to plant migration (D'Antonio and Vitousek 1992).

The status of fire-intolerant sagebrush and its communities is threatened not only by wildfire and the incursion of exotic annuals, but also by the encroachment of native conifers, in part due to fire control and northerly movement of Mojave vegetation in response to warming temperatures (Bradley 2009, 2010; Ford and others, Chapter 6 this volume). Nielson and others (2005) simulated climate change impacts on potential future distribution of the sagebrush ecosystem. The greatest warming scenario reduced the system to 20 percent of its current area within the Twenty-First Century. Currently, about 350 species of conservation concern are associated with the sagebrush ecosystem (Wisdom and others 2005) and 20 percent of the systems flora and fauna are considered imperiled (Center for Science, Economics and Environment 2002). Thus, major species losses can be expected if current trends continue.

Proposed research and management to meet these threats are: expanded research on biocontrol and other control methods for cheatgrass and other invasives (Runyun and others, Chapter 7 this volume); adaptation of native plants coexisting with invasives (Mealor and others 2004; Leger 2008), species specific seed zones (Erickson and others 2004); deployment of pooled seed sources, including accessions that will pre-adapt vegetation to expected changes in climatic conditions (Johnson and others 2010); management to reduce bottlenecks to species migration, and assisted succession (Friggens and others, Chapter 8 this volume).

Genetic Responses to Climate Change

Plant fitness, the ability to produce viable offspring, is often dependent on attunement to climate. Three types of biological responses from an organism can direct attunement: phenotypic plasticity, dispersal, and genetic change. These responses are fundamentally different biological processes occurring at different temporal scales, but all responses could potentially interact with each other and impact an organism's capacity to genetically adapt to climate change (Davis and others 2005; Visser 2008; Reed and others 2010).

- Phenotypic plasticity is defined as the capacity of a particular genotype to produce varied phenotypes in response to different environments (Pigliucci 2001). Phenotypic plasticity operates within a generation, the shortest time scale of the three responses. It can be temporary (non-heritable) or inherited through some epigenetic mechanisms, the changes in gene expression by means other than DNA substitutions (Bird 2007). Epigenetic mechanisms could have important implications on how we assess plant vulnerabilities to climate change. For example, if a plant species possesses phenotypic plasticity in climatically adapted traits, this species may be more resilient under climate change.

- Dispersal of propagules (e.g., seed and pollen) can lead to gene flow. These dispersal processes can create a shift in gene frequencies and introduce novel genotypes from different populations, potentially affecting fitness. Dispersal occurs on a multi-generation temporal scale, yet the rate and distance propagules travel can have implications on plant species capacity to respond to a changing climate.

- Genetic change, the process of creating novel genes by mutation in the coding or regulatory DNA sequence that undergoes natural selection, occurs at the longest temporal scale. In this sense, a mutation could also include gene or whole genome duplications (i.e., polyploidy), which are common in some angiosperm lineages (Fawcett and Van de Peer 2010). These temporal scales are all dependent on the life history characteristics of the particular species. Species with short generation times will likely respond at a faster rate than those that have longer generation times (i.e., annuals are more likely to have higher fitness that perennials). Unfortunately, this benefits many invasive plant species that are annuals.

Genetic changes that affect the fitness of an organism can shape ecological processes, such as fecundity, mortality, and dispersal (reviewed in Carroll and others 2007; Kinnison and Hairston 2007). For example, a novel genotype that conveys fitness advantage to drought tolerance would increase in frequency in a climate that becomes arid, leading to higher survival, fecundity, and dispersal rates for individuals possessing this genotype. If arid conditions persist, strong selection pressure for drought tolerance could change the gene frequencies in a population over several generations. Conversely, if no drought tolerance genes exist, mortality and low fecundity could create a smaller population size. Genetic drift, stochastic changes in gene frequencies, could lead to the loss of genetic diversity, increasing the risk of extirpation of the population. A similar scenario was recently shown empirically in the flower phenology of field mustard (*Brassica rapa*). Franks and others (2007) demonstrated that flower phenology in this species responded to a five-year drought by earlier flowering and that the ancestors (i.e., pre-drought plants) had significantly reduced survival rates compared to contemporary plants.

Natural selection caused by climate is spatially dependent, especially for widely distributed species. The process can create variable plant trait responses or ecotypes across the landscape (Turesson 1925). Therefore, climatic selection has been demonstrated to be a major factor in intraspecific genetic adaptation (Langlet 1936; Savolainen and others 2007). Much of this research, completed in common garden studies of trees species, has shown that the adaptive strategies among species are not the same. For example, Douglas-fir (*Pseudotsuga menziesii*) is highly variable in growth phenology and populations have a narrow threshold for cold hardiness. The variability in this trait is mainly associated with winter temperatures and frost dates (St. Clair and others 2005). In contrast, western white pine (*Pinus monticola*) exhibits little adaptive variation to cold hardiness despite having a similar species distribution as Douglas-fir. In western white pine, cold hardiness is apparently a phenotypically plastic trait. However, for western white pine, variation in growth is strongly associated with the amount of growing season precipitation (Rehfeldt and others 1984; Richardson and others 2009). These genecological studies illustrate that ecologically similar plant species may have vastly different adaptive strategies to cope with climatic stresses and that populations within these species will respond differently under climate change.

Genetic Tools for Addressing Climate Change

Knowledge of intraspecific and population-level responses to climate change are essential for the restoration of plant species. Once associations between genetic traits and climate variables can be established, as previously discussed, genecological modeling can be used to define contemporary seed zones and predict future seeds zones using GCM scenarios (e.g., Rehfeldt and others 2002; Rehfeldt 2004; St. Clair and Howe 2007). While GCMs scenarios are not without assumptions (IPCC 2007), modeling intraspecific adaptive genetic variation in the future is instructive for identifying geographical regions of current and future on-site and off-site conservation and planning for the potential movement of desirable genotypes. However, most genecology research has been completed for forest trees and little knowledge exists for desert or species.

Molecular genetic approaches have served a different purpose to that of common garden trials of adaptive traits. Since molecular markers are generally neutral (i.e., not influenced directly by natural selection), they are valuable in assessing range-wide genetic diversity and structure. Measures of genetic diversity provide a means to assess the relative fitness of populations and the level of inbreeding (Reed and Frankham 2003). Therefore, low levels of genetic diversity suggest the effective population size is or has been experiencing a bottleneck. Further losses to population size could result in leading to a greater risk of extirpation.

Molecular markers can also reflect past biogeographic distributions and demographic changes. Isolated populations from past glacial cycles are often inferred from patterns of genetic variation. Therefore, molecular markers are indirectly tied to past climate events. For example, organellar DNA markers were used to elucidate putative glacial refugia and post-glacial colonization in whitebark pine (*Pinus albicaulis*). Richardson and others (2002) showed that Holocene warming provided whitebark pine with opportunities to establish contact zones and genetic introgression from previously isolated populations. Other studies have shown that present-day genetic patterns are supported by bioclimatic modeling of predicted Pleistocene climate (Rebernig and others 2010). Much of the research using molecular markers on temperate plants show similar patterns of post-glacial colonization, such that the higher proportions of genetic diversity and structure are found in the lower latitudes of a species' distribution (Hampe and Petit 2005). The skewed distribution of genetic diversity may make species more vulnerable to climate warming since lower latitude populations are generally at higher risk of extirpation.

Popular population genetic techniques such as microsatellites and amplified fragment length polymorphisms have been instrumental in identifying vulnerable plant taxa and populations by elucidating genetic diversity and structure. However, these techniques have limitations in the amount of detectable genetic variation and applications to other areas of genetic research. Next-generation sequencing technology has the capacity to sequence millions of 50 to 500 base pair fragments of genomic DNA or RNA that can uncover hundreds of thousands of single nucleotide polymorphisms (Mardis 2008). Researchers can develop these polymorphisms into thousands of molecular markers for discerning genetic relationships. The capabilities of next-generation sequencing have been compared to existing data generated from traditional sequencing methods in Fishers (*Martes pennanti*). Knaus and others (2011) discovered distinct populations of this rare carnivore in California that was unresolved in the previous genetic data. Such findings will a have an impact on how this species will be managed. In addition to providing more accuracy in discerning genetic relationships, next-generation sequencing offers greater versatility to address questions in plant-climate interactions.

Two different molecular approaches have the capability to elucidate the relationships between genotype and phenotypes, bridging the gap between physiological/phenotypic plant responses and the underlying genotypic mechanisms.

- RNA sequencing: a process of transcriptome profiling (i.e., sequencing all expressed RNA transcripts in a sample) using next-generation sequencing technology. In this approach, RNA sequences are decoded and levels of gene expression can be estimated by transcript copy number (Wang and others 2009)
- Association genetics: an approach to identify a gene or genes involved with a phenotype by determining a pattern of presence and absence between molecular markers and a trait using groups of plants or plant populations with differing phenotypes (Neale and Savolainen 2004; Ingvarsson and Street 2010)

Research involving next-generation sequencing can improve our understanding of processes and mechanisms involved with creating variable traits and physiological responses important to climatic adaptation.

Potential Plant Vulnerabilities

Based on the available research and the previous discussion, inferences can be drawn about the general plant characteristics that may increase vulnerabilities to climate change. While the details on criteria for assessing and scoring vulnerabilities are discussed elsewhere (Friggens and others, Chapter 8 this volume), we provide a list of characteristics that are potentially influential to the success or failure of plant species under climate change.

- Habitat specialists: Many habitat specialists and narrow endemics could be at high risk to climatic extirpation. Examples include the hanging garden flora previously discussed. These plants species are limited in their movement because similar habitats are rare or nonexistent. For managers, long-term seed banking may be the only option for preservation of these species.
- Plant dependencies on other organisms: Plants that rely on other organisms for their reproduction (e.g., pollinators and seed dispersers) or survival (e.g., mycorrhizal fungi) could be more vulnerable to climate change (Brantley and Ford, Chapter 3 this volume). Understanding the relationships of these plants and their associates is an important step to increase the chances for successful restoration or movement of plant species.
- Life history characteristics: Generation time, fecundity, and dispersal capabilities are important life history characteristics when considering vulnerability. Species with long generation times, low seedset, and limited dispersal capabilities are typically vulnerable to climate change. Unfortunately, these life histories also describe many of our nativet species (Runyon and others, Chapter 7 this volume).
- Adaptive genetic strategies: Plants have different adaptive genetic strategies. Plants that have more narrowly defined adapted populations will require more attention to the movement of seed to the appropriate seed zones. Therefore, plants with narrowly defined adapted populations are more likely to experience maladaptation with climate change.
- Genetic diversity: The extant genetic structure and diversity within a species can be a major influence on vulnerability to climate change. Genetic diversity affects a spectrum of adaptive responses a plant species can possess. Therefore, reduced diversity could impact fitness, making a species more vulnerable to climate change.

Table 4-1. Research areas for mitigating climate change impact on grassland, shrubland and desert ecosystems of western North America.

Research focus	Details	Benefits
Bioclimatic modeling	Assessment of which climate variables can be important to species distributions based on presence/absence data (Friggens and others, Chapter 1 this volume)	Predicts current and future species distributions
Genecological modeling	Intraspecific genetic relationship with climate	Used to develop current and future seed zones
Climate/disturbance interactions	Relationships between disturbance agents (insects, disease, fire) and climate (Ford and others, Chapter 6 this volume)	Key to elucidating climate interaction with disturbances
Climate/invasives interactions	Understanding relationships between invasive species, natives, and climate change (Runyon and others, Chapter 7 this volume)	Offers insights into how climate affects invasive species interactions with natives
Autecology/climate relationships	Climate impacts to breeding systems, seed dispersers, and pollinators (Brantley and Ford, Chapter 4 this volume)	Identifies unseen vulnerabilities with pollinator/dispersal agents
Molecular genetics	Use of DNA or other markers to assess intraspecific genetic structure and diversity	Identifies unique populations and areas of high genetic diversity

Research Needs

The impacts of climate change on the flora inhabiting grassland, shrublands, and desert ecosystems of western North America remain largely unknown. Accurate assessments of plant species' potential vulnerabilities to climate change hinge on research needs spanning multiple disciplines to resolve their complexity (table 4-1). Understanding of these vulnerabilities can then be developed into plans and technologies for conservation and restoration (Friggens and others, Chapter 8 this volume). At the heart of these complex problems are several key principals: (1) recognizing changes in plant species and communities and whether or not climate is the root cause, (2) understanding species vulnerabilities under climate change, (3) accurate prediction of the movement of plant communities to plan for the future, and (4) mitigating these changes by fostering regeneration or assisting the dispersal of appropriately adapted plant materials.

Literature Cited

Anonymous. 2007. Glen Canyon National Park Rare Plants. Available: http://www. nps.gov/glca/naturescience/rareplants.htm.

Beckage, B., B. Osborne, D. G. Gavin, C. Pucko, T. Siccama and T. Perkins. 2008. A rapid upward shift of a forest ecotone during 40 years of warming in the Green Mountains of Vermont. Proceedings of the National Academy of Sciences 105: 4197-4202.

Berg, E. E., J. D. Henry, C. L. Fastie, A. D. De Volder and S. M. Matsuoka. 2006. Spruce beetle outbreaks on the Kenai Peninsula, Alaska, and Kluane National Park and Reserve, Yukon Territory: relationship to summer temperatures and regional differences in disturbance regimes Forest Ecology and Management 227: 219-232.

Betancourt, J. L., T. R. V. Devender and P. S. Martin, eds. 1990. Packrat Middens: The last 40,000 Years of Biotic Change. University of Arizona Press, Tucson, AZ.

Biesmeijer, J. C., S. P. M. Roberts, M. Reemer, R. Ohlemuller and others. 2006. Parallel declines in pollinators and insect-pollinated plants in Britain and the Netherlands. Science 313: 351-354.

Bird, A. 2007. Perceptions of epigenetics. Nature 447: 396-398.

Bradley, B. A. 2009. Regional analysis of the impacts of climate change on cheatgrass invasion shows potential risk and opportunity. Global Change Biology 15: 196-208.

Bradley, B. A. 2010. Assessing ecosystem threats from global and regional change: hierarchical modeling of risk to sagebrush ecosystems from climate change, land use and invasive species in Nevada, USA. Ecography 33: 198-208.

Breshears, D. D., N. S. Cobb, P. M. Rich, K. P. Price and others. 2005. Regional vegetation die-off in response to global-change-type drought. Proceedings of the National Academy of Sciences 102: 15144-15148.

Brooks, M. L. and D. Pyke. 2001. Invasive plants and fire in the deserts of North America. In: Galley, K. E. M. and T. P. Wilson, eds. Proceedings of the invasive species workshop: The role of fire in the control and spread of invasive species. Fire Conference 2000: The First National Congress on Fire Ecology, Prevention and Management. Misc. Publ. No. 11, Tall Timbers Research Station, Tallahassee, FL: 1-14.

Brown J. H. and A. C. Gibson. 1983. Biogeography. C. V. Mosby, St. Louis, MI. 634 p.

Carroll, S. P., A. P. Hendry, D. N. Reznick and C. W. Fox. 2007. Evolution on ecological time-scales. Functional Ecology 21: 387-393.

Center for Sciences, Economics and Environment. 2002. The state of the nation's ecosystems: Measuring the Lands, Water and Living Ecosystems of the United States. Cambridge, UK: Cambridge University Press. Available: http: //www. heinzctr.org/ecosystem/index.html.

Cleland, E. E., I. Chuine, A. Menzel, H. A. Mooney and M. D. Schwertz. 2007. Shifting plant phenology in response to global change. Trends in Ecology and Evolution 22: 357-365.

Crimmins, T. M., M. A. Crimmins and C. D. Bertelsen. 2009. Flowering range changes across an elevation gradient in response to warming summer temperatures. Global Change Biology 15: 1141-1152.

D'Antonio, C. M. and T. M. Vitousek. 1992. Biological invasions by exotic grasses, the grass/fire cycle, and global change. Annual Review of Ecology and Systematics 23: 63-87.

Dale, V. H., L. A. Joyce, S. McNulty, R. P. Neilson and others. 2001. Climate change and forest disturbances. Bioscience 51: 723-734.

Davis, M., R. Shaw and J. Etterson. 2005. Evolutionary responses to changing climate. Ecology 86: 1704-1714.

Erickson, V. J., N. L. Mandel and F. C. Sorensen. 2004. Landscape patterns of phenotypic variation and population structuring in a selfing grass, *Elymus glaucus* (blue wildrye). Canadian Journal of Botany 82: 1776-1789.

Esque, T. C. and C. R. Schwalbe. 2002. Alien annual plants and their relationships to fire and biotic change in Sonoran desertscrub. Pages 165-194. In: B. Tellman, ed. Invasive Exotic Species in the Sonoran Region. Arizona-Sonora Desert Museum and the University of Arizona Press, Tucson, AZ.

Fawcett, J. A. and Y. Van de Peer. 2010. Angiosperm polyploids and their road to evolutionary success. Trends in Evolutionary Biology. Page-press. Available: http://www.pagepress.org/journals/index.php/eb/article/viewArticle/eb.2010.e3/2215

Garrett, K. A., S. P. Dendy, M. N. Frank, M. N. Rouse and S. E. Travers. 2006. Climate change effects on plant disease: genomes to ecosystems. Annual Review Phytopathology 44: 489-509.

Franks, S., S. Sim and A. Weis. 2007. Rapid evolution of flowering time by an annual plant in response to a climate fluctuation. Proceedings of the National Academy of Sciences 104 (4): 1278-1282.

Hampe, A. and R. J. Petit. 2005. Conserving biodiversity under climate change: the rear edge matters. Ecology Letters 8: 461-467.

Ingvarsson, P. K. and N. R. Street. 2010. Association genetics of complex traits in plants. New Phytologist, Tansley review, 189(4): 909-922.

Intergovernmental Panel on Climate Change [IPCC]. 2007. In: Solomon, S., D. Qin, M. Manning, Z. Chen, M. Marquis, K. B. Avery, M. Tignor and H. L. Miller, eds. Climate change 2007: The physical science basis. Contribution of Working Group I to the Fourth Assessment Report of the Intergovernmental Panel on Climate Change. Cambridge University Press, Cambridge, UK. 996 p.

Iverson, L. R. and A. M. Prasad. 1998. Predicting abundance of 80 tree species following climate change in the eastern United States. Ecological Monographs 68: 465-485.

Johnson, G. R., L. Stritch, P. Olwell, S. Lambert, M. E. Horning and R. Cronn. 2010. What are the best seed sources for ecosystem restoration on BLM and USFS lands? Native Plant Journal. 11(2): 117-131.

Johnston, M. C. 1977. Brief resume of botanical, including vegetation, features of the Chihuahuan Desert region with special emphasis on their uniqueness. In: Wauer, R. H. and D. H. Risking, eds. Transactions of the symposium on the biological resources of the Chihuahuan Desert region, United States and Mexico. October 17-18, 1974, Alpine, TX. Proceedings and Transactions Series no. 3. Washington, DC: USDI National Park Service: 335-359.

Kelly, A. E. and M. L. Goulden. 2008. Rapid shifts in plant distribution with recent climate change. Proceedings of the National Academy of Sciences 105: 11823-11826.

Kinnison, M. T. and N. G. Hairston. 2007. Eco-evolutionary conservation biology: contemporary evolution and the dynamics of persistence. Functional Ecology 21: 444-454.

Knaus, B. J., R. Cronn, A. Liston, K. Pilgrim and M. K. Schwartz. 2011. Mitochondrial genome sequences illuminate maternal lineages of conservation concern in a rare carnivore. BMC Ecology 11: 10.

Langlet, O. 1936. Studier over tallens fysiologiska variabilitet och dess samband med klimatet. Medd Statens Skogsforsoksanstalt 29: 219-470.

Ledig, F. T., G. E. Rehfeldt, C. Sáenz-Romero and C. Flores-López. 2010. Projections of suitable habitat for rare species under global warming scenarios. Journal of Botany 97: 970-987.

Leger, E. A. 2008. The adaptive value of remnant native plants in invaded communities: an example from the Great Basin. Ecological Applications 18: 1226-1235.

Mardis, E. R. 2008. The impact of next-generation sequencing technology on genetics. Trends in Genetics 24: 133-141.

Mealor, B. A., A. L. Hild and N. L. Shaw. 2004. Native plant community composition and genetic diversity associated with long-term weed invasions. Western North American Naturalist 64: 503-513.

Memmott, J., P. G. Craze, N. M. Waser and M. V. Price. 2007. Global warming and the disruption of plant-pollinator interactions. Ecology Letters 10: 710: 717.

Meyer, S. E. 1986. Ecology of gysophile endemism in the eastern Mojave Desert. Ecology 67: 1303-1313.

Neale, D. B. and O. Savolainen. 2004. Association genetics of complex traits in conifers. Trends in Plant Science 9: 325-330.

Neilson, R. P., J. M. Lenihan, D. Bachelet and R. J. Drapek. 2005. Climate change implications for sagebrush ecosystems. Transactions of the 70th North American Wildlife and Natural Resources Conference 70: 145-159.

Petit, R. J., I. Aguinagalde, J.-L. de Beaulieu, C. Bittkau and others. 2003. Glacial refugia: hotspots but not melting pots of genetic diversity. Science 300: 1563-1565.

Pigliucci, M. 2001. Phenotypic Plasticity: Beyond Nature and Nurture. Johns Hopkins University Press, Baltimore, MD. 333 p.

Rebernig, C. A., G. M. Schneeweiss, K. E. Bardy, P. Schonswetter and others. 2010. Multiple Pleistocene refugia and Holocene range expansion of an abundant southwestern American desert plant species (*Melampodium leucanthum*, Asteraceae). Molecular Ecology 19: 3421-3443.

Reed, D. and R. Frankham. 2003. Correlation between fitness and genetic diversity. Conservation Biology 17: 230-237.

Reed, T. E., D. E. Schindler and R. S. Waples. 2011. Interacting effects of phenotypic plasticity and evolution on population persistence in a changing climate. Conservation Biology 25: 56-63.

Rehfeldt, G. E. 2004. Interspecific and intraspecific variation in *Picea engelmannii* and its congeneric cohorts: biosystematics, genecology, and climate change. Gen. Tech. Rep. RMRS-GTR-134. Fort Collins, CO: U.S. Department of Agriculture, Forest Service, Rocky Mountain Research Station. 18 p.

Rehfeldt, G. E., N. L. Crookston, M. V. Warwell and J. S. Evans. 2006. Empirical analyses of plant-climate relationships for the western United States. International Journal of Plant Sciences 167: 1123-1150.

Rehfeldt, G. E., D. E. Ferguson and N. L. Crookston. 2009. Aspen, climate, and sudden decline in the western USA. Forest Ecology Management 258: 2353-2364.

Rehfeldt, G. E., R. J. Hoff and R. J. Steinhoff. 1984. Geographic patterns of genetic variation in *Pinus monticola*. Botanical Gazette 145: 229-239.

Rehfeldt, G. E., N. M. Tchebakova, Y. I. Parfenova, W. R. Wykoff, N. A. Kuzmina and L. I. Milyutin. 2002. Intraspecific responses to climate in *Pinus sylvestris*. Global Change Biology 8: 912-929.

Richardson, B. A. and Meyer, S. E. 2012. Paleoclimate effects and geographic barriers shape regional population genetic structure of blackbrush (*Coleogyne ramosissima*: Rosaceae). Botany 90: 293-299.

Richardson, B. A., S. J. Brunsfeld and N. B. Klopfenstein. 2002. DNA from bird-dispersed seed and wind-disseminated pollen provides insights into postglacial colonization and population genetic structure of whitebark pine (*Pinus albicaulis*). Molecular Ecology 11: 215-227.

Richardson, B. A., G. E. Rehfeldt and M. S. Kim. 2009. Congruent climate related genecological responses from molecular markers and quantitative traits for western white pine (*Pinus monticola*). International Journal of Plant Sciences 170: 1120-1131.

Savolainen, O., T. Pyhäjärvi and T. Knürr. 2007. Gene flow and local adaptation in trees. Annual Review of Ecology Evolution and Systematics 38: 595-619.

Sivinski, R., R. K. Lowrey and P. Knight. 1996. New Mexico vascular plant diversity. New Mexico Journal of Science 36: 60-78.

Soja, A. J., N. M. Tchebakova, H. F. French, M. D. Flannigan and others. 2007. Climate-induced boreal forest change: predictions versus current observations. Global and Planetary Change 56: 274-296.

Springer, C. J. and J. K. Ward. 2007. Flowering time and elevated atmospheric CO_2. New Phytologist 176: 243-255.

St. Clair, J. B. and G. T. Howe. 2007. Genetic maladaptation of coastal Douglas-fir seedlings to future climates. Global Change Biology 13: 1441-1454.

St. Clair, J. B., N. L. Mandel and K. W. Vance-Borland. 2005. Genecology of Douglas fir in western Oregon and Washington. Annals of Botany 96: 1199-1214.

Thomas, C. D. 2010. Climate, climate change and range boundaries. Diversity and Distributions 16: 488-495.

Thompson, R. S. and K. H. Anderson. 2000. Biomes of western North America at 18,000, 6,000, and 0 ^{14}C yr B.P. reconstruction from pollen packrat midden data. Journal of Biogeography 27: 555-584.

Turesson, G. 1925. The plant species in relation to habitat and climate. Hereditas 6: 147-234.

Tylianakis, J. M., R. K. Didham, J. Bascompte and D. A. Wardel. 2008. Global change and species interactions in terrestrial ecosystems. Ecology Letters 11: 1351-1363.

Visser, M. E. Keeping up with a warming world: assessing the rate of adaptation to climate change. Proceedings of the Royal Society B 22: 649-659.

Wang, Z., M. Gerstein and M. Snyder. 2009. RNA-Seq: a revolutionary tool for transcriptomics. Nature Reviews Genetics. 10: 57-63.

Warshall, P. 1995. The Madrean sky island archipelago: a planetary overview. In: DeBano, L. F., G. J. Gottfried, R. H. Hamre and C. B. Edminster, tech. cords. Biodiversity and management of the Madrean Archipelago: the sky islands of southwestern United States and northwestern Mexico. September 19-23, 1994, Tucson, AZ. Gen. Tech. Rep. RM-GTR-264. Fort Collins, CO: U.S. Department of Agriculture, Forest Service, Rocky Mountain Forest and Range Experiment Station: 6-18.

Waser, N. M. 1979. Pollinator availability as a determinant of flowering time in ocotillo (*Fouquieria spendens*). Oecologia 39: 107-121.

Welsh, S. L. 1989. On the distribution of Utah's hanging gardens. The Great Basin Naturalist 49: 1-30.

Wisdom, M. J., M. M. Rowland and L. H. Suring. 2005. Habitat threats in the sagebrush ecosystem: methods of regional assessment and applications in the Great Basin. Lawrence, KS: Alliance Communications Group. 301 p.

Woods, A., K. D. Coates and A. Hamann. 2005. Is an unprecedented dothistroma needle blight epidemic related to climate change? Bioscience 55: 761-768.

Chapter 5

Climate Change, Animal Species, and Habitats: Adaptation and Issues

Deborah M. Finch[1], D. Max Smith[1], Olivia LeDee[2], Jean-Luc E. Cartron[3], and Mark A. Rumble[4]

[1] U.S. Forest Service, Rocky Mountain Research Station; Grassland, Shrubland, and Desert Ecosystems Program; Forestry Sciences Laboratory, Albuquerque, New Mexico

[2] Department of Forest and Wildlife Ecology, University of Wisconsin, Madison, Wisconsin

[3] Dryland Institute, New Mexico Office, Albuquerque, New Mexico

[4] U.S. Forest Service, Rocky Mountain Research Station; Grassland, Shrubland, and Desert Ecosystems Program; Forest and Grassland Research Laboratory, Rapid City, South Dakota

Executive Summary

Because the rate of anthropogenic climate change exceeds the adaptive capacity of many animal and plant species, the scientific community anticipates negative consequences for ecosystems. Changes in climate have expanded, contracted, or shifted the climate niches of many species, often resulting in shifting geographic ranges. In the Great Basin, for example, projected increases in temperature could decrease ability of sagebrush to compete with warm-desert shrubs, leading to a shift in community composition.

Individualistic plant responses to climate change such as altered germination, flowering, and fruiting phenologies influence timing of reproduction and migration of animal species. Changes in timing of production of seeds, fruits, insects, and other prey items may result in a disconnect between timing of food availability and timing of migratory bird arrival or peak period of animal reproduction.

Increasing water scarcity, river and wetland drying, and further disruption of water flow regimes in the Interior West are likely to become overriding conservation issues, particularly given that riparian areas are known to have unusually high biological diversity and often harbor endangered species. Because of its dependence on ground and surface water, riparian vegetation is sensitive to hydrological effects of climate change. Changes in timing and magnitude of snowmelt have already been documented in western mountains. Water scarcity and river drying will negatively impact riparian habitats and wetlands, causing changes in vegetation composition and habitat structure and altering, in some cases eliminating, wildlife habitat.

Wildfire frequency is likely to increase due to changes in temperature and precipitation and invasion of combustible exotic species such as cheatgrass (*Bromus tectorum*). The interrelation among temperatures, moisture, biological invasions, and fire could trump direct impacts of climate change, leaving species and ecosystems with even less time to adapt.

Research priorities include the need to assess vulnerability of wildlife species, habitats, and ecosystems to climate change and to identify habitats and ecosystems where impacts are high and conservation actions are necessary. Improved understanding of climate change effects on habitats prone to fire, invasive species, insects, and diseases will enable habitat management planning and conservation. New methods and decision support tools are needed for protecting vulnerable populations and habitats and/or or assisting their migration in relation to shifting ecosystems.

We describe the current and potential future responses of terrestrial animal species and habitats to climate change in the Great Basin, Great Plains, and Southwest. With its extensive ecological, landscape-scale research background, RMRS and its partners and cooperators have an opportunity to play a leading role studying the complex interactions of climate change and other stressors affecting the ecosystems and species within these regions.

Introduction

Greenhouse gas emissions will continue to increase for at least the next few decades as fossil fuels remain the primary source of global energy (IPCC 2007a), resulting in further warming of our climate system. Depending on the emissions scenario, the IPCC projects an end of century increase in average global surface temperature of 1.8 °C B1 (low emissions scenario) to 4.0 °C A1FI (high emissions scenario) (IPCC 2007a).

Because the rate of anthropogenic climate change exceeds the adaptive capacity of many animal and plant species, the scientific community anticipates "predominantly negative consequences" for ecosystems (IPCC 2007b).

For plants and animals, the impacts of climate change may be direct (e.g., water stress) or indirect (e.g., change in interspecific interactions). Species with a strong life history linkage to ambient conditions are susceptible to the direct impacts of climate change. For these species, altered weather-climate conditions are of concern: advanced timing of spring conditions, spatial shift in climate niche, heat stress, drought, and frequent, heavy precipitation events; for species that are specialists, dependent upon narrow habitat requirements or few interspecific interactions, the indirect impacts of climate change are of particular concern (LeDee and others 2011). These species are susceptible to changes in the availability and quality of habitat and the intensity and duration of interactions with other species. In turn, these changes may alter their behavior, distribution, development, reproduction, and/or survival.

We describe the current and potential future responses of terrestrial animal species and habitats to climate change in the Great Basin, Great Plains, and Southwest.

The Great Basin

Overview of Climatic Conditions and Habitats

In the Interior West, the Great Basin hydrographic region occupies most of Nevada, much of the western half of Utah, and a portion of southeastern Idaho. The physiographic region identified as the Great Basin Desert extends beyond these boundaries to include portions of Wyoming, Arizona, and New Mexico (Shreve 1942; MacMahon 1979). Observed changes in climate and hydrology of the Great Basin include 5 to 10% decreases and increases in annual average precipitation in parts of Nevada and Idaho, 5 to 20% increases in precipitation in Utah, and a 20-day advance in spring snowmelt date (U.S. GCRP 2009). IPCC climate models predict average temperature to increase by 1.7 to 3.3 °C in Nevada and Utah (EPA 1998a, 1998b). Following is a discussion of animal species vulnerability and adaptation to these changes in several Great Basin habitats.

Sagebrush uplands. The big sagebrush (*Artemisia tridentata*) species complex characterizes at least 45 percent of the land area in Great Basin (West 1983). Sagebrush shrublands provide nesting sites for breeding passerine birds, breeding and wintering habitat for diurnal raptors, foraging sites for pronghorn (*Antilocapra americana*), and year-round habitat for small mammal communities (Hanley and Hanley 1982; Ryser 1985; Katzner and Parker 1997; Bradford and others 1998; Wisdom and others 2005). Wisdom and others (2005) identified 13 wildlife species as sagebrush-obligates or sagebrush associates. Two of these species, the greater sage-grouse (*Centrocercus urophasianus*) and pygmy rabbit (*Brachylagus idahoensis*), have been petitioned for Federal listing as threatened or endangered. Both feed on sagebrush during certain periods of the year and rely on plant or soil structure provided by sagebrush stands for nests and burrows (Wallestad and others 1975; Green and Flinders 1980; Katzner and Parker 1997; Gabler and others 2001; Himes and Drohan 2007).

Riparian zones. Riparian vegetation, found in areas where surface or groundwater is available to support phreatophytic species, covers a very small percentage of the Great Basin and can take many forms, such as woodlands, shrublands, and grass-sedge meadows (Thomas and others 1979; Dobkin and others 1995, 1998). Numerous species of birds use western riparian vegetation for nesting, migrating, and wintering habitat (Knopf and others 1988). Riparian vegetation is particularly important for Neotropical migrant birds, many of which have declining populations (Ryser 1985; Ammon 2002; Arsenault 2002). Several riparian-obligate mammal species, such as beaver (*Castor canadensis*) and muskrat (*Ondatra zibethicus*), declined due to trapping or habitat loss in the Nineteenth Century, but populations have recently recovered in some areas (Thomas and others 1979; National Audubon Society 2000).

Wetlands and Lakes. Great Basin streams drain to inland bodies of water that form productive wildlife habitat. The relative scarcity of water in the region makes wetlands and lakes attractive to wildlife species, most notably migratory waterbirds (Ryser 1985; Oring and Reed 1996). These bodies of water vary in depth, salinity, and presence of aquatic vegetation, but all play important roles in wildlife conservation. Many lakes and wetlands are identified as globally important breeding habitat for waterbirds, including the American white pelican (*Pelecanus erythrorhynchos*); waterfowl; and shorebirds, including species of concern such as the snowy plover (*Charadrius alexandrines*, Cornely 1982; Knopf and Kennedy 1980; Jehl 1986; Neel and Henry 1996; Warnock and other 1998; Manning and Paul 2003). Wetlands and lakes are used by impressive numbers of migratory waterbirds for stopover and staging areas (Boula 1985; Jehl 1986; Oring and Reed 1996; Warnock and other 1998; Jehl and others 2002; Manning and Paul 2003) and are an important component of bald eagle (*Haliaeetus leucocephalus*) winter habitat (Isaacs and Anthony1987).

Key Future Issues Associated With Climate Change and Adaptation

Sagebrush-steppe/salt desert scrub. Sagebrush is more frost tolerant than woody species growing at lower elevations and latitudes in the arid west (Beatley 1975). Projected increase in temperatures could decrease ability of sagebrush to compete with warm-desert shrubs, leading to a shift in community composition. Under climate change projections, sagebrush shrublands are expected to recede in range as warm-desert vegetation encroaches from the north and woodlands encroach from higher elevations due to increases in precipitation (Neilson and others 2005; Rehfeldt and others 2006; Friggens and others, Chapter 1 this volume). In addition, wildfire frequency is likely to increase due to changes in temperature and precipitation and invasion of combustible exotic species such as cheatgrass. This change in fire regime facilitates a shift from native shrubland to exotic grassland (Knapp 1996; Chambers and others 2007), which has already been shown to have negative consequences for shrubland reptiles, birds, and mammals (Reynolds 1979; Knick and Rotenberry 2002; Knick and others 2003; Wisdom and others 2005). In addition to fire, climate change has the potential to increase frequency of insect outbreaks, which could alter vegetation composition as well (Chambers 2008).

Little is known about potential for natural adaptation to climate change by Great Basin upland wildlife (Chambers 2008). What is certain, however, is that populations of sagebrush-obligate species, such as greater sage-grouse and pygmy rabbits, would not be capable of adapting to loss of sagebrush in their range because it provides essential food and cover, and would therefore be restricted to areas where sagebrush is likely to persist (Aldridge and others 2008). Sage-grouse also avoid areas where woodlands have encroached on shrublands (Atamian and others 2010; Doherty and others 2010). Humans could facilitate adaptation to climate change impacts by maintaining landscape connectivity to ensure that sagebrush-obligate species can move from unsuitable habitat and colonize available sites.

The impact of interactions between climate change and other disturbance agents can result in increased stress on ecosystems. For example, sagebrush ecosystems stressed by climate change in combination with cheatgrass invasions may be less resistant and more susceptible to fire with consequences for sagebrush-dependent species.

Riparian zones. Because of its dependence on ground and surface water, riparian vegetation is sensitive to hydrological effects of climate change. Changes in timing and magnitude of snowmelt have already been documented in western mountains (Cayan and others 2001; Mote and others 2005; Stewart and others 2005; Barnett and others 2008; Pierce and others 2008). These changes disrupt flood regimes and riparian plant reproduction in the Great Basin (Melack and others 1997; Webb and other 2007). Along with changes in hydrology, increased temperatures and fire frequencies increase mortality of native riparian trees such as cottonwood (*Populus* spp.) and aspen (*Populus tremuloides*), which provide important foraging and nesting sites for birds (Dobkin and others 1995; van Mantgem and others 2009; Allen and others 2010; Liu and others 2010).

Riparian-nesting birds have been extirpated from Great Basin riparian zones following losses of native vegetation from grazing and streamflow regulation (National Audubon Society 2000; Wright and Chambers 2002; Webb and others 2007). In many cases, exotic vegetation, which is more tolerant of altered conditions, has replaced native species along watercourses (Knopf and others 1988). Though some species of migratory and breeding birds have successfully adapted to use exotic vegetation, others require native vegetation for nesting (Hunter and others 1987; Stoleson and Finch 2001; Sogge and others 2008; van Riper and other 2008; Walker 2008). As the majority of research has focused on birds, information is clearly needed to determine adaptation potential of riparian amphibians, reptiles, and mammals to climate change in the Great Basin.

Wetlands and lakes. Water levels of Great Basin wetlands and lakes regularly fluctuate in response to temperature, precipitation, and water diversion (Neel and Henry 1996; Manning and Paul 2003). These and other stressors can lead to reductions in aquatic prey for waterbirds (Sada and Vinyard 2002). Long-term changes in precipitation patterns would affect water levels, which would impact many migratory bird species (Ryser 1985). Rising temperatures and increasingly frequent droughts, predicted under climate change scenarios for the western United States (RMRS 2009), could increase salinity in many lakes, altering availability of invertebrate prey (Boula 1985). Alternately, precipitation totals and storm intensity are expected to increase as well (Neilson and others 2005; Chambers 2008), which could decrease salinity and impact availability of invertebrate prey during critical periods for migratory birds.

Animals using Great Basin lakes and wetlands have few opportunities for adaptation if bodies of water disappear or fluctuate beyond levels of optimal salinity, apart from changing migratory paths or breeding locations. Future research into natural or human-facilitated adaptation is needed to conserve migratory bird populations in the face of climate change.

The Great Plains

Overview of Climatic Conditions and Habitats

Since the 1960s, average temperature in the Great Plains has increased 0.8 °C (U.S. GCRP 2009). Extreme high temperatures are more frequent and extreme low temperatures less frequent than in previous decades (DeGaetano and Allen 2002); in addition, heat waves (≥3 days extreme high temperatures) increased in frequency over the last 50 years (DeGaetano and Allen 2002). Precipitation in the Great Plains, sensitive to global land surface-atmosphere-ocean interactions, is characteristically variable; this interannual variation is particularly high in spring and summer (Ruiz-Barradas and Nigam 2005; Ruiz-Barradas and Nigam 2010). The high natural variability in precipitation across years and seasons decreases the capacity to detect changes in this climate parameter. For example, in the Central Great Plains, after two decades of dry conditions (1961 to 1980), annual precipitation increased 12% in the subsequent two decades (Garbrect and others 2004). Although patterns in temperature and precipitation are of interest to natural resource managers, a climate condition of particular concern in the region is drought. Widespread, severe, multi-year droughts, such as those of the 1930s and 1950s, are a regular element of the Great Plains system (Woodhouse and Overpeck 1998; Schubert and others 2004). Altered wind patterns, an increase in drought affected areas, and sea-level rise are among a list of changes associated with the enhanced greenhouse gas effect (IPCC 2007a).

By mid-century, average temperatures in the Great Plains may increase 1.1 °C to 3.3 °C; by the end of the century, global climate models project average temperatures to increase 1.4 °C to 7.2 °C (U.S. GCRP 2009). The projected increases in average temperature are greatest under scenarios with higher emissions of greenhouse gases (U.S. GCRP 2009). Climate projections indicate that the Northern Great Plains will experience the greatest warming in the region (U.S. GCRP 2009). In the Northern Great Plains, precipitation is likely to increase (5 to 20% lower emissions scenario; 5 to >40% higher emissions scenario); the Southern Great Plains may experience precipitation declines from 5 to 20% lower emissions scenario; 5 to >40% higher emissions scenarios (U.S. GCRP 2009). Higher maximum temperatures, high minimum temperatures, more hot summer days, and more heavy precipitation events are very likely by the end of the Twenty-First Century (Easterling and others 2000). Drought conditions are projected to increase in frequency, severity, and spatial extent (IPCC 2007b), including in the vulnerable Great Plains region (Woodhouse and Overpeck 1998). Again, the enhanced greenhouse gas effect is associated with a suite of climatic changes (i.e., increased storm intensity, fire, and flooding).

Habitats. The Great Plains are vast with topographic features ranging from steep mesas to rolling hills (Vinton and Collins 1997). The region is characterized by diverse terrestrial habitats. While shortgrass prairie is the dominant native vegetation in the arid western Great Plains, tallgrass prairie is dominant in the mesic, eastern region of the Great Plains (Vinton and Collins 1997). Cool-season grasses and forbs are the dominant native vegetation in the northern Great Plains (Vinton and Collins 1997).

These native grasslands host a diverse array of birds, mammals, reptiles, and invertebrates. In the northern Great Plains, thousands of shallow wetlands also dot the landscape; this swath of wetlands, called the Prairie Potholes, is an important source of stopover and breeding habitat for waterfowl. In the river drainages of the northern Great Plains, riparian woodlands provide important, structurally complex habitat for wildlife in the region (Rumble and Gobeille 2004, 1998). Although they cover less than 2% of the landscape, riparian woodlands host more than 50% of the animal species in the region (Theobald and others 2010).

Key Future Issues Associated With Climate Change and Adaptation

Climate-induced changes in vegetation will impact the distribution and abundance of animals on the landscape. For the Great Plains, projections of future vegetation do not indicate major declines in the total amount of grassland (see Friggens and others, Chapter 1 this volume), but the distribution may shift northwestward (Rehfeldt and others 2006). The projected increase in drought conditions will likely alter grassland composition and productivity, disturbance requirements, and erosion (Clark and others 2002). For example, woody vegetation in mixed and shortgrass prairie only occurs in areas of moisture compensation (Mack 1981; Girard and others 1989). These changes, particularly drought conditions, will likely exacerbate the major declines in grassland-dependent bird species (George and others 1992). Wetlands are highly sensitive to changes in hydrology and elevated temperatures; climate change alters the timing and availability of water resulting in changes in wetland species and habitat structure (Burkett and Kusler 2000; Winter 2000). For this reason, the Prairie Pothole region is considered highly vulnerable to future climate conditions (Johnson and others 2010). The likely result is major declines in waterfowl production (Sorenson and others 1998), particularly in the western Prairie Pothole region (Johnson and others 2010). In riparian systems of the western United States, reduced precipitation, early snowmelt, and higher temperatures will alter the timing and magnitude of stream flow; the result will likely be decreases in vegetation cover and particular species requiring moist soil conditions (Theobald and others 2010). In turn, this will lead to declines in the diverse animal species dependent on the riparian zone for reproduction and survival.

Earlier spring conditions (e.g., snowmelt, warm temperatures, and ice-out) cue some species to initiate migration and reproduction earlier in the year (Parmesan and Yohe 2003). For example, in a study of 44 migratory bird species, researchers found that more than 50% arrive earlier to breed in the Northern Prairie region; the trend is correlated with local climate and is most notable for species associated with aquatic habitats (e.g., blue-winged teal [*Anas discors*], northern shoveler [*Anas clypeata*], and Wilson's phalarope [*Steganopus tricolor*]) (Swanson and Palmer 2009). Large, rapid fluctuations in temperature are characteristic of spring; early arrival may expose migrants to more extreme cold snaps, low food availability, and other inhospitable conditions. Shifts in timing of resource availability in response to changes in rainfall patterns may also affect migrating birds. Altered snow conditions may also affect migrations of elk (Benkobi and others 2005) and deer and elk attendance by displaying sage-grouse (Bradbury and others 1989; Swanson 2009).

The geographic region where temperature and precipitation patterns are suitable for a species to persist is called its climate niche (Pearson and Dawson 2003). While a climatic niche describes "suitable" habitat, it does not mean that a species will not be able to inhabit an area that is considered climatically unsuitable in the future. Modeled shifts in a species climatic niche are not necessarily a perfect representation of the species future distribution. Changes in climate may expand, contract, or shift the climate niches of species (Parmesan and Yohe 2003). Under future climate conditions, bird species in the Great Plains, such as the Baird's sparrow (*Ammodramus bairdii*), may experience considerable reductions in their potential distributional area (Peterson 2003). Although some species may shift their distribution, agriculture and other landscape alterations will likely restrict these range shifts (Vos and others 2008).

For some species, high ambient temperatures may lead to heat stress or death. The regal fritillary (*Speyeria idalia*) is an endangered butterfly native to the mixed and tallgrass prairies of the central United States. Like most insects, it is sensitive to subtle, brief changes in temperature. High summer temperatures, especially in combination with intense solar radiation, may be lethal for eggs and larvae (Kopper and others 2000). The greater prairie-chicken (*Tympanuchus cupido*) is "especially vulnerable" to climate change (North American Bird Conservation Initiative 2010) and heat stress may result in juvenile mortality (Flanders-Wanner and others 2004). Heat stress may also impact reproduction (Finch 1983) and survival in song birds.

Warmer temperatures and changes in precipitation will likely increase the frequency and severity of disease outbreaks (Harvell and others 2002). Type C and E botulism, a disease of increasing concern for waterfowl, is more prevalent is shallow, warm waters (Rocke and Samuel 1999). Under such conditions (projected for the Great Plains), there may be more frequent outbreaks that result in massive waterfowl mortality.

Water availability determines the distribution and abundance of all living organisms; few species tolerate dry conditions. The northern leopard frog (*Rana pipiens*), a species of conservation concern in the Great Plains and western United States, is in widespread decline across its range (Smith and Keinath 2007). The local extinction of the species in montane regions of Colorado is attributed to severe drought conditions in the mid-1970s (Corn and Fogelman 1984). Under future climate scenarios, drought conditions are projected to increase in frequency, severity, and spatial extent (IPCC 2007a) with potentially large declines in amphibian populations (McMenamin and others 2008).

Flooding is a relatively common cause of reproductive failure in birds, particularly waterbirds (Burger 1982). In the Platte River area of the Great Plains, flooding in response to heavy precipitation is an established source of nest failure and chick mortality for the threatened Great Plains piping plover (*Charadrius melodus*) and endangered interior least tern (*Sterna antillarum athalassos*); in 1990, all surveyed nests for both species were inundated and resulted in extensive mortality (Sidle and others 1992). For populations already in decline, additional mortality is cause for management concern.

Although climate change and its associated impacts (e.g., conversion of land for biofuel production) will exacerbate declines in many animal populations and initiate major shifts in vegetation communities, some animal and plant species will likely benefit. Individual plants and animals may exhibit behavioral or phenotypic plasticity, altering their behavior or phenotype to minimize negative impacts or benefit from the novel conditions (e.g., Charmantier and others 2008; Kearney and others 2009). In addition, some animal and plant populations with high genetic diversity will exhibit flexibility, adapting to altered climatic conditions (Rice and Emery 2003). Given the varying responses of species, monitoring, research, and vulnerability assessments will be needed to prioritize management activities and allocate limited time and resources to meet conservation goals.

The American Southwest

Overview of Climatic Conditions and Habitats

The American Southwest is already experiencing pronounced climate change impacts that can be measured: 93% of New Mexico's watersheds have experienced increasing annual trends in moisture stress during 1970 to 2006; snowpack in New

Mexico's major mountain ranges has declined over the past two decades in 98% of all sites analyzed; and the timing of peak streamflow from snowmelt in the state is an average of one week earlier than in the mid-Twentieth Century (Enquist and others 2008).

The Southwest is characterized by general water scarcity compounded by cyclical droughts. It is also experiencing rapid human population growth resulting in increasing water use conflicts. As a result of all these factors, many southwestern natural communities are particularly at risk from global climate change (e.g., Hurd and Coonrod 2007). Most climate models for the Southwest predict pronounced temperature increases, particularly in the summer, coupled with more frequent, more severe droughts and possibly an overall drier climate from reduced winter precipitation (Meehl and others 2007; Seager and others 2007). Water is expected to become increasingly scarce (in part from increased evaporative rates), with lower soil moisture, reduced base river flow, reduced river basin recharge (Serrat-Capdevilla and others 2007), and decreased reservoir levels (Milly and others 2008). Climate and hydrological models also show reduced snowpack and earlier snow melt, which, in turn, will further alter river flow regimes (Barnett and others 2008; Pierce and others 2008; Bonfils and others 2008; Enquist and others 2008).

The ecological importance of riparian areas and wetlands is disproportionate to their size on the southwestern landscape, as they concentrate much of the regional wildlife (e.g., Carothers and others 1974; Ohmart and Anderson 1982; Rosenberg and others 1982; Hunter and others 1988; Krueper 1996; Cartron and others 2000). These naturally fragile ecosystems have already been heavily impacted by river regulation, groundwater pumping, woodcutting, overgrazing, mining, and invasive non-native plants (e.g., Knopf and others 1988; Unitt 1987; Ohmart 1994; Cartron and others 2000; Finch and Stoleson 2000). While some of the wildlife may increasingly rely on riparian areas, further shifting predation and competition equilibria, diminishing river flows, and river basin recharge may strongly threaten the regeneration of native riparian trees and other vegetation (Lytle and Merritt 2004), leading to large-scale loss and fragmentation of riparian and wetland ecosystems.

Key Future Issues Associated With Climate Change and Adaptation

Although the size of southwestern grasslands, shrublands, and deserts may not decrease over the long term (Rehfeldt and others 2006), their floristic composition may be drastically altered from individualistic species responses to climate change (Rehfeldt and others 2006) and from biological invasions occurring at an increasing pace (see Archer and Predick 2008).

Lizard species richness is unusually high in the southwestern United States, and consequently, many conservationists are alarmed about the potential for population extinctions in the Southwest because lizards comprise a group of species already showing severe impacts of climate change worldwide (Sinervo and others 2010). For instance, 12% of local populations of 48 lizard species in Mexico have already disappeared because of warmer temperatures, and up to 20% could go extinct by 2080 if these trends continue. Surveys of 200 Mexican locations indicated the temperature has changed too rapidly for the lizards to keep pace (Sinervo and others 2010). Similar results were found at other locations around the world. By modeling extinction risk, the research team learned that climate change is occurring too rapidly for lizards to compensate with physiological adaptations to higher body temperatures.

Severe droughts, in combination with increased incidences of fire, are predicted to accelerate the pace of invasions by certain non-native plant species (e.g., tamarisk) in southwestern environments. Ecosystems that are not adapted to fire (e.g., riparian woodlands and the Sonoran Desert) are particularly at risk. Risk of conversion of some ecosystems to monocultures of non-native plants is high, with resulting impacts on associated wildlife.

Of particular concern in the Sonoran Desert has been the spread of buffelgrass (*Pennisetum ciliare*) and Lehmann lovegrass (*Eragrostis lehmanniana*), introducing wildfires into an ecosystem not adapted to them (Finch and others 2010). The spread of buffelgrass and Lehmann lovegrass, fostered by drought and a positive feedback response to fire, illustrates the potential for climate change, biological invasions, and fire to interact synergistically (e.g., Cox and Ruyle 1998). The potential consequences for invasions by these exotic species are changes in food resources and structure of wildlife habitats.

Individualistic responses to climate change and seasonal latitudinal and/or elevational movements of wildlife species have the potential to create temporally mismatched phenologies between flowering plants and pollinators (Memmott and others 2007), an important issue for hummingbirds and bats in the Southwest.

As water availability, plant species composition, and habitat types in the Southwest change in response to warming, there will likely be matching changes in accessibility of some ecosystem services as well as changes in conservation targets. In a dual context of water scarcity and human population growth, climate change impacts are likely to lead to increasingly frequent clashes between economic interests and conservation efforts. Conservation and restoration efforts to mitigate or minimize climate change along southwestern rivers will likely be increasingly limited due to higher priorities in water allocation, such as irrigation for agriculture. Water allocations and natural flows are critical for supporting aquatic and riparian habitats in the Southwest. Wildlife populations associated with floodplain riparian areas and wetlands are expected to become increasingly impacted by drier weather and associated habitat changes coupled with higher water demands from growing human populations (Finch and others 2011). Increased movements of wildlife populations seeking to adapt to changing conditions and scarcity of water may increase conflicts with humans in urban-wildlife interfaces or in recreational areas. Drought typically promotes reduced crops of seeds, berries, and other sources of food for wild animals, resulting in a higher frequency of conflicts between humans and wildlife (e.g., bears) as wildlife expand their search efforts by entering campgrounds and urban fringe areas.

Amphibian and fish species may be especially vulnerable to climate change because of their dependency on vulnerable aquatic ecosystems (Bagne and others 2011). Further loss, degradation, and fragmentation of riparian areas, particularly riparian woodlands, may not only affect breeding and wintering populations of many bird species but may also disrupt migration (loss of stopover habitat) and precipitate further population declines of species such as the endangered southwestern willow flycatcher (*Empidonax traillii extimus*), which requires moist habitats (Finch and Stoleson 2000), and yellow-billed cuckoo (*Coccyzus americanus*), which requires large patches of suitable riparian wooded habitat. Increased aridity of rivers and streams is known to foster the spread of tamarisk, an exotic woody plant that is replacing southwestern riparian habitats dominated by native cottonwoods and willows. Increasing aridity also promotes increased fire risk. Tamarisk rebounds more quickly after fire than native species, leading to habitat conversion to a tamarisk-dominated community (Smith and others 2009) with a different habitat structure that promotes a different wildlife species composition (Smith and others 2007).

Endemic and rare species and remnant faunas found in patchy habitats are prevalent in the southwestern United States. As air temperatures increase and water availability and soil moisture decrease, remnant and isolated habitats (e.g., the Madrean oak and Sky Islands of southeastern Arizona and southwestern New Mexico) are especially vulnerable to impacts. If local habitats wink out, sedentary animal species may be unable to travel to similar habitats elsewhere and risk local extinctions (Coe and others 2012; Davison and others 2012).

Management Practices in the Interior West

How should we manage wildlife under a changing climate? The novelty of climate change means that we do not have tried-and-true adaptation strategies. Furthermore, because local conditions define what is appropriate and feasible, we should not expect a universal answer. However, the emerging consensus among scientists, managers, and stakeholders is that proper stewardship can maintain the resilience of natural systems to change (Halpin 1997). Although some argue this is a business as usual approach (Heller and Zavaleta 2009), such strategies will reduce existing stressors and increase the ability for animals and plants to cope with the direct and indirect impacts of climate change (table 5-1).

To manage wildlife and habitats faced with climate change, Federal, state, and private natural resources managers will need new information that projects where habitats and populations will change and will persist. Assessments of vulnerability to climate change at the species, habitat, ecosystem, and landscape levels will enable managers to identify target areas and species for conservation and management actions (Glick and others 2011; Bagne and others 2011).

Table 5-1. Best practices to maintain ecosystem resilience to climate impacts and examples of implementation in the Great Plains.

Best practice	Regional examples
Reduce existing threats	The Conservation Reserve Program provides more than 10 million acres of suitable habitat for many grassland species in the region. The program provides habitat for species displaced by conversion to agriculture, the dominant regional land use.
Practice adaptive management	Grazing in sensitive vegetation communities can compact soils and reduce regeneration of species like green ash or cottonwood. Managers can monitor effects of grazing and modify grazing management plans to ensure forage and community resources are not over utilized.
Evaluate land acquisition, including connectivity	The U.S. Geological Survey North Dakota Gap Analysis Project is an example of habitat-based planning for species that are poorly represented in an existing reserve network.
Consider natural disturbance regimes	Current grazing management guidelines include annual adjustments based on precipitation patterns. Research will be needed to predict the effects of increased reoccurring drought cycles on resource availability.
Build capacity via agency and university partnerships	Landscape Conservation Cooperatives are building partnerships with regional agencies, universities, and stakeholder to address climate change and other stressors in the region.
Engage the public in education and outreach activities	Youth environmental education programs provide a venue to engage the public on the topic of climate change. For example, the U.S. Forest Service sponsors the Kids in the Woods Program that provides conservation training. It also publishes a youth magazine called *Natural Inquirer* and a children's series known as *The Investigator*. Environmental education can offer positive opportunities to individuals who want to engage on the climate change issue (e.g., developing urban wildlife habitat or pollinator gardens).

Top Research Priorities

- Assess vulnerability of wildlife species, habitats, and ecosystems to climate change in grasslands, shrublands, and deserts of the Interior West (Glick and others 2011; Bagne and others 2011).
- Identify "hot spots" of management concern where high concentrations of vulnerable species are likely to be impacted by climate change, and partner with managers to develop action plans.
- Develop methods for protecting vulnerable populations and habitats and/or or assisting their migration relative to shifting ecosystems.
- Evaluate and identify critical sagebrush, grassland, and desert habitats and corridors that are likely to persist in coming decades so these lands can be managed for obligate, endemic, and endangered species and for maintaining biological diversity.
- Improve understanding of climate change effects on habitats prone to fire, invasive species, insects, and diseases to enable habitat planning and conservation (Chambers 2008).
- Determine whether and how wildlife species and communities can adapt to climate-induced changes in vegetation composition and prey availability.
- In riparian areas and other fragile ecosystems, evaluate changing wildlife species assemblages (including migration) and competition and predation pressures as a function of the interactions between climatic and hydrological conditions, spread of invasive plants, and fire frequency and intensity.
- Evaluate changing distributions and phenologies of hummingbird (and bat) nectar resources within the context of climate change and invasive species (top priority identified by Western Hummingbird Partnership 2010).
- Develop decision support tools, models, and website applications for conserving vulnerable wildlife and their habitats and biological diversity.

Strengths of RMRS Research Background for Proposed Research

The USDA Forest Service RMRS has developed a climate change strategy specifying priorities in research aimed at water, wildland fire, and terrestrial ecosystems (USDA FS RMRS 2010). In relation to this strategy, RMRS researchers are uniquely poised to address wildlife, habitat, and adaptation issues in response to climate change. Station scientists have developed a system for assessing vulnerability of species to climate change known as SAVS (Bagne and others 2011) that can be modified and adapted for broader application. Current and past research projects have focused on changes in habitat composition, distributions of invasive and native species, wildlife habitat use, population demographics, and populations of sensitive and endangered species under climate change scenarios. Station researchers in the Great Basin specialize in the development of native plant materials useful for habitat restoration and for sustaining critical plant species and ecosystems. Studies on the effects of fire, invasive species, and other disturbances on sagebrush, grassland, and riparian ecosystems comprise a major focal area of the RMRS GSD Ecosystems Program.

Partners, Collaborators, and Sponsors

Current and potential cooperators include Federal, state, and municipal agencies such as USDA Forest Service Regions 1, 2, 3, and 4 and western research stations, USGS Climate Change and Science Centers, Bureau of Land Management, U.S. Fish and Wildlife Service, Bureau of Reclamation, state wildlife management agencies, state conservation districts, and city open space divisions. Science and management collaborations with Department of the Interior Landscape Conservation Cooperatives have become an important RMRS focus. Developing research partnerships with USFWS Joint Ventures has potential to address climate change impacts on wildlife. Collaboration with Mexican researchers, governmental agencies, and non-Government organizations will serve several needs: (1) climate conditions and species assemblages in tomorrow's Southwest may have their analogs in today's Mexico; (2) some compounding threats to southwestern ecosystems may spread from Mexico (insect diseases; invasive plants originally from Africa and other tropical or subtropical regions), particularly those elevating the risk of fire; and (3) some conservation tools and strategies could be tested first in Mexico. RMRS is already working with The Nature Conservancy's Southwest Climate Change Initiative to identify opportunities to address global climate change adaptation challenges in New Mexico, Arizona, Utah, and Colorado. Other non-Government partners where relationships have already been established include National Wildlife Federation, Sky Island Alliance, Western Hummingbird Partnership, Partners in Flight, Western Elk Foundation, Nature Serve, National Wild Turkey Foundation, National Wildlife Foundation, and some industry partners such as wind energy corporations.

Literature Cited

Aldridge, C. L., S. E. Nielsen, H. L. Beyer, M. S. Boyce and others. 2008. Range-wide patterns of sage-grouse persistence. Diversity and Distributions 14: 983-994.

Allen, C. D., A. K. Macalady, H. Chenchouni, D. Bachelet and others. 2010. A global overview of drought and heat-induced tree mortality reveals emerging climate change risks for forests. Forest Ecology and Management 259: 660-684.

Ammon, E. M. 2002. Changes in the bird community of the lower Truckee River, Nevada, 1868-2001. Great Basin Birds 5: 13-20.

Archer, S. R. and K. I. Predick. 2008. Climate change and ecosystems of the southwestern United States. Rangelands: June 2008: 23-28.

Arsenault, D. 2002. Nevada Partners in Flight All Bird Monitoring Plan. Reno, NV: Lahontan Audobon Society.

Atamian, M. T., J. S. Sedinger, J. S. Heaton and E. J. Blomberg. 2010. Landscape-level assessment of brood-rearing habitat for greater sage-grouse in Nevada. Journal of Wildlife Management 74: 1533-1543.

Bagne, K. E., D. M. Finch and M. M. Friggens. 2011. Vulnerability of amphibians to climate change: implications for rangeland management. In: Feldman, S. R. and M. B. Sacido, eds. IX International Rangeland Congress: Diverse Rangelands for a Sustainable Society. April 3-10, 2011; Rosario, Argentina. IRC 2001 Congress. 159 p.

Bagne, K. E., M. M. Friggens and D. M. Finch. 2011. A system for assessing vulnerability of species (SAVS) to climate change. Gen. Tech. Rep. RMRS-GTR-257. Fort Collins, CO: U.S. Department of Agriculture, Rocky Mountain Research Station. 28 p.

Barnett, T. P., D. W. Pierce, H. G. Hidalgo, C. Bonfils and others. 2008. Human-induced changes in the hydrology of the western United States. Science 319: 1080-1083.

Beatley, J. C. 1975. Climates and vegetation pattern across the Mohave/Great Basin Desert transition of southern Nevada. American Midland Naturalist 93: 53-70.

Benkobi, L., M. Rumble, C. Stubblefield, R. Gamo and J. Millspaugh. 2005. Seasonal migration and home ranges of female elk in the Black Hills of South Dakota and Wyoming. The Prairie Naturalist 37: 151-166.

Bonfils, C., B. D. Santer, D. W. Pierce, H. G. Hidalgo and others. 2008. Detection and attribution of temperature changes in the mountainous western United States. Journal of Climate 21(23): 6404-6424.

Both, C., S. Bouwhuis, C. M. Lessells and M. E. Visser. 2006. Climate change and population declines in a long-distance migratory bird. Nature 441: 81-83.

Boula, K. M. 1985. Foraging ecology of migrant waterbirds, Lake Abert, Oregon. Thesis, Oregon State University.

Bradbury, J. W., S. L. Vehrencamp and R. M. Gibson. 1989. Dispersion of displaying male sage grouse. I. Patterns of temporal variation. Behavioral Ecology and Sociobiology 24: 1-14.

Bradford, D. F., S. E. Franson, A. C. Neale, D. T. Heggem, G. R. Miller and G. E. Canterbury. 1998. Bird species assemblages as indicators of biological integrity in Great Basin rangeland. Environmental Monitoring and Assessment 49: 1-22.

Burger, J. 1982. An overview of proximate factors affecting reproductive success in colonial birds: concluding remarks and summary of panel discussion. Colonial Waterbirds 5: 58-65.

Burkett, V. and J. Kusler. 2000. Climate change: potential impacts and interactions in wetlands of the United States. Journal of the American Water Resources Association 36: 313-320.

Carothers, S. W., R. R. Johnson and S. W. Aitchison. 1974. Population structure and social organization of southwestern riparian birds. American Zoologist 14: 97-108.

Cartron, J.-L. E., S. H. Stoleson, P. L. L. Stoleson and D. W. Shaw. 2000. Riparian areas. Pages 281-328. In: Jemison, R. and C. Raish, eds. Livestock Management in the American Southwest: Ecology, Society and Economics. Elsevier Science, Amsterdam, Netherlands.

Cayan, D. R., S. A. Kammerdiener, M. D. Dettinger, J. M. Caprio and D. H. Peterson. 2001. Changes in the onset of spring in the western United States. Bulletin of the American Meteorological Society 82(3): 399-415.

Chambers, J. C. 2008. Climate change and the Great Basin. Gen. Tech. Rep. RMRS-GTR-204. Fort Collins, CO: U.S. Department of Agriculture, Forest Service, Rocky Mountain Research Station.

Chambers, J. C., B. A. Roundy, R. R. Blank, S. E. Meyer and A. Whittaker. 2007. What makes Great Basin sagebrush ecosystems invasible by *Bromus tectorum*? Ecological Monographs 77: 117-145.

Clark, J. S., E. C. Grimm, J. J. Donovan, S. C. Fritz, D. R. Engstrom and J. E. Almendinger. 2002. Drought cycles and landscape responses to past aridity on prairies of the northern Great Plains, U.S.A. Ecology 83: 595-601.

Coe, S., D. M. Finch and M. M. Friggens. 2012. An assessment of climate change and the vulnerability of wildlife in the Sky Islands of the Southwest. Gen. Tech. Rep. RMRS-GTR-273. Fort Collins, CO: U.S. Department of Agriculture, Forest Service, Rocky Mountain Research Station. 208 p.

Corn, P. S. and J. C. Fogleman. 1984. Extinction of montane populations of the northern leopard frog (*Rana pipiens*) in Colorado. Journal of Herpetology 18: 147-152.

Cornely, J. E. 1982. Waterfowl production at Malheur National Wildlife Refuge 1942-1980. U.S Fish and Wildlife Publications 38: 559-571.

Cox, J. R. and G. B. Ruyle. 1998. The influence of climate, soil and grazing on the distribution of Lehmann lovegrass. Pages 150-157. In: Tellman, B., D. M. Finch, C. Edminster and R. Hamre, eds. The future of arid grasslands: identifying issues, seeking solutions. October 9-13, 1996; Tucson, Arizona. Proc. RMRS-P-3. Fort Collins, CO: U.S. Department of Agriculture, Forest Service, Rocky Mountain Research Station. 392 p.

Davison, J. E., S. Coe, D. Finch, E. Rowland, M. Friggens and L. J. Graumlich. 2012. Bringing indices of species vulnerability to climate change into geographic space: an assessment across the Coronado National Forest. Biodiversity and Conservation 21: 189-204.

Dobkin, D. S., A. C. Rich, J. A. Pretare and W. H. Pyle. 1995. Nest-site relationships among cavity-nesting birds of riparian and snowpocket aspen woodlands in the northwestern Great Basin. Condor 97: 694-707.

Dobkin, D. S., A. C. Rich, J. A. Pretare and W. H. Pyle. 1998. Habitat and avifaunal recovery from livestock grazing in a riparian meadow system of the northwestern Great Basin. Conservation Biology 12: 209-221.

DeGaetano, A. T. and R. J. Allen. 2002. Trends in twentieth-century temperature extremes across the United States. Journal of Climate 15: 3188-3205.

Doherty, K. E., D. E. Naugle and B. L. Walker. 2010. Greater sage grouse nesting habitat: the importance of managing at multiple scales. Journal of Wildlife Management 74: 1544-1553.

Easterling, D., G. Meehl, C. Parmesan, S. Changnon, T. Karl and L. Mearns. 2000. Climate extremes: observations, modeling, and impacts. Science 289: 2068-2074.

Enquist, C. A. F., E. H. Girvetz and D. F. Gori. 2008. Conservation implications of emergent moisture stress due to recent climate changes in New Mexico. A climate change vulnerability assessment for biodiversity in New Mexico, part III. Climate Change Ecology and Adaptation Program, The Nature Conservancy in New Mexico. Available: http://nmconservation.org/dl/CC_report2_final.pdf.

Finch, D. 1983. Seasonal variation in nest placement of Abert's towhees. Condor 85: 111-113.

Finch, D. M., K. E. Bagne, M. M. Friggens, D. M. Smith and K. M. Brodhead. 2011. A review of climate change effects on terrestrial rangeland birds. In: Feldman, S. R., G. E. Oliva and M. B. Sacido, eds. IX International Rangeland Congress: Diverse Rangelands for a Sustainable Society. April 3-10, 2011; Rosario, Argentina. IRC 2001 Congress. 68 p.

Finch, D. M., M. Friggens and K. Bagne. 2011. Case study 3: species vulnerability assessment for the Middle Rio Grande, New Mexico. In: Glick, P., B. A. Stein and N. A. Edelson, eds. Scanning the conservation horizon: a guide to climate change vulnerability assessment. Washington, DC: National Wildlife Federation: 96-103.

Finch, D. M., D. Pearson, J. Wunderle and W. Arendt. 2010. Terrestrial animals as invasive species and as species at risk from invasions. In Dix, M. E. and K. Britton, eds. A dynamic invasive species research vision: opportunities and priorities 2009-2029. Gen. Tech. Rep. WO-79/83. Washington, DC: U.S. Department of Agriculture, Forest Service Research and Development: 43-54.

Finch, D. M. and S. H. Stoleson, eds. 2000. Status, ecology, and conservation of the southwestern willow flycatcher. Gen. Tech. Rep. RMRS-60. Ogden, UT: U.S. Department of Agriculture, Forest Service, Rocky Mountain Research Station.

Flanders-Wanner, B., G. White and L. McDaniel. 2004. Weather and prairie grouse: dealing with effects beyond our control. Wildlife Society Bulletin 32: 22-34.

Gabler, K. I., L. T. Heady and J. W. Laundre. 2001. A habitat suitability model for pygmy rabbits (*Brachylagus idahoensis*) in southeastern Idaho. Western North American Naturalist 61: 480-489.

Garbrect, J., M. Van Liew and G. O. Brown. 2004. Trends in precipitation, streamflow, and evapotranspiration in the Great Plains of the United States. Journal of Hydrologic Engineering 9: 360-367.

George, T. L., A. C. Fowler, R. L. Knight and L. C. McEwen. 1992. Impacts of a severe drought on grassland birds in western North Dakota. Ecological Applications 2: 275-284.

Girard, M., H. Goetz and A. Bjugstad. 1989. Native woodland types of southwestern North Dakota. Res. Pap. RM-281. Fort Collins, CO: U.S. Department of Agriculture, Forest Service, Rocky Mountain Forest and Range and Experiment Station. 36 p.

Glick, P., B. A. Stein and N. A. Edelson, eds. 2011. Scanning the conservation horizon: a guide to climate change vulnerability assessment. National Wildlife Federation, Washington, DC. 168 p.

Green, J. S. and J. T. Flinders. 1980. Habitat and dietary relationships of the pygmy rabbit. Journal of Range Management 33: 136-142.

Halpin, P. 1997. Global climate change and natural-area protection: management responses and research directions. Ecological Applications 7: 828-843.

Hanley, T. A. and K. A. Hanley. 1982. Food resource partitioning by sympatric ungulates on Great Basin rangeland. Journal of Range Management 35: 152-158.

Harvell, C. D., C. E. Mitchell, J. R. Ward, S. Altizer and others. 2002. Climate warming and disease risks for terrestrial and marine biota. Science 296: 2158-2162.

Heller, N. and E. Zavaleta. 2009. Biodiversity management in the face of climate change: a review of 22 years of recommendations. Biological Conservation 142: 14-32.

Himes, J. G. and P. J. Drohan. 2007. Distribution and habitat selection of the pygmy rabbit, *Brachylagus idahoensis*, in Nevada (USA). Journal of Arid Environments 68: 371-382.

Hunter, W. C., R. D. Ohmart and B. W. Anderson. 1987. Status of breeding riparian-obligate birds in southwestern riverine systems. Western Birds 18: 10-18.

Hunter, W. C., R. D. Ohmart and B. W. Anderson. 1988. Use of exotic saltcedar (*Tamarix chinensis*) by birds in arid riparian systems. Condor 90: 113-123.

Hurd, B. H. and J. Coonrod. 2007. Climate change and its implications for New Mexico's water resources and economic opportunities. Technical Report 45, New Mexico State University. Available: https://portal.azoah.com/oedf/documents/08A-AWS001-DWR/Omnia/20070700%20Hurd%20and%20Coonrod%20Climate%20Change%20NM%20Water.pdf.

Intergovernmental Panel on Climate Change [IPCC]. 2007a. Climate change 2007: synthesis report. Contribution of Working Groups I, II and III to the Fourth Assessment Report of the Intergovernmental Panel on Climate Change. [Core Writing Team, Pachauri, R. K. and Reisinger, A. eds.]. IPCC, Geneva, Switzerland.

Intergovernmental Panel on Climate Change [IPCC]. 2007b. Climate change 2007: impacts, adaptation and vulnerability. Contribution of Working Group II to the Fourth Assessment Report of the Intergovernmental Panel on Climate Change, Parry, M. L., O. F. Canziani, J. P. Palutikof, P. J. van der Linden and C. E. Hanson, eds. Cambridge University Press, Cambridge, UK.

Isaacs, F. B. and R. G. Anthony. 1987. Abundance, foraging, and roosting of bald eagles in the Harney Basin, Oregon. Northwest Science 61: 114-121.

Jehl, J. R. 1986. Biology of red-necked phalaropes (*Phalaropus lobatus*) at the western edge of the Great Basin in fall migration. Great Basin Naturalist 46: 185-197.

Jehl, J. R, Jr., W. S. Boyd, D. S. Paul and D. W. Anderson. 2002. Massive collapse and rapid rebound: population dynamics of eared grebes (*Podiceps nigricollis*) during an ENSO event. Auk 199: 1162-1166.

Johnson, W. C., B. Werner, G. Guntenspergen, R. Voldseth and others. 2010. Prairie wetland complexes as landscape functional units in a changing climate. BioScience 60: 128-140.

Katzner, T. E. and K. L. Parker. 1997. Vegetative characteristics and home ranges used by pygmy rabbits (*Brachylagus idahoensis*) during winter. Journal of Mammalogy 78: 1063-1072.

Knapp, P. A. 1996. Cheatgrass (*Bromus tectorum* L.) dominance in the Great Basin Desert: history, persistence, and influences to human activities. Global Environmental Change 6: 37-52.

Knick, S. T., D. S. Dobkin, J. T. Rotenberry, M. A. Schroeder, W. M. Vander Haegen and C. van Riper, III. 2003. Teetering on the edge or too late? Conservation and research issues for avifauna of sagebrush habitats. Condor 105: 611-634.

Knick, S. T. and J. T. Rotenberry. 2002. Effects of habitat fragmentation on passerine birds breeding in intermountain shrubsteppe. Studies in Avian Biology 25: 130-140.

Knopf, F. L., R. R. Johnson, T. Rich, F. B. Samson and R. C. Szaro. 1988. Conservation of riparian ecosystems in the United States. Wilson Bulletin 100: 272-284.

Knopf, F. L. and J. L. Kennedy. 1980. Foraging sites of white pelicans nesting at Pyramid Lake, Nevada. Western Birds 11: 175-180.

Kopper, B., R. Charlton and D. Margolies. 2000. Oviposition site selection by the regal fritillary, *Speyeria idalia*, as affected by proximity of violet host plants. Journal of Insect Behavior 13: 651-665.

Krueper, D. J. 1996. Effects of livestock management on southwestern riparian systems. Pages 281-301. In: Shaw, D. W. and D. M. Finch, eds. Desired future conditions for southwestern riparian ecosystems: bringing interests and concerns together. Gen. Tech. Rep. RM-272. Fort Collins, CO: U.S. Department of Agriculture, Forest Service, Rocky Mountain Forest and Range Experiment Station.

LeDee, O., K. Martin, D. McFarland, M. Meyer, A. Paulios, C. Ribic, D. Sample, and T. Van Deelen. 2011. Wildlife working group report. In: Wisconsin's changing climate: impacts and adaptation. Wisconsin Initiative on Climate Change Impacts. Available: http://www.wicci.wisc.edu/.

Liu, Y., J. Stanturf and S. Goodrick. 2010. Trends in global wildfire potential in a changing climate. Forest Ecology and Management 259: 685-697.

Lytle, D. A. and D. M. Merritt. 2004. Hydrologic regimes and riparian forests: a structured population model for cottonwood. Ecology 85: 2493-2503.

Mack, S. 1981. Hardwood ravines and associated vegetation in west-central North Dakota. Thesis. North Dakota State University, Fargo. 168 p.

MacMahon, J. A. 1979. North American deserts: their floral and faunal components. In: R. A. Perry and D. W. Goodall, eds. Arid-land Ecosystems: Structure, Functioning, and Management Vol. 1. International Biological Program 16. Cambridge: Cambridge University Press: 21-81.

Manning, A. E. and D. S. Paul. 2003. Migratory waterbird use of the Great Salt Lake ecosystem. Great Basin Birds 6: 5-17.

McMenamin, S. K., E. A. Hadly and C. K. Wright. 2008. Climatic change and wetland desiccation cause amphibian decline in Yellowstone National Park. Proceedings of the National Academy of Sciences 105: 16988-16993.

Meehl, G. A., T. F. Stocker, W. D. Collins, P. Friedlingstein and others. 2007. Global climate projections. In: Solomon, S., D. Qin, M. Manning, Z. Chen, M. Marquis, K. B. Averyt, M. Tignor and H. L. Miller, eds. Climate Change 2007: The Physical Basis. Contribution of Working Group I to the Fourth Assessment Report of the Intergovernmental Panel on Climate Change Cambridge University Press, Cambridge, UK: 747-845.

Melack, J. M., J. Dozier, C. R. Goldman, D. Greenland, A. M. Milner and R. J. Naiman. 1997. Effects of climate change on inland waters of the Pacific Coastal Mountains and western Great Basin of North America. Hydrological Processes 11: 971-992.

Memmott, J., P. G. Craze, N. M. Waser and M. V. Price. 2007. Global warming and the disruption of plant pollinator interactions. Ecology Letters 10: 710-717.

Milly, P. C. D., J. Betancourt, M. Falkenmark, R. M. Hirsch and others. 2008. Stationarity is dead: whither water management? Science 319(5863): 573-574.

Mote, P. W., A. F. Hamlet, M. P. Clark and D. P. Lettenmaier. 2005. Declining mountain snowpack in western North America. Bulletin of the American Meteorological Society 86(1): 39-49.

National Audubon Society. 2000. Jordan River Natural Conservation Corridor Report.

Neel, L. A. and W. G. Henry. 1996. Shorebirds of the Lahontan Valley, Nevada, USA: a case history of western Great Basin shorebirds. International Wader Studies 9: 15-19.

Neilson, R. P., J. M. Lenihan, D. Bachelet and R. J. Drapek. 2005. Climate change implications for sagebrush ecosystems. Transactions of the Wildlife and Natural Resources Conference 70: 145-159.

North American Bird Conservation Initiative, U.S. Committee. 2010. The state of the birds 2010 report on climate change, United States of America. Washington, DC: U.S. Department of the Interior.

Ohmart, R. D. 1994. The effects of human-induced changes on the avifauna of western riparian habitats. Studies in Avian Biology 15: 273-285.

Ohmart, R. D. and B. W. Anderson. 1982. North American desert riparian ecosystems. Pages 433-479. In: G. L. Bender, ed. Reference Handbook on the Deserts of North America. Greenwood Press, Westport, CT.

Oring, L. W. and J. M. Reed. 1996. Shorebirds of the western Great Basin of North America: overview and importance to continental populations. International Wader Studies 9: 6-12.

Parmesan, C. and G. Yohe. 2003. A globally coherent fingerprint of climate change impacts across natural systems. Nature 421: 37-42.

Pearson, R. G. and T. P. Dawson. 2003. Predicting the impacts of climate change on the distribution of species: are bioclimate envelope models useful? Global Ecology and Biogeography 12: 361-371.

Peterson, A. T. 2003. Projected climate change effects on Rocky Mountain and Great Plains birds: generalities of biodiversity consequences. Global Change Biology 9: 647-655.

Pierce, D. W., T. P. Barnett, H. G. Hidalgo, T. Das and others. 2008. Attribution of declining western U.S. snowpack to human event. Journal of Climate 21(23): 6425-6444.

Rehfeldt, G. E., N. L. Crookston, M. V. Warwell and J. S. Evans. 2006. Empirical analyses of plant-climate relationships for the Western United States. International Journal of Plant Science 167: 1123-1150.

Reynolds, T. D. 1979. Response of reptile populations to different land management on the Idaho National Engineering Laboratory Site. Great Basin Naturalist 39: 255-262.

Rocke, T. E. and M. D. Samuel. 1999. Water and sediment characteristics associated with avian botulism outbreaks in wetlands. Journal of Wildlife Management 63: 1249-1260.

Rosenberg, K. V., R. D. Ohmart and B. W. Anderson. 1982. Community organization of riparian breeding birds: Response to an annual resources peak. Auk 99: 260-274.

Ruiz-Barradas, A. and S. Nigam. 2005. Warm-season precipitation variability over the US Great Plains in observations, NCEP and ERA-40 reanalyses, and NCAR and NASA atmospheric simulations. Journal of Climate 18: 1808-1830.

Ruiz-Barradas, A. and S. Nigam, 2010. Great Plains precipitation and its SST links in 20th Century climate simulations, and 21st and 22nd Century climate projections. Journal of Climate 23: 6409-6429.

Rumble, M. and J. Gobeille. 1998. Avian use of successional cottonwood (*Populus deltoides*) woodlands along the middle Missouri River. American Midland Naturalist 152: 165-177.

Rumble, M. and J. Gobeille. 2004. Bird community relationships to succession in green ash (*Fraxinus pennsylvanica*). American Midland Naturalist 140: 372-381.

Ryser, F. A., Jr. 1985. Birds of the Great Basin. University of Nevada Press, Reno.

Sada, D. W. and G. L. Vinyard. 2002. Anthropogenic changes in biogeography of Great Basin aquatic biota. Smithsonian Contributions to the Earth Sciences 33: 277-293.

Schubert, S., M. Suarez, P. Pegion, R. Koster and J. Bacmeister. 2004 Causes of long-term drought in the U.S. Great Plains. Journal of Climate 17: 485-503.

Schroeder, M. A. and L. A. Robb. 1993. Greater prairie-chicken (*Tympanuchus cupido*). In: A. Poole, ed. The Birds of North America Online. Ithaca: Cornell Lab of Ornithology. Available: http://bna.birds.cornell.edu/bna/species/036.

Seager, R., M. Ting, I. Held, Y. Kushnir and others. 2007. Model projections of an imminent transition to a more arid climate in southwestern North America. Science 316: 1181-1184.

Serrat-Capdevila, A., J. B. Valdés, J. G. Pérez, K. Baird, L. J. Mata and T. Maddock III. 2007. Modeling climate change impacts—and uncertainty—on the hydrology of a riparian system: the San Pedro Basin (Arizona/Sonora). Journal of Hydrology 347: 48-66.

Shreve, F. 1942. The desert vegetation of North America. Botanical Review 8: 195-246.

Sidle, J. G., D. E. Carlson, E. M. Kirsh and J. J. Dinan. 1992. Flooding: mortality and habitat renewal for least terns and piping plovers. Colonial Waterbirds 15: 132-136.

Sinervo, B., F. Méndez-de-la-Cruz, D. B. Miles, B. Heulin and others. 2010. Erosion of lizard diversity by climate change and altered thermal niches. Science 328 (5980): 894-899

Smith, B. E. and D. A. Keinath. 2007. Northern leopard frog (*Rana pipiens*): a technical conservation assessment. [Online]. U.S. Department of Agriculture, Forest Service, Rocky Mountain Region. Available: http://www.fs.fed.us/r2/projects/scp/assessments/northernleopardfrog.pdf.

Smith, D. M., D. M. Finch, C. Gunning, R. Jemison and J. F. Kelly. 2009. Post-wildfire recovery of riparian vegetation during a period of water scarcity in the Southwestern USA. Fire Ecology 5: 38-55.

Smith, D. M., J. F. Kelly and D. M. Finch. 2007. Avian nest box selection and nest success in burned and unburned southwestern riparian forest. Journal of Wildlife Management 71: 411-421.

Sogge, M. K., S. J. Sferra and E. H. Paxton. 2008. Tamarix as habitat for birds: implications for riparian restoration in the southwestern United States. Restoration Ecology 16(1): 146-154.

Sorenson, L., R. Goldberg, T. Root and M. Anderson. 1998. Potential effects of global warming on waterfowl populations breeding in the northern Great Plains. Climatic Change 40: 343-369.

Stewart, I. T., D. R. Cayan and M. D. Dettinger. 2005. Changes toward earlier streamflow timing across western North America. Journal of Climate 18(8): 1136-1155.

Stoleson, S. H. and D. M. Finch. 2001. Breeding bird use of and nesting success in exotic Russian olive in New Mexico. Wilson Bulletin 113: 452-455.

Swanson, C. 2009. Ecology of greater sage-grouse in the Dakotas. Dissertation, South Dakota State University. 168 p.

Swanson, D. and J. Palmer. 2009. Spring migration phenology of birds in the northern Prairie region is correlated with local climate change. Journal of Field Ornithology 80: 351-363.

Theobald, D., D. Merritt and J. Norman, III. 2010. Assessment of threats to riparian ecosystems in the western U.S. Prepared for the Western Environmental Threats Assessment Center, Prineville, OR. Available: http://warnercnr.colostate.edu/~davet/WesternRiparianThreatsAssessment2010.pdf.

Thomas, J. W., C. Maser and J. E. Rodiek. 1979. Wildlife habitats in managed rangelands—the Great Basin of southeastern Oregon: riparian zones. Gen. Tech. Rep. PNW-80. Portland, OR: U.S. Depsrtment of Agriculture, Forest Service, Pacific Northwest Forest and Range Experimental Station.

Unitt, P. 1987. *Empidonax traillii extimus*: An endangered subspecies. Western Birds 18: 137-162.

USDA Forest Service, Rocky Mountain Research Station [USDA FS RMRS]. 2010. 2009 Climate change research strategy. Fort Collins, CO: U.S. Department of AgricultureForest Service, Rocky Mountain Research Station. Available: http://www.fs.fed.us/rmrs/docs/climate-change/climate-change-research-strategy.pdf.

U.S. Environmental Protection Agency [USEPA]. 1998a. Climate change and Nevada. EPA 236-F-98-007o.

U.S. Environmental Protection Agency [USEPA]. 1998b. Climate change and Utah. EPA 236-F-98-007z.

U.S. Global Change Research Program [USGCRP]. 2009. Global climate change impacts in the United States. T. R. Karl, J. M. Melillo and T. C. Peterson, eds. Cambridge University Press.

van Mantgem, P. J., N. L. Stephenson, J. C. Byrne, L. D. Daniels and others. 2009. Widespread increase of tree mortality rates in the western United States. Science 323: 521-524.

van Riper, C., III, K. L. Paxton, C. O'Brien, P. B. Shafroth and L. J. McGrath. 2008. Rethinking avian response to *Tamarix* on the lower Colorado River: a threshold hypothesis. Restoration Ecology 16: 155-167.

Vinton, M. and S. Collins. 1997. Landscape gradients and habitat structures in native grasslands of the central Great Plains in Ecology and conservation of Great Plains vertebrates. F. Knopf and F. Samson, eds. Springer-Verlag, New York.

Vos, C. C., P. Berry, P. Opdam, H. Baveco and others. 2008. Adapting landscapes to climate change: examples of climate-proof ecosystem networks and priority adaptation zones. Journal of Applied Ecology 45: 1722-1731.

Walker, H. A. 2008. Floristics and physiognomy determine landbird response to tamarisk (*Tamarix ramosissima*) invasion in riparian areas. Auk 125(3): 520-531.

Wallestad, R. O., J. G. Peterson and R. L. Eng. 1975. Foods of adult sage grouse in central Montana. Journal of Wildlife Management 39: 628-30.

Warnock, N., S. M. Haig and L. W. Oring. 1998. Monitoring species richness and abundance of shorebirds in the western Great Basin. Condor 100: 589-600.

Webb, R. H., Leake, S. A. and R. M. Turner. 2008. The ribbon of green: change in riparian vegetation on the southwestern United States. University of Arizona Press, Tucson.

West, N. E. 1983. Temperate Deserts and Semi-deserts. Elsevier Publishing, Amsterdam, The Netherlands.

Western Hummingbird Partnership. 2010. Western Hummingbird Partnership Action Plan. Available: http://www.hummonnet.org/pdf/201006whp_actionplan.pdf [accessed October 13, 2010].

Winter, T. C. 2000. The vulnerability of wetlands to climate change: a hydrologic landscape perspective. Journal of the American Water Resources Association 36: 305-311.

Wisdom, M. J., M. M. Rowland and L. H. Suring, eds. 2005. Habitat Threats in the Sagebrush Ecosystem: Methods of Regional Assessment and Application in the Great Basin. Allen Press, Lawrence, Kansas.

Woodhouse, C. and J. Overpeck. 1998. 2000 Years of drought variability in the central United States. Bulletin of the American Meteorological Society 79: 2693-2714.

Wright, J. M. and J. C. Chambers. 2002. Restoring riparian meadows currently dominated by Artemisia using alternative state concepts-above-ground vegetation response. Applied Vegetation Science 5: 237-246.

Chapter 6

Disturbance and Climate Change in the Interior West

Paulette L. Ford[1], Jeanne K. Chambers[2], Sharon J. Coe[1,3], and Burton C. Pendleton[1]

[1] U.S. Forest Service, Rocky Mountain Research Station; Grassland, Shrubland, and Desert Ecosystems Program; Forestry Sciences Laboratory, Albuquerque, New Mexico

[2] U. S. Forest Service, Rocky Mountain Research Station; Grassland, Shrubland, and Desert Ecosystems Program; Forestry Sciences Laboratory, Reno, Nevada

[3] School of Renewable Natural Resources, University of Arizona, Tucson, Arizona

Executive Summary

Within the continental United States, average annual temperature increased during the Twentieth Century by approximately 0.65 °C. The most extreme warming occurred throughout the northern and western United States (IPCC 2007a; Williams and others 2010). Disturbances such as fire, drought, grazing, urbanization, and energy development are predicted to have a heightened impact on the western United States under a changing climate. For example, extreme drought conditions accompanied by rising temperatures characterized the American Southwest during the past decade (Floyd and others 2009). Key future issues to consider are:

- Longer and more severe droughts.
- Longer periods of dry conditions leading to increased potential for "mega fires."
- Increased ecosystem susceptibility to insect pests and disease.
- Increased susceptibility of ecosystems to invasion of non-native species.
- Changes in the relationships among plants, water, nutrients, and soils on grazed lands.
- Increased effects of grazing on greenhouse gas (GHG) levels.
- Increased conflicts over use of freshwater for native ecosystems and for growing human populations.
- Changes in precipitation runoff and potential for changes in flooding patterns.
- Increased concern over the potential for fire as human development extends the wildland-urban interface.
- Increased disturbance associated with domestic fuel exploration and production.

Some examples of research the RMRS GSD Program is conducting to address many of these key issues are:

- Studies of the response of Great Basin upland and riparian plant communities to climate change and anthropogenic disturbance and the implications for future responses to climate and management activities.
- Methods for maintaining and restoring riparian communities and their ecosystem services based on an understanding of the effects of climate change.
- Understanding the interacting effects of climate and fire on successional processes at landscape scales.

- Plant-climate relationships in the western United States and the effects of climate change on those relationships and on the landscape distribution of key species and communities.
- The interacting effects of climate change and livestock grazing on rangeland resources of the United States.
- The role of climate variation on historic fire regimes at local to sub-continental scales.
- The effects of climate and land use factors on successional dynamics and ecological threshold crossings in grassland ecosystems and the use of this information for state-and-transition models.
- The effects of climate on pinyon-juniper woodlands in western landscapes over the last 150 years.

However, there are gaps in our knowledge base. Some major research needs are:

- Improved methods for post-fire restoration of arid ecosystems and of ecosystems dominated by fire-adapted exotic grasses.
- Ecosystem recovery after fire, including effects of livestock grazing and re-seeding and re-planting of plant species.
- Relationships of weather and climate patterns to past and present fire regimes at local scales.
- Regional climate change predictions and improved capacity to predict ecological responses.
- Interactions among the primary climate change variables: precipitation regimes, elevated CO_2 and increased temperature.
- The most appropriate and least impactful sites for energy development.
- Appropriate plant materials for use in reclamation and restoration of disturbed sites under expected climate change scenarios.
- Effects of large solar generating facilities and wind-power developments on migration corridors, seed movement, and potential off-site effects of chemical dust control agents.

Our research sponsors, collaborators, and partners include: universities, The National Forest Service, Bureau of Land Management, Agricultural Research Service, Natural Resources Conservation Service, U.S. Geological Survey, Bureau of Indian Affairs, U.S. Fish and Wildlife Service, National Park Service, National Science Foundation, Long Term Ecological Research Network, state and municipal governments, tribal governments, Joint Fire Science Program, Department of Defense, Department of Energy, Bureau of Reclamation, non-Governmental organizations and other RMRS programs.

Introduction

We examine the interactions between climate change and natural and anthropogenic disturbances in grassland, shrubland, and desert ecosystems of the Interior West. Disturbances such as fire, drought, grazing, urbanization, and energy development are predicted to have a heightened impact on the western United States under a changing climate. We identify key issues related to these predictions, and provide examples of research that the RMRS GSD Ecosystems Program is conducting to address many of these predictions, as well as identify future research needs.

Interaction of Climate Change and Fire

Climate change is predicted to have multiple effects on fire regimes in grassland, shrubland and desert ecosystems. Current climate change models predict increased temperatures that will result in higher evaporative potential and heat stress across the western United States (Bates and others 2008). Predicted changes in precipitation are less certain, but it is likely that the southwestern United States and central Rockies will exhibit decreased annual precipitation.

Key Issues

Increases in spring and summer temperatures of ~0.9 °C and a one to four week earlier melting of snowpacks have been related to increased fire activity across the West (Westerling and others 2006). Since 1986, the length of the active wildfire season has increased by 78 days and the average burn duration of large fires has increased from 7.5 to 37.1 days (Westerling and others 2006). Earlier snowmelt at high elevations and lack of snow retention at mid elevations in GSD ecosystems (Mote and others 2005) is resulting in longer periods of dry conditions and, when coupled with hot, dry, and windy weather, provides the conditions for wildfire.

The number of days of high fire danger (based on the energy release component index) is increasing and the Great Basin and the Southwest are among the regions most affected (Brown and others 2004). Extremely dry conditions result in more erratic fire behavior, with large flame lengths, torching, crowning, and blowups (Brown and others 2004). Mega fires, or large-scale fires that significantly exceed those of recent decades, are now occurring in GSD ecosystems as evidenced by the 264,260-ha burn in the Murphy Complex wildfire in Idaho and Nevada and 146,901-ha burn in the Milford Flat wildfire in Utah in 2007 (Chambers and Pellant 2008).

Relationships among climate and fire regimes differ among the Bailey's ecoregions (Bailey 1995) due to a diversity of vegetation types and historic fire regimes.

- In most mountainous ecoregions, low precipitation, high temperatures, and a high Palmer's Drought Severity Index in seasons prior to and including the fire season are associated with higher burn areas due to low fuel moisture, increased probability of ignition, and higher potential for fire spread (Westerling and others 2006; Littel and others 2009).

- In southwestern and arid ecoregions, precipitation in seasons prior to the fire season is more highly associated with burn area than warmer temperatures or drought the year of fire due to the importance of fine fuel production (Littel and others 2009).

- In the Great Basin, prior year relationships are even more important and burn area is associated solely with warm, wet conditions in winter or spring one or more years prior to the fire season. A warming climate with less snowpack and a higher proportion of rain at low to mid elevations in mountainous ecoregions may result in increases in area burned at these elevations due to decreased water availability and longer growing seasons (Littel and others 2009).

- In southwestern and arid ecoregions, increasing aridity may result in a decrease in area burned due to a reduction in fine fuels.

Current ecological conditions within different ecoregions influence the responses to climate-induced changes in fire regimes. In arid and semi-arid shrublands and deserts, invasion of exotic grasses with higher flammability and fire spread than native species is increasing both fire frequency and extent.

- In the Mojave and western Sonoran Deserts, invasion of the winter annual grasses *Bromus madritensis* subsp. *rubens* and *Schismus barbatus* is resulting in frequent and large fires in ecosystems that seldom burned in the past (Brooks and McPherson 2006).
- In the eastern Sonoran Desert, invasion of exotic perennial grasses such as *Eragrostis lehmanniana* and *Pennisetum ciliare* are resulting in increased fire frequency and size (Brooks and McPherson 2008).
- In cold desert shrublands, invasion of exotic annual grasses, especially cheatgrass (*Bromus tectorum)*, is increasing fine fuels and fire spread and resulting in conversion of diverse shrublands to near monocultures with greatly increased fire frequency and size (Knapp 1996).
- In many arid and semi-arid grassland ecosystems, expansion and dominance of woody species is resulting in significant decreases in fire frequency and lower resilience to fire (Van Auken 2000).

In these topographically diverse ecosystems, a warmer and drier climate will likely increase the susceptibility of higher-elevation and more mesic ecosystems to invasion by exotic grasses that are currently constrained to lower elevation systems, thus, increasing the risk of wildfire (Chambers and others 2007). Lower-elevation ecosystems may become less susceptible to invasion due to hotter and drier conditions that exceed the ecological amplitude of the invader. As a consequence, active restoration may be necessary (Bradley and others 2009).

Research Needs

- Relationships of weather and climate patterns to past and present fire regimes at local scales.
- Ecological factors and management strategies that increase ecological resistance to exotic species invasions.
- Ecological factors and fire and fuels management strategies that increase ecological resilience to fire at landscape scales and prevent threshold crossings.
- Effects of changes in fire regimes and fuels management on watershed function (erosion, water quality and quantity, and biotic organisms).
- Effects of fire and fuels management on riparian ecosystems, stream channels, and aquatic habitat.
- Improved methods for post-fire restoration of arid ecosystems and ecosystems dominated by fire-adapted exotic grasses.
- Effects of livestock grazing on ecosystem recovery after fire.

Effects of Drought

Recent climate change predictions indicate increasing periods of drought for the western United States (Bates and others 2008). Decreased annual precipitation in the southwestern United States and central Rockies coupled with increased evapotranspiration due to higher temperatures will increase the potential for longer and more severe droughts across most of the western United States. In addition, the Interior West is one of three areas where heat waves are predicted to become more frequent, more intense, and longer lasting (IPCC 2007b). Since 1950, the western United States has already experienced up to four more days per decade with extreme high temperatures.

Differential effects of climate change on GSD ecosystems may increase susceptibility of some ecosystems to the effects of drought and heat waves. For example, earlier snowmelt and a lower proportion of precipitation falling as snow will decrease the extent of snow cover and result in lower snow water equivalent at mid elevations in mountainous regions (Mote and others 2005). A decrease in snow water equivalent and increase in the amount of solar radiation absorbed on snow-free surfaces (Mote and others 2005) may exacerbate the effects of drought and heat waves on ecosystems at these elevations.

Increases in the severity and frequency of drought have the potential to significantly increase the level of stress experienced by native ecosystems. Drought typically results in reductions in plant primary production and water use, mortality of immature plants (seedlings) and animals, and increased susceptibility to insects or disease (Hanson and Weltzin 2000).

Severe or prolonged drought can eventually result in mortality of adult plants despite adaptations to arid conditions (Breshears and others 2005). Changes in biogeochemical cycling can occur, and reductions in plant cover can significantly increase soil erosion (Rapport and Whitford 1999).

Drought can increase the susceptibility of ecosystems to invasion of non-native species, especially under elevated CO_2 conditions (Smith and others 2009). However, prolonged drought or drought that occurs at the margin of a species range can result in mortality of non-native invaders such as *Bromus tectorum* (Jeanne Chambers, personal observation). Drought also can alter fire regimes but effects differ among ecoregions (Westerling and others 2006; Littel and others 2009).

- In most mountainous ecoregions, drought conditions in seasons prior to and including the fire season are associated with larger burn areas.
- In southwestern and arid ecoregions, precipitation in seasons prior to the fire season is more highly associated with burn area than warmer temperatures or drought the year of fire due to the importance of fine fuel production (Littel and others 2009). However, prolonged drought can decrease production of fine fuels and may decrease the probability of fire.

The ecological conditions and anthropogenic stressors of GSD ecosystems can influence their responses to drought and heat waves. Many GSD ecosystems, including hot desert grasslands (Rapport and Whitford 1999), cold desert shrublands (Chambers and Wisdom 2009) and hot desert shrublands (Smith and others 2009), have undergone significant transformations as a result of overgrazing by livestock, agriculture, mining, energy production, urban, suburban and exurban development, recreation, and road development. A high proportion of these ecosystems have crossed ecological thresholds or are at risk of crossing thresholds to less desirable alternative states than existed prior to Anglo-American settlement. Severe or prolonged drought has the potential to result in additional threshold crossings and novel alternative states.

The potential for large-scale die-offs of key species and the consequences for ecosystems can be illustrated by recent, widespread mortality of *Pinus edulis* in the Southwest. In 2002 to 2003, 40 to 80% of *P. edulis*, a dominant, overstory tree species, suffered mortality in a four-state region of the Southwest after 15 months of soil water depletion (Breshears and others 2005). Mortality of the trees resulted from subcontinental drought and anomalously high temperatures. The proximal cause of mortality was apparent infestation by bark beetles, which is often related to drought-induced water stress (Allen and Breshears 1998). The die-off was not constrained to *P. edulis*;

a dominant herbaceous species *Boutelua gracilis* exhibited a 50% reduction in live basal cover at one of the study sites. Interrelated effects included large changes in near-ground solar radiation (Martens and others 2000), runoff and erosion (Allen and Breshears 1998), and genetic structure of *Pinus edulis* on the landscape (Mitten and Duran 2004).

The potential for regional vegetation die-off under global-change-type drought remains a pivotal uncertainty in projections of climate change impacts (IPCC 2001). Regional mortality of key species has the potential to rapidly alter vegetation composition, associated ecosystem properties, and land surface conditions for decades.

Research Needs

- Regional climate change predictions and improved capacity to predict ecological responses.
- Experiments that examine the interactions of the primary climate change variables: precipitation regimes, elevated CO_2, and increased temperature.
- Patterns of response of key species over environmental gradients.
- Interactive effects of soil moisture and temperature on competitive interactions.
- Effect of precipitation and drought on secondary succession and carbon sequestration.
- Role of drought in increasing/decreasing susceptibility to invasion by exotic plant species.
- Role/importance of precipitation seasonality, serial correlation, and extremes on ecosystem structure and function.
- Role of precipitation on nutrient cycling and feedbacks to plant production.
- The level of drought that kills key native perennial species.

Grazing and Climate Change

Rangelands are defined as lands where native vegetation is predominantly grasses, shrubs, or open woodlands, and includes grasslands, shrublands, savannas, and most desert, tundra, meadow, wetland, and riparian ecosystems (Kauffman and Pyke 2001). Rangelands provide important ecosystem services such as biological diversity, wildlife habitat, soil conservation, and GHG sequestration (Ritten and others 2010). Globally, livestock grazing is an important factor affecting ecosystem integrity as it occurs on more area than any other land use. It has been considered the most widespread influence on native ecosystems in western North America (Fleischner 1994). Grazing can reduce biological diversity and ecosystem integrity through removal of vegetation; trampling of soils, vegetation, and biological soil crusts; redistribution of nutrients; and dispersal of exotic plant species and pathogens (Kauffman and Pyke 2001). Many arid grasslands evolved in the presence of large mammalian herbivores (Brown and MacDonald 1995), and thus the intensity of grazing is an important consideration when evaluating past, current, and future effects of grazing on plant species in grasslands (Loeser and others 2007). Also, these effects can be influenced by drought (Loeser and others 2007); therefore, drought should be considered when evaluating the results of grazing studies. In addition, carefully managed grazing may provide opportunities for reducing the density of non-native plant species if such species are consumed by livestock (Kleppel and LaBarge 2011). In another example, targeted cattle grazing on rangeland dominated by cheatgrass reduced cheatgrass cover and, in turn, reduced rate of spread of prescribed fire in the northern Great Basin (Diamond and others 2009).

A variety of studies have addressed issues related to grazing under a changing climate, with topics ranging broadly from quantifying the impact of grazing on GHG levels (Wolf and others 2010) to evaluating potential direct impacts on animals from nutritional stress (Craine and others 2010). Relatively few studies have addressed the impacts of both grazing and climate change on native species of animals and plants. Research results are more readily available that address how grazed lands may change in their ability to support grazing as a livelihood in the future. Furthermore, there is a shortage of work aimed specifically at arid and semi-arid lands in the western United States. Some of the issues that are expected to face managers of public lands where grazing occurs are:

- Changes in the relationships among plants, water, nutrients, and soils on grazed lands are expected to occur under climate change.
- Determining appropriate stocking rates for maintenance of ecosystem function and long-term conservation of rangelands will become more difficult.
- Determining how grazing may affect GHG levels.

Hatfield and others (2008) identified several ecological processes that have the potential to be affected by climate change that relate to grazing: growing season length and plant phenology, net primary production, species composition, and nitrogen cycle feedbacks.

Effects are expected to vary by region. The spatial and temporal distribution of precipitation is a primary driver in the ecology of rangelands (Hatfield and others 2008). The water content of soil and the relationship of water to plants are influenced by levels of CO_2 and ambient temperature. Warming is expected to lead to an earlier onset of green-up in spring and a longer growing season (Badeck and others 2004), but species are expected to vary in their responses to these phenomena. In some areas, modeling efforts have suggested that the spring growing season may shorten (Cullen and others 2009). Furthermore, precipitation variability and increased CO_2 may cause deviations from the overall patterns set by temperature.

Climate change and increased atmospheric CO_2 concentrations are considered to have had an influence on the expansion of shrublands over the past couple hundred years (Hatfield and others 2008). Shrub encroachment into grasslands reduces forage for livestock and wildlife (Burkinshaw and Bork 2009). On the other hand, estimates of future suitable climate in western states covered in this review suggest that changes will favor an increase in area possessing conditions that would support semi-desert grasslands (Friggens and others, Chapter 1 this volume). The threat of soil erosion on grazed lands increases in periods of years with reduced precipitation (Washington-Allen and others 2010). Herbivory by native herbivores can alter plant community responses to warming (Post and Pedersen 2008), yet experimental manipulations aimed at the potential consequences of climate change on rangelands often have not incorporated native herbivory.

Overall, nutrient and water cycles on grazed lands are complex. Del Grosso (2010) pointed out that the results from various studies demonstrate that "generalizations about how changes in climate and land management affect element cycling are often confounded."

Concerns exist over how to make appropriate stocking decisions in the face of climate change (Ritten and others 2010; Tietjen and Jeltsh 2007). The long-term sustainability of rangelands depends on appropriate range management. Variable range production, caused in large part by stochastic precipitation, is already complex, with stocking decisions often made before growing season precipitation is known (Ritten and others 2010). Semi-arid and arid regions show high variability in mean annual rainfall (references in Tietjen and Jeltsh 2007). Rainfall directly influences primary productivity, which, in turn, significantly influences the carrying capacity of a given system for livestock. If net primary productivity is reduced, the carrying capacity is reduced and overgrazing is exacerbated (Tietjen and Jeltsh 2007). An increase in grazing pressure can lead to the reduction of palatable grasses and herbs and an increase in unpalatable grasses and herbs and woody plants (references in Tietjen and Jeltsh 2007).

Craine and others (2010) indicated that "predictions of how forage quality will be affected by changes in temperature and precipitation are varied and conflicting." The increased threat of drought severity, frequency, and duration under climate change increases the complexity of making sound stocking rate decisions (Ritten and others 2010; Popp and others 2009). Sustainable management of arid and semi-arid rangelands is expected to depend heavily on how well rangeland managers understand important ecological processes (Popp and others 2009).

Livestock production contributes to GHG emissions. On a global level, livestock are considered to produce 37% of the global anthropogenic methane (CH_4) through digestive processes (Neely and others 2009), though others have put that value closer to 50% (Morrison 2009). Nitrous oxide, also a GHG, is released mostly as a side-effect of using nitrogen fertilizer or animal manure (Morrison 2009), although high levels of grazing are thought to increase nitrous oxide emissions because grazing increases the rate of nitrogen cycling (Del Grosso 2010).

Recent evidence suggests that grazing can reduce such emissions in semi-arid grasslands that experience soil freeze-thaw cycles in spring (Wolf and others 2010). Options exist in terms of more efficient use of grazing lands and manure to reduce GHG emissions (Gill and others 2010).

The value of rangeland soils in carbon sequestration has been identified as important on a national and an international level (Brown and others 2010; Follett and Reed 2010; Neely and others 2009), particularly as degradation of rangeland reduces the ability of the soils to sequester carbon. Worldwide, grazing lands have been estimated as reducing approximately 20% of the CO_2 released annually into the atmosphere from global deforestation and land use changes (Follett and Reed 2010).

Research Needs

- Continue efforts to improve predictions about future trends of vegetation dynamics under climate change and various management alternatives on grazed lands.
- Increase the scale at which field experiments are conducted (i.e., more large-scale studies) and ensure that rigorous experimental design is employed. Craine and others (2010) noted that climate change experiments are generally too small to allow grazing to be adequately characterized.
- More research on understanding the mechanisms driving observed changes in rangelands with respect to temperature, precipitation, soil cycles, etc. Nutrient cycles on rangelands (carbon, nitrogen, temperature, water, and soil) are critically important as they affect plant growth and quality of forage, which, in turn, influence stocking rates.
- Increase research focus beyond grasslands to grazing in deserts and shrublands.
- Incorporate interactions of invasive plant species and fire behavior in models and field studies.

- Develop decision-support tools to help managers evaluate how stocking rates may need to be adjusted under the threat of climate change.

Population Growth, Development, and Climate Change

The population of the United States continues to increase. In 2000, the population of the United States was 281 million people (U.S. Census Bureau 2000a), and between 1990 and 2000, the U.S. population increased by 33 million people, the largest census-to-census increase recorded in the census history. Growth rates in the West (Montana, Wyoming, Colorado, New Mexico, and the seven states to the west) were higher than the national rate during this period at 20%.

Increasingly, human populations are concentrated in cities. Globally, almost all of the expected population growth is projected to occur in urban areas (Alig and others 2004). In the United States, according to the 2000 census, 79% of the population lived in urban areas (defined as all "urbanized areas" of 50,000 or more people, and "urban clusters" of 2500 to 49,999 people; U.S. Census Bureau 2000b). In each of the 12 states considered by this assessment, there was an increase in the percentage of the population that lived in urban areas between 1960 and 1990.

Population growth creates increased demands on natural resources, such as water and wood products, as well as energy products (coal, oil, natural gas, etc.). Clumping development into urban areas can reduce certain kinds of energy demands (e.g., housing and work locations may be closer) but can negatively impact agricultural output from the loss of farmlands and can lead to fragmentation of forests and other adjacent landscapes (Alig and others 2004).

Key Issues

There are a variety of ways in which climate change will interact with factors that arise from a growing population that increasingly will be concentrated in cities, including: changes in the availability of freshwater, changes in precipitation runoff and potential for changes in flooding, increased energy demands, and ex-urban development.

Increases in population place increasing demands on freshwater resources. While predictions vary as to future changes in the timing and total amount of precipitation according to model and region, the IPCC predicts an increase in precipitation in northern areas and a decrease in southern areas of the western half of North America (Christensen and others 2007). Thus, in southern areas, inputs of freshwater from precipitation are likely to decrease, and increasing demands for freshwater for human consumption (from increased population) will worsen existing impacts on native flora and fauna.

- Summer and autumn flows in river basins supplied by snowmelt water are predicted to be reduced (Kundzewicz and others 2008).
- Alterations to streamflow will differ by region due to variation in the degree to which precipitation and temperature change as well as variation in the characteristics of individual hydrologic basins (DeWalle and others 2000).

Changes to the timing of peak flows in spring are likely to alter freshwater availability for municipalities and exacerbate issues of water storage in reservoirs (Bartolino and Cunningham 2003). The High Plains Aquifer lies under portions of eight states and has supported irrigation of agricultural lands; in some areas, water levels have dropped greater than 30 m since pre-pumping periods (Bartolino and Cunningham 2003). In

Tucson and Phoenix, groundwater levels have dropped 91 to 152 m in some places and riparian vegetation has been lost; similar problems exist in Las Vegas, Nevada.

An increase in population leads to an increase in the demand for energy. In 2006, the three top sources of energy in the United States were petroleum, natural gas, and coal (McDonald and others 2009). McDonald and others (2009) evaluated the land-use intensity of different types of energy production that are expected to increase in the United States based on the Energy Information Administration forecast for energy production by 2030, particularly if legislation passes to implement a system of cap-and-trade to regulate emissions:

- The type of energy development expected to impact the most total area (km²) is biofuel development. Biofuels and biomass burning of energy crops take up the most space per unit power (320 to 375 km²/TW hr/yr, and 433 to 654 km²/TW hr/yr, respectively).
- Wind and solar power have intermediate values of space required per unit of power. Wind power was estimated to account for a relatively small percentage of the new land area impacted between 2006 and 2030.
- Nationally, future energy development is likely to impact temperate deciduous forests and temperate grasslands the most.
- Regardless of whether cap-and-trade policy is implemented, MacDonald and others (2009) estimated that by 2030, the total new area affected by energy production in the United States will be greater than 206,000 km² (more than the area of Nebraska).

This loss of land to energy development will directly impact native species of flora and fauna. Furthermore, some forms of energy production require substantial amounts of water, which leads to additional indirect impacts.

Urban residents worldwide tend to produce less GHG than residents elsewhere in the same countries (Dodman 2009). In the United States in 2001, urban households drove less on average; for households with vehicles, urban households traveled on average ~21,000 miles, whereas rural households traveled on average ~28,000 miles (U.S. EIA 2005). However, in cities that experience a substantial heat island effect, residents may use more energy in summer to maintain cool temperatures indoors. Increasing development reduces natural areas that are likely to be critical as plant and animal communities change due to temperature and precipitation changes. The impacts of fire as human development extends into suburbs and the wildland urban interface need to be considered along with impacts from population growth on natural areas adjacent to large population centers.

Research Needs

- Continue research on regional-scale predictions of changes in precipitation under climate change.
- Identify streams, rivers, and associated riparian areas at greatest risk from altered streamflow and changes in water quality due to human-induced freshwater consumption and reduced precipitation.
- Identify policies that could be implemented to conserve water, either through reduced consumption and/or re-use by industrial and residential consumers.
- Identify regionally specific recommendations on locating new development to reduce energy consumptions and minimize impacts to natural areas.

Energy Development and Climate Change

There is an almost universal consensus among the international scientific community that GHG must be reduced in order to slow the rate of global warming (Abbasi and Abbasi 2000; Dincer 2000). As fossil fuel costs and the impact of their use have become more readily apparent, there has been increased industry investment and Government support for the development of renewable energy sources (Kunz and others 2007). Renewable alternative energy sources include nuclear power, biomass energy (Abbasi and Abbasi 2010), solar power, and wind power. Traditional oil, coal, and natural gas exploration and production occur within the boundaries of GSD and will continue for the foreseeable future.

In the western United States, the sprawl of energy development will have a potentially greater impact than in other areas of the country due to several factors, including the availability of large tracts of Government-owned land, high solar radiation, a fast-growing population, space available for new transmission corridors, and public acceptance of alternative energy production. Climate change velocities are also expected to be highest in low-elevation communities such as deserts, temperate grasslands, and shrublands (Loarie and others 2009). Development of alternative energy sources has far surpassed our understanding of their environmental impacts. It is important that we understand the potential environmental impacts of alternative energy development in order to mitigate undesirable effects.

Key Issues

Traditional energy production using fossil fuels can be expected to continue well into the Twenty-First Century. The geographic area covered by RMRS includes significant sources of these fuels as well as uranium deposits. Disturbances associated with fuel exploration and production include: drill pads, roads, pipeline corridors, open pits, mine tailings, and wind turbine sites.

While considerable research has already been focused on techniques for reclaiming these sites, the current goal of restoring historic communities may no longer be viable. Given the predicted ecotone and community shifts under climate change projections, large areas within the western states may no longer support present ecosystems (Saxon and others 2005), significantly complicating the selection of plant materials for restoration (Hufford and others 2010). Researchers must identify and develop new plant materials that better tolerate increasing drought and high temperatures and are competitive with invasive species (Hufford and others 2010).

Energy production from biomass, termed "biofuels," has been touted as a way to reduce reliance on fossil fuels and reduce GHG emissions. Biofuels are considered carbon neutral because they use recently fixed carbon as opposed to the ancient carbon of fossil fuels (Abbasi and Abbasi 2010). Key considerations in the conversion of large acreages to biofuel production are:

- Biomass production is not "nutrient neutral," and large production may not be sustainable due to soil degradation and depletion of nutrients (Abbasi and Abbasi 2010).
- Use of crop plants and agricultural lands traditionally used for food production for biofuels competes with feed and food demands, increasing world prices and decreasing supplies of foodstuffs.
- Alternatives include the use of non-food energy crops, such as crop residues, hydrocarbon-rich plants, organic waste products, weeds, and fast-growing grasses and woody species (Schmer and others 2008; Abbasi and Abbasi 2010).

- Additional mitigation may come from use of degraded rangeland and abandoned cropland for biofuel production rather than diverting existing agricultural lands needed for food production (Fargione and others 2010).

Construction of alternative energy-generating facilities is a high priority for utility companies, state and Federal governments, and the public. The arid Southwest contains a large amount of Federal lands that also receive significant amounts of solar radiation, and the majority of large-scale solar facilities are slated for development on these lands. Six new solar facilities were approved on Federal land in Nevada and California in October 2010 (USA Today 2010). The largest is 2830 ha (greater than 10 square miles) and larger facilities are being considered (USGS 2010). The solar facilities are approved for construction on the fast track, though extensive environmental assessment will not be completed prior to breaking ground (USGS 2010). While new solar facilities are significantly more efficient than traditional power plants and produce far fewer CO_2 emissions, they are not without environmental impacts in their construction and operation. Limited experience with large-scale solar facilities means that there is little on-the-ground experience regarding these potential impacts (Tsoutsos and others 2005; McDonald and others 2009). The U.S. Department of the Interior has identified 24 solar energy zones in six western states that have high potential for solar energy development and have limited environmental impacts. The zones will facilitate more rapid solar energy development. The final number and size of the solar energy zones will be determined in 2012 (BLM 2011). Some issues to consider are:

- Facilities must be kept free of vegetation in order to prevent the possibility of heat-induced wildfires, resulting in large areas devoid of vegetation.
- Dust emissions from construction, and resulting un-vegetated areas and roads will likely increase. Little is known regarding potential off-site movement of chemical dust-control agents or their effect on surrounding vegetation.
- The impact of solar energy development on wildlife has not been well researched. Effects on migration corridors as well as effects on resident species are largely unknown (USGS 2010).
- Service roads may serve as transmission corridors for exotic plant species.
- Attention during the planning, construction, and operation phases could minimize potential environmental impacts (Tsoutsos and others 2005).

Wind energy is increasingly important as a means of alternative energy production. As with solar installations, new and much larger wind farms are planned or under development. Wind-generating turbines are installed in linear arrays on ridge tops, in canyons, along coastlines, and offshore. Smaller-scale development occurs in more urban settings. The technology to develop energy from wind on a large scale is more mature than that of large-scale solar development. Several studies have been conducted on wildlife impacts, but questions still remain.

- Habitat types most likely affected by wind energy production are temperate conifer forests and temperate grasslands (McDonald and others 2009).
- As with fossil fuel production, impacts on wildlife from wind turbines will largely come from habitat fragmentation, species avoidance behavior, and bird and bat mortality rather than from direct effects from installation (McDonald and others 2009).
- Our understanding of potential impacts of proposed large-scale wind farms, especially offshore, is severely lacking (Drewitt and Langston 2006).
- Recent monitoring studies indicate large numbers of bat fatalities associated with wind energy facilities (Kunz and others 2007).

- Potential effects on birds include collision mortality, displacement due to disturbance, altered migration flyways or local flight paths, and habitat change or loss (Drewitt and Langston 2006).

Research Needs

- Background research to help managers and companies select the most appropriate and least impactful sites for energy development.
- Rigorous, long-term studies of the environmental impacts of large-scale power development, including pre-construction assessments where possible.
- Development of appropriate plant materials for use in reclamation and restoration of disturbed sites under expected climate change scenarios.
- Identification of biomass materials suitable for use in small-scale rural applications as well as development of high-yield, non-food energy crops.
- Research to examine the impact of large, solar generating facilities and wind farms on migration corridors and seed movement and potential off-site effects of chemical dust control agents.
- Multi-year monitoring and hypothesis-based research on causes of bat and bird mortality (Kunz and others 2007), particularly in the Southwest where data are lacking.
- Development of education programs to teach citizens the economic and ecological value of energy efficiency and conservation as a step in reducing energy development sprawl in the western United States.

Literature Cited

Abbasi, S. A. and N. Abbasi. 2000. The likely adverse environmental impacts of renewable energy sources. Applied Energy 65: 121-144.

Abbasi, T. and S. A. Abbasi. 2010. Biomass energy and the environmental impacts associated with its production and utilization. Renewable and Sustainable Energy Reviews 14: 919-937.

Alig, R. J., J. D. Kline and M. Lichtenstein. 2004. Urbanization on the US landscape: looking ahead in the 21st century. Landscape and Urban Planning 69: 219-234.

Allen, C. D. and D. D. Breshears. 1998. Drought-induced shift of a forest-woodland ecotone: rapid landscape response to climate variation. Proceedings of the National Academy of Science 95: 14839-14842.

Badeck, F.-W., A. Bondeau, K. Bottcher, D. Doktor and others. 2004. Response of spring phenology to climate change. New Phytologist 162: 295-309.

Bailey, R. G. 1995. Descriptions of the ecoregions of the United States, 2nd edition. Miscellaneous Publication No. 1391. Washington, DC: U.S. Department of Agriculture, Forest Service. 108 p.

Bartolino, J. R. and W. L. Cunningham. 2003. Ground-water depletion across the nation. U.S. Geological Survey Fact Sheet 103-03. Available: http://pubs.usgs.gov/fs/fs-103-03/JBartolinoFS(2.13.04).pdf.

Bates, B. C., Z. W. Kundzewicz, S. Wu and J. P. Palutikof, eds. 2008. Climate Change and Water. IPCC Secretariat, Geneva. 210 p.

Bureau of Land Management, U.S. Department of the Interior. 2011. Solar Energy Zones, October 3, 2011. Available: http://www.BLM.gov.

Bradley, B. A., M. Oppenheimer and D. S. Wilcove. 2009. Climate change and plant invasions: restoration opportunities ahead? Global Change Biology 15: 1511-1521.

Breshears, D. D., N. S. Cobb, P. M. Rich, K. P. Price and others. 2005. Regional vegetation die-off in response to global-change-type drought. Proceedings of the National Academy of Science 102: 15144-15148.

Brooks, M. L. and G. McPherson. 2008. Ecological role of fire and causes and ecological effects of altered fire regimes in the southwest. Pages 8-1 to 8-3. In: HydroGeoLogic. Proceedings from the Southwest Region Threatened, Endangered, and At-Risk Species Workshop, October 22-25, 2007; Tucson, AZ.

Brown, J., J. Angerer, S. W. Salley, R. Blaisdell and J. W. Stuth. 2010. Improving estimates of rangeland carbon sequestration potential in the U.S. Southwest. Rangeland Ecology and Management 63: 147-154.

Brown, J. H. and W. McDonald. 1995. Livestock grazing and conservation on southwestern rangelands. Conservation Biology 9: 1644-1647.

Brown, T. J., B. L. Hall and A. L. Westerling. 2004. The impact of Twenty-First Century climate change on wildland fire danger in the western United States: an application perspective. Climate Change 62: 365-388.

Brun, S. E. and L. E. Band. 2000. Simulating runoff behavior in an urbanizing watershed. Computers, Environment, and Urban Systems 24: 5-22.

Burkinshaw, A. M. and E. W. Bork. 2009. Shrub encroachment impacts the potential for multiple use conflicts on public land. Environmental Management 44: 494-504.

Chambers, J. C. and M. Pellant. 2008. Climate change impacts on northwestern and intermountain US rangelands. Rangelands 30: 29-33.

Chambers, J. C., B. A. Roundy, R. R. Blank, S. E. Meyer and A. Whittaker. 2007. What makes Great Basin sagebrush ecosystems invasible by *Bromus tectorum*? Ecological Monographs 77: 117-145.

Chambers, J. C. and M. J. Wisdom. 2009. Research and management issues associated with land cover and land use change in the Great Basin. Restoration Ecology 17: 707-714.

Christensen, J. H., B. Hewitson, A. Busuioc, A. Chen and others. 2007. Regional climate projections. In: Solomon, S., D. Qin, M. Manning, Z. Chen, M. Marquis, K. B. Averyt, M. Tignor and H. L. Miller, eds. Climate Change 2007: The Physical Science Basis. Contribution of Working Group I to the Fourth Assessment Report of the Intergovernmental Panel on Climate Change Cambridge University Press, Cambridge, United Kingdom.

Craine, J. M., A. J. Elmore, K. C. Olson and D. Tolleson. 2010. Climate change and cattle nutritional stress. Global Change Biology 16: 2901-2911.

Cullen, B. R., I. R. Johnson, R. J. Eckard, G. M. Lodge and others. 2009. Climate change effects on pasture systems in south-eastern Australia. Crop and Pasture Science 60: 933-942.

Del Grosso, S. J. 2010. Grazing and nitrous oxide. Nature 464: 843-844.

DeWalle, D. R., B. R. Swistock, T. E. Johnson and K. J. McGuire. 2000. Potential effects of climate change and urbanization on mean annual streamflow in the United States. Water Resources Research 36: 2655-2664.

Diamond, J. M., C. A. Call and N. Devoe. 2009. Effects of targeted cattle grazing on fire behavior of cheatgrass-dominated rangeland in the northern Great Basin, USA. International Journal of Wildland Fire 18: 944-950.

Dincer, I. 2000. Renewable energy and sustainable development: a crucial review. Renewable and Sustainable Energy Reviews 4: 157-175.

Dodman, D. 2009. Blaming cities for climate change? An analysis of urban greenhouse gas emission inventories. Environment and Urbanization 21: 185-201.

Drewitt, A. L. and R. H. W. Langston. 2006. Assessing the impacts of wind farms on birds. Ibis 148: 29-42.

Fargione, J. E., R. J. Plevin and J. D. Hill. 2010. The ecological impact of biofuels. Annual Review of Ecology and Systematics 41: 351-377.

Fleischner, T. L. 1994. Ecological costs of livestock grazing in western North America. Conservation Biology 8: 629-644.

Floyd, M. L., M. Clifford, N. S. Cobb, D. Hanna and others. 2009. Relationship of stand characteristics to drought-induced mortality in three Southwestern piñon-juniper woodlands. Ecological Applications 19(5): 1223-1230.

Follett, R. F. and D. A. Reed. 2010. Soil carbon sequestration in grazing lands: social benefits and policy implications. Rangeland Ecology and Management 63: 4-15.

Gill, M., P. Smith and J. M. Wilkinson. 2010. Mitigating climate change: the role of domestic livestock. Animal 4: 323-333.

Hanson, P. J. and J. F. Weltzin. 2000. Drought disturbance from climate change: response of United States forests. Science of the Total Environment 262: 205-220.

Hatfield, J., K. Boote, P. Fay, L. Hahn and others. 2008. Agriculture. In: The effects of climate change on agriculture, land resources, water resources, and biodiversity. A Report by the U.S. Climate Change Science Program and the Subcommittee on Global Change Research. Washington, DC. 362 p.

Hufford, K., K. Hansen, R. Coupal and P. Stahl. 2010. Trajectories of restoration: climate change and seed sourcing in the Intermountain West. Unpublished report.

Intergovernmental Panel on Climate Change [IPCC]. 2001. Climate change 2001: synthesis report. A Contribution of Working Groups I, II, and III to the Third Assessment Report of the Intergovernmental Panel on Climate Change. Watson, R. T. and Core Writing Team, eds. Cambridge University Press, New York.

Intergovernmental Panel on Climate Change [IPCC]. 2007a. Synthesis report. A Contribution of Working Groups I, II, and III to the Fourth Assessment Report of the Intergovernmental Panel on Climate Change. Cambridge University Press, Cambridge, UK.

Intergovernmental Panel on Climate Change [IPCC]. 2007b. Regional climate projections. Prepared by R. Alley and others. In: S. Solomon and others, eds. Climate Change 2007: The Physical Science Basis. Contribution of Working Group I to the Fourth Assessment Report of the Intergovernmental Panel on Climate Change. Cambridge University Press, Cambridge, U.K.

Kauffman, J. B. and D. A. Pyke. 2001. Range ecology, global livestock influences. Pages 33-52. In: Levin, S., ed. Encyclopedia of Diversity, Vol. 5. San Diego, CA: Academic Press.

Kleppel, G. S. and E. LaBarge. 2011. Using sheep to control purple loosestrife (*Lythrum salicaria*). Invasive Plant Science and Management 4: 50-57.

Knapp, P. A. 1996. Cheatgrass (*Bromus tectorum*) dominance in the Great Basin Desert. Global Environmental Change 6: 37-52.

Kundzewicz, Z. W., L. J. Mata, N. W. Arnell, P. Döll and others. 2008. The implications of projected climate change for freshwater resources and their management. Hydrological Sciences 53: 3-10.

Kunz, T. H., E. B. Arnett, W. P. Erickson, A. R. Hoar and others. 2007. Ecological impacts of wind energy development on bats: questions, research needs, and hypotheses. Frontiers in Ecology and Environment 5: 315-324.

Littell, J. S., D. McKenzie, D. L. Peterson and A. L. Westerling. 2009. Climate and wildfire area burned in the western U.S. ecoprovinces, 1916-2003. Ecological Applications 19: 1003-1021.

Loarie, S. R., P. B. Duffy, H. Hamilton, G. P. Asner, C. B. Field and D. D. Ackerly. 2009. The velocity of climate change. Nature 462: 1052-1055.

Loesser, M. R. R., T. D. Sisk and T. E. Crews. 2007. Impact on grazing intensity during drought in an Arizona grassland. Conservation Biology 21: 87-97.

Martens, S. N., D. D. Breshears and C. W. Meyer. 2000. Ecological Modeling 126: 79-93.

McDonald, R. I., J. Fargione, J. Kiesecker, W. M. Miller and J. Powell. 2009. Energy sprawl or energy efficiency: climate policy impacts on natural habitat for the United States of America. PLoS ONE 4(8): 1-22.

Mitton, J. B. and K. L. Duran. 2004. Genetic variation in piñon pine, *Pinus edulis*, associated with summer precipitation. Molecular Ecology 13: 1259-1264.

Morrison, K. 2009. Towards greener grazing. Nature Reports 3: 104-106.

Mote, P. W., A. F. Hamlet, M. P. Clark and D. P. Lettenmair. 2005. Declining mountain snowpack in western North America. Bulletin of the American Meteorological Association 86: 39-49.

Neely, C., S. Bunning and A. Wilkes. 2009. Review of evidence on drylands pastoral systems and climate change: Implications and opportunities for mitigation and adaptation. Land and Water Discussion Paper 8. Food and Agriculture Organization of the United Nations. Rome, Italy.

Popp, A., S. Domptail, N. Blaum and F. Jeltsch. 2009. Land use experience does not qualify for adaptation to climate change. Ecological Modeling 220: 694-702.

Post, E. and C. Pedersen. 2008. Opposing plant community responses to warming with and without herbivores. Proceedings of the National Academy of Sciences 105: 12353-12358.

Rapport, D. J. and W. G. Whitford. 1999. How ecosystems respond to stress. Bioscience 49: 193-203.

Ritten, J. P., W. M. Frasier, C. T. Bastian and S. T. Gray. 2010. Optimal rangeland stocking decisions under stochastic and climate-impacted weather. American Journal of Agricultural Economics 92: 1242-1255.

Saxon, E., B. Baker, W. Hargrove, F. Hoffman and C. Zganjar. 2005. Mapping environments at risk under different climate change scenarios. Ecology Letters 8: 53-60.

Schmer, M. R., K. P. Vogel, R. B. Mitchell and R. K. Perrin. 2008. Net energy of cellulosic ethanol from switchgrass. Proceedings of the National Academy of Sciences 105: 464-469.

Smith, S. D., T. N. Charlet, L. K. Fenstermaker and B. A. Newingham. 2009. Effects of global change on Mojave desert ecosystems. Pages 31-56. In: Webb, R. H., L. F. Fenstermaker, J. S. Heaton, D. L. Hughson, E. V. McDonald and D. M. Miller, eds. The Mojave Desert: Ecosystem Processes and Sustainability. University of Nevada Press.

Tietjen, B. and F. Jeltsh. 2007. Semi-arid grazing systems and climate change: a survey of present modeling potential and future needs. Journal of Applied Ecology 44: 425-434.

Tsoutsos, T., N. Frantzeskaki and V. Gekas. 2005. Environmental impacts from the solar energy technologies. Energy Policy 33: 289-296.

U.S. Census Bureau. 2000a. All across the U.S.A.: population distribution and composition, 2000. Population profile of the United States: 2000 (Internet release). Chapter 2. Available: http://www.census.gov/population/www/pop-profile/files/2000/chap02.pdf.

U.S. Census Bureau. 2000b. U.S. population living in urban vs. rural areas. Available: http://www.fhwa.dot.gov/planning/census/cps2k.htm.

U.S. Energy Information Administration. 2005. Table A2. U.S. per household vehicle-miles traveled, vehicle fuel consumption and expenditures, 2001. Available: http://www.eia.doe.gov/emeu/rtecs/nhts_survey/2001/tablefiles/page_a02.html.

USA Today. 2010. Solar project gets OK for Mojave Desert. USA Today 10/26/2010: 3A.

U.S. Geological Survey [USGS]. 2010. Natural resource needs related to climate change in the Great Basin and Mojave Desert. Workshop, April 20-22, 2010; Las Vegas, NV. Available: www.wr.usgs.gov/workshops/ccw2010/abstracts.html [12/01/2010].

Van Auken, O. W. 2000. Shrub invasions of North American semiarid grasslands. Annual Review of Ecology and Systematics 31: 197-215.

Washington-Allen, R. A., N. E. West, R. D. Ramsey, D. H. Phillips and H. H. Shugart. 2010. Retrospective assessment of dryland soil stability in relation to grazing and climate change. Environmental Monitoring and Assessment 160: 101-121.

Westerling, A. L., H. G. Hidalgo, D. R. Cayan and T. W. Swetnam. 2006. Warming and earlier spring increase U.S. forest wildfire activity. Science 313: 940-943.

Williams, A. P., C. D. Allen, C. I. Miller, T. W. Swetnam and others. 2010. Forest responses to increasing aridity and warmth in the southwestern United States. Proceedings of the National Academy of Sciences 107: 21289-21294.

Wolf, B., X. Zheng, N. Brüggemann, W. Chen and others. 2010. Grazing-induced reduction of natural nitrous oxide release from continental steppe. Nature 464: 881-884.

Chapter 7

Invasive Species and Climate Change

Justin B. Runyon[1], Jack L. Butler[2], Megan M. Friggens[3], Susan E. Meyer[4], and Sharlene E. Sing[1]

[1] U.S. Forest Service, Rocky Mountain Research Station; Grassland, Shrubland, and Desert Ecosystems Program; Forestry Sciences Laboratory, Bozeman, Montana

[2] U.S. Forest Service, Rocky Mountain Research Station; Grassland, Shrubland, and Desert Ecosystems Program; Forest and Grassland Research Laboratory, Rapid City, South Dakota

[3] U.S. Forest Service, Rocky Mountain Research Station; Grassland, Shrubland, and Desert Ecosystems Program; Forestry Sciences Laboratory, Albuquerque, New Mexico

[4] U.S. Forest Service, Rocky Mountain Research Station; Grassland, Shrubland, and Desert Ecosystems Program; Shrub Sciences Laboratory, Provo, Utah

Executive Summary

Invasive species present one of the greatest threats to the health and sustainability of ecosystems worldwide. Invasive plants, animals, and diseases are known to have significant negative effects on biological diversity and the ecological structure and functions of native ecosystems. Moreover, the economic cost imposed by invasive species is enormous—the damage inflicted to natural resources and costs of control measures is an estimated $137 billion each year in the United States. Climate change can fundamentally alter the behavior, spread, and harm caused by invasive species and the effectiveness of control methods. If we are to keep pace with and effectively limit the spread and damage caused by invasive species, it is critical to understand and predict how climate change will affect species invasions and the efficacy of the tools used to combat these invasions. To better identify research needs, we review the current state of knowledge pertaining to climate change impacts on several key topics, including invasive plants, their biocontrol, and wildlife disease.

Climate change is expected to alter the distribution and spread of invasive plants but in largely unknown ways. The climate models used to predict future distributions of invasive plants (e.g., cheatgrass) are limited by a lack of knowledge about, and consideration of, the ecology, genetics, etc., of the plant. Moreover, climate change may favor and convert non-native species considered benign today into the noxious weeds of tomorrow, but we are unable to predict which species might be favored. There is evidence that the physiology and competitive ability of invasive plants will be favored more than native plants, particularly in arid ecosystems, but in complex ways that are poorly understood.

Biological control—one of few tools proven effective against widespread invasive plants—will be affected by climate change in a number of ways. Like invasive plants, the range and spread of biocontrol insects are likely to be altered. Of particular concern is the potential for climate change to disrupt the temporal or spatial synchrony between biocontrol agents and their invasive host plants. There is also evidence that climate-induced changes in plant chemistry will alter plant-insect interactions in important ways (e.g., how much an insect eats) and could ultimately affect population levels of insects and invasive plants. However, we know next to nothing about the potential consequences of these predicted changes for successful use of this powerful management tool.

Climate change can alter wildlife disease dynamics with potentially severe consequences for the affected species and entire ecosystems. For example, increased temperatures and altered precipitation patterns can increase the range and abundance of vector species (e.g., mosquitoes and ticks) and thus the frequency of vector borne disease outbreaks, including West Nile Virus. Climate-induced changes can further promote disease by affecting host susceptibility to infection. However, climate change could limit the spread of some pathogens. Research is needed to understand how climate change will impact disease emergence and spread to prioritize and inform management actions.

Climate change will modify invasive species and the tools used to manage them. Our understanding of how and in what direction climate change will drive such changes is insufficient to adequately predict and respond. However, climate-induced changes are likely to be complex and will need to be examined on a case by case basis until more generalized frameworks can be developed. This review will guide development of important research questions, the answers to which will better position us to devise and apply meaningful management options to address invasive species in both present and future climates.

Introduction

Biological invasions threaten the integrity of many ecosystems and are considered second only to habitat destruction in their effects on biodiversity and on landscapes as a whole. For example, invasive plants currently infest approximately 100 million acres of land in the United States and are spreading at the rate of several million acres per year. However, climate change has the potential to greatly alter the behavior of invaders and their interactions with other organisms, with important consequences for invaders' management. A better understanding of what these climate-induced changes will be is critical to adapt, develop, and successfully apply management strategies to control invasive species.

Invasive species are defined here as any native or non-native species that causes or is likely to cause social, economic, or ecological harm. This chapter is divided into three sections: the first covers climate change effects on invasive plants and their competitive interactions with other plants. The second deals with potential impacts on biocontrol of invasive plants, including direct effects on biocontrol agents and their interactions with invasive plants. The third summarizes climate change effects on wildlife disease.

Climate Change Effects on Invasive Plants

Non-native plants are now a common theme of many ecosystems throughout the United States (Pimentel and others 2000), including places established specifically to protect native species and communities (Allen and others 2009). Although the exact number of plants introduced into the United States is unknown, published estimates range from 4000 (Stein and Flack 1996) to 5000 species (Morse and others 1995). In comparison, there are approximately 17,000 species of native plants in the United States (Stein and Flack 1997). At present, only a small proportion of the 4000 to 5000 non-native species are classified as invasive, adversely impacting native species, communities, and ecosystems (Hiebert 1997; Skinner and others 2000). The overall impact of existing invasive species may increase or decrease under several scenarios of global change driven by greenhouse-gas influenced climate change, increasing carbon dioxide (CO_2) concentration, increasing nitrogen (N) deposition, and altered disturbance regimes (Dukes and Mooney 1999; Bradley and others 2010). Furthermore, the larger proportion of non-native species considered benign and maintained artificially as ornamentals represent a substantial pool of potentially damaging species should environmental conditions shift in their favor as a result of one or more of the elements of global change (Sutherst 2000).

Although alterations of climatic patterns will undoubtedly exert a major influence on the distribution of invasive plants (Blumenthal and others 2008; Hellmann and others 2008), studies that report the responses of invasive plants to climate change in an ecosystem context are limited (Dukes and Mooney 1999). However, Bradley and colleagues (Bradley 2009; Bradley and others 2009) have examined the effects of variable future climate scenarios on cheatgrass (*Bromus tectorum* L.) for the interior western United States using bioclimatic envelope modeling approaches based on Atmosphere-Ocean General Circulation Models (AOCGM). Cheatgrass is an invasive winter annual brome species that, along with red brome (*Bromus rubens* L. or *Bromus madritensis* ssp. *rubens* [L.]), dominate millions of hectares of former shrublands in semi-arid and arid habitats throughout the Interior West (Brooks and others 2004; Chambers and others 2007). Both species facilitate their own increase and spread through their effect on fire return frequency (*Bromus* spp. invasions provide abundant, highly flammable fine fuel); cycles of frequent burning can create near-monocultures of these grasses over large areas (Mack and D'Antonio 1998; Brooks and others 2004). Using the climate of the area currently occupied as a guide, Bradley (2009) and Bradley and others (2009) identified major variables that predict cheatgrass presence: annual precipitation, summer precipitation, and spring precipitation, with lesser effects of winter temperature. Modeling potential distribution given current climatic conditions indicated that sizeable areas (Wyoming, for example) may become available as climatically suitable habitat. AOCGM models generally predict that the Great Basin region will experience both reduced total precipitation and reduced spring precipitation, but the models vary widely in their predictions for summer precipitation. Consequently, the outcome of bioclimatic envelope modeling of future cheatgrass distribution is very much dependent on the AOCGM model used; both major increases (45%) and major decreases (70%) in future climatically suitable area have been predicted (Bradley 2009). The high uncertainty of these largely precipitation-based predictions is, in part, due to the inherent difficulty in projecting future precipitation (compared to temperature).

Bioclimatic envelope modeling is a valuable tool for predicting species response to climate change, but these models assume that species distribution is static under a given set of climatic conditions (see Friggens and others, Chapter 1 this volume). Bradley and colleagues (2009) used a presence-only approach that makes no a priori assumptions about the climate unsuitability of areas not known to be occupied, and their model does not take into account the fact that cheatgrass is known to be rapidly expanding its range into novel habitats. These researchers have documented range expansion into montane, extreme salt desert, and warm desert environments, many of which are likely outside the defined bioclimatic envelope (e.g., Ramakrishnan and others 2006; Leger and others 2009; Scott and others 2010). Furthermore, the bioclimatic envelope model as used by Bradley and others (2009) does not take into account another very important fact, namely that not all cheatgrass is created equal. Research has confirmed that the invasion of novel habitats involves unique biotypes (inbreeding lines) of cheatgrass that have suites of adaptive traits that preadapt them to specific environments (Ramakrishnan and others 2004, 2006; Merrill and others, in review).

This genetic variability, combined with highly dispersible seeds, creates the possibility that biotypes preadapted to areas with changed climates could rapidly replace cheatgrass biotypes that have become locally maladapted. This shift would be transparent to a casual observer, as there are few or no morphological markers for identifying these unique biotypes. In essence, these shifts involve evolutionary change in response to climate change, a possibility that is rarely considered and difficult to include in modeling scenarios.

At the plant level, increased atmospheric CO_2 concentration has a positive impact on plant photosynthesis and growth, although the relative response varies considerably among species (Hunt and others 1991). Previous research indicates relatively strong responses of invasive plants to elevated CO_2 in competition-free environments (Ziska 2003; Dukes 2000), and studies are available that demonstrate higher rates of photosynthesis for invasive plant species when compared to their native counterparts (Pattison and others 1998; Baruch and Goldstein 1999; Durand and Goldstein 2001). However, Dukes (2000) concluded after an extensive review that, while a large number of invasive species respond strongly to elevated CO_2, the overall responses were not statistically different from the responses of non-invasive plants within the same functional group.

Studies that experimentally compare the physiological responses of invasive plants to elevated CO_2 to their native constituents are limited (Sasek and Strain 1991; Dijkstra and others 2010a; Song and others 2009). In an environmentally controlled experiment involving monocultures of three invasive species and three co-occurring native species, Song and others (2009) reported that elevated CO_2 resulted in significantly higher photosynthetic rates and increased biomass for the invasive species compared to the native species tested. Similarly, Sasek and Strain (1991) found that Japanese honeysuckle (*Lonicera japonica*), a non-native species, produced significantly more biomass under CO_2 enrichment than did coral honeysuckle (*Lonicera sempervirens*), a related native species. These authors suggested that this may convey an advantage for invasive species under increasing atmospheric CO_2, although such responses may differ in diverse, competitive environments (Bazzaz and McConnaughay 1992). For example, Dijkstra and others (2010) evaluated the effects of elevated CO_2 on a mix of five native semi-arid grassland species and one invasive plant species under greenhouse conditions. They found that species' responses to elevated CO_2 and supplemental water depended on whether the species were grown in a monoculture or in a mixture. Specifically, *Linaria dalmatica*, the invasive species used in that study, responded positively to elevated CO_2 when grown in a monoculture but negatively when grown in mixtures that included the five native species.

In mixed species competition, the response of a functional group, including invasive plants, to elevated CO_2 may depend upon how CO_2 indirectly alters competition for other resources (Bazzaz and McConnaughay 1992; Patterson 1995). Increased CO_2 also decreases transpirational water loss, which can improve season-long soil moisture conditions, and invasive species that can take advantage of the additional moisture may become more abundant (Dukes and Mooney 1999). Elevated CO_2-induced increases in water use efficiency are predicted to be greater in arid ecosystems because of the increased availability of a very limited resource (Smith and others 2000; Morgan and others 2004). The direct effect of atmospheric CO_2 enrichment on annual bromes (cheatgrass and red brome) has been investigated in both greenhouse and free air carbon enrichment (FACE) studies (Smith and others 1987, 2000). The general conclusion from these studies is that annual bromes have a larger positive growth response to CO_2 enrichment than associated native herbaceous species, which should increase annual brome competitive advantage as atmospheric CO_2 levels increase.

Elevated CO_2-induced increases in soil moisture can enhance plant N uptake, which is important for sustained increases in plant productivity associated with increased atmospheric CO_2 (Dijkstra and others 2008, 2010a). However, Dijkstra and others (2010b) reported that N availability decreased with increasing CO_2-induced soil moisture, while warming increased soil inorganic N and plant N uptake.

Anthropogenic-caused increases in N deposition is a component of global change that receives limited attention with respect to its potential impact on non-forested ecosystems (Vitousek 1994) where slow-growing native species adapted to low nutrient poor soils are likely to be the most impacted by increasing N (Milchunas and Laurenroth 1995; Tilman 1987). Fertilization experiments in N-limited ecosystems demonstrate that increased N concentrates plant diversity into one or a few N-responsive plants (Tilman 1987; Vitousek 1994 and references within), which likely includes many non-native species found in several North American grasslands. Stohlgren and others (1999) reported that much of the variation in non-native species richness could be explained by the total percentage N in the soil; however, more recent research indicates that elevated CO_2 could ameliorate the negative effect of N enrichment on species richness (Reich 2009).

In summary, predicting the specific effects of global change on current and potential invasive plants is a significant challenge because the complex matrix of interacting elements associated with global change often produces inconsistent patterns (Bradley and others 2010) and also because invasive plants already represent a significant component of global change (Vitousek 1994). Overall, the evidence indicates that invasive plants will be favored by many of the elements associated with global change. This may be especially true for non-forested ecosystems of the Interior West that are typically water and nutrient limited. However, applying general patterns to specific species invading specific sites is difficult, and more site-specific research is needed in non-forested ecosystems that simultaneously evaluate multiple elements of global change, including the effects of extreme events (Bradley and others 2010). For example, more research is needed on the population genetic structure of both cheatgrass and red brome, including the initiation of large reciprocal seeding experiments to determine whether differences in adaptive phenotypes associated with inbreeding lines that have distinctive marker genotypes result in differential establishment, survival, growth, and fecundity in contrasting environments. Additionally, GSD Ecosystem researchers need to respond to restoration opportunities where the distribution and abundance of invasive plants are contracting because of global change.

Climate Change Effects on Biocontrol

Direct Impacts on Biocontrol Agents

Biocontrol intentionally reunites, for the purposes of pest population regulation in an invaded or adopted range, the species targeted for control with co-evolved and host-specific natural enemies originating from their common native range. The establishment, abundance, and distribution of invasive plants (weeds) and the co-evolved, host-specific herbivorous insects known as their biological control (or biocontrol) agents are fundamentally mediated by habitat suitability, competition, and natural enemies (Holt and Barfield 2009). Long-term shifts in seasonal temperature and coupled precipitation patterns anticipated under climate change in turn have the potential to alter species abundance and distribution (Walther and others 2009). Studies specifically evaluating how climate change may affect weed biocontrol are scarce (but see Sims-Chilton and others 2010; Watt and others 2010). Under these circumstances, extrapolation from generic ("herbivorous insects" or "invasive species") or multi-trophic (e.g., "host-specific invasive pest" or "rare indigenous species") case studies can be useful. In addition, results reported from studies of invasive or conservation-targeted species are effective for inferring many direct and indirect potential climate change impacts on non-native weeds and their arthropod biocontrol agents.

Bale and others (2002) provided a comprehensive review of key direct effects—insect herbivore development, survival, range, and abundance—as influenced by the increased temperatures predicted under global climate change. Hellmann and others (2008) identified probable consequences of climate change for invasive species and developed testable hypotheses for invasive species responses to specific climate change consequences. Monitoring for changes in the geographic distribution of host-specific herbivorous insect species across latitudinal and elevational gradients was identified as a robust methodology for accurately sensing climate change impacts (Andrew and Hughes 2005; Hodkinson and Bird 1998).

Because many of the plant species targeted for classical weed biocontrol in temperate regions of the United States originated in Eurasia, the simplistic assumption might be made that increasing temperatures in North America will generally benefit biocontrol agents that have been collected from a comparatively warmer native range. Studies evaluating ecological sorting along altitude-influenced thermal gradients indicate that insect physiological responses to temperature, specifically thermal tolerance thresholds, can profoundly affect agent demographics via temperature-mediated fecundity (Dangles and others 2008) and distribution (Hodkinson and Bird 1998). The results of a meta-analysis of insect species range margins suggests that although genetic diversity tends to decline during colonization of new habitats, there could be a positive feedback between range expansion and an increase in traits that accelerate range expansion through adaptations specifically affecting dispersal, metabolic rate, and changes in habitat associations (Hill and others 2011).

Increased temperatures projected under climate change could substantially extend the core area and edge-of-range distributions for both weed biocontrol agents and their host plants, especially for Eurasian species established in northern temperate locales. Thomas and others (1999) determined that a 2 to 3 °C rise in mean spring and summer temperature increased available suitable habitat and the length of time that successional habitat could be occupied, and decreased the effective distance between suitable habitat patches in northern temperate locations. Davis and others (1998) asserted that accurate predictions of species range and abundance cannot be based on physiological response to temperature alone (called "climate mapping") but should also consider climatic influences on species dispersal and inter-specific interactions. Bradley and others (2009) cautioned that climate change could result in contractions of invasive plant ranges as well as range expansions.

The probability that a species will reach locations that have, under the influence of global warming, changed from unsuitable to suitable habitat patches depends on the interaction of dispersal ability and behavioral responses with environmental structural components (Gaston 2009). Fox and others (1999) determined that positive effects of winter warming on St. John's wort (*Hypericum perforatum* L.) would be ephemeral and readily neutralized by a projected increase in summertime herbivory if winter warming was followed by summer drought; the authors concluded that St. John's wort would not likely benefit from the warmer temperatures predicted under global warming, particularly at the northern extent of its range. The guild structure of herbivores colonizing *Acacia falcata* growing within or transplanted at sites 208 km beyond its current range was similar even though the transplant sites were 1.2 and 5.5 °C warmer; this was not the case for the guild structure of herbivores collected from a related host species *A. leptostachya* growing at transplant sites outside the current range (Andrew and Hughes 2007).

The internal temperature of ectotherms, including all plants and most insect species, is regulated by ambient environmental temperature (Gutierrez and others 2008). Ectothermic metabolic rate, dictated by body mass and body temperature, is therefore highly susceptible to alterations in habitat thermal properties (Dillon and others 2010; Gillooly and others 2001). Response to changing climatic conditions is restricted to dispersal, phenotypic plasticity, or adaptation (Holt 1990). Phenological alterations resulting from the increased length of temperate growing seasons can facilitate the development of asynchrony in key interspecific interactions (van Asch and others 2007; Cobbold and Powell 2010; Fabiana and others 2010). Hegland and others (2009) pointed out that asynchrony in insect-plant interactions can be temporal or spatial in nature, and, in extreme cases, could lead to trophic decoupling and food web scale disruptions characterized by a mismatch in abundance of consumers and their food sources.

Much of the research conducted in Interior West grasslands, shrublands, and desert ecosystems concerns function and productivity in dryland habitats. The interaction of environmental (e.g., climate change) and anthropogenic (e.g., management practices) drivers profoundly affects dryland function and productivity (Chambers and Pellant 2008). Productivity, in terms of increased plant photosynthesis, biomass, and water use efficiency, is predicted to increase, especially for alien invasive species, in U.S. arid ecosystems under higher atmospheric levels of CO_2 associated with climate change (Ziska 2003; Smith and others 2000). Species interactions, and not only direct effects of climate change, were shown to influence grassland productivity and species diversity (Suttle and others 2007). Drylands are susceptible to dominance by non-native transformer species (i.e., species capable of significantly altering ecosystems over a wide area) (Richardson and others 2000). Transformer species such as *Bromus tectorum* (cheatgrass; downy brome) and *Linaria dalmatica* (Dalmatian toadflax) (D'Antonio and others 2004) are targets of biocontrol research by scientists in the GSD Ecosystems Program of RMRS. Biocontrol, used alone or as part of an adaptive integrated weed management strategy, may significantly reduce unintended negative, non-target impacts to surrounding desirable vegetation. Conventional herbicide treatments have been correlated with secondary invasions of weeds such as cheatgrass (Pearson and Ortega 2009) and an increase in the proportion of bare or unvegetated ground (Barnes 2007); the ability of dryland vegetation communities to rebound after herbicide applications is likely to be compromised under climate change and may increase the frequency, intensity, and persistence of desertification. Verstraete and others (2009) paraphrased the United Nations Convention to Combat Desertification definition of desertification as: "any form of degradation in drylands...where degradation refers to a persistent reduction in the bundle of services provided to humans by the ecosystem under considerations, thus encompassing both social and biophysical considerations."

Impacts on Plant-Herbivore Interactions

The success or failure of biocontrol is largely determined by the outcomes of interactions between individual plants and biocontrol agents (herbivores). That is, herbivory at the individual level can have negative effects on a plant's growth and reproduction, which can, in turn, impact the abundance, distribution, and dynamics of entire plant populations (Maron and Crone 2006). For biocontrol to be deemed successful, individual herbivory must lead to population-level reductions in the target weed. However, climate change has the potential to fundamentally alter interactions between plants and herbivores, which could alter broader population-level outcomes and the success of biocontrol. Another primary route by which climate change is predicted to affect herbivory is by modifying plant chemistry—the central factor regulating plant-herbivore interactions. Major climate change factors, most notably elevated CO_2 and temperature, can potentially affect the susceptibility or resistance of plants to herbivory (e.g., by altering leaf nutrients and defensive compounds); however, little is known about how these changes may affect individual plant-insect interactions or broader community dynamics. A better understanding of how climate change will impact relationships between invasive plants and their biocontrol agents is needed to predict and advance biocontrol efficacy in a rapidly changing climate.

The most obvious way climate change can affect interactions between plants and insects is by altering the basic nutritional value of plants. Most studies show that herbivores consistently respond to CO_2-induced changes in their host plants by consuming more foliage (Coviella and Trumble 1999). For example, elevated CO_2 generally causes an increase in plant growth (the "fertilizer effect") and increases in the ratio of C:N in plant tissues, which reduces the nutritional quality for N-limited insects (Coviella and Trumble 1999). As a result, insects must eat more to compensate for less N content (Coviella and Trumble 1999; Dermody and others 2008; Johnson and McNicol 2010). Another route by which increased CO_2 can affect insect feeding is by increasing sugars in plant leaves. For example, soybean plants grown in elevated CO_2 conditions contain 31% more sugars than plants grown in ambient air and, as a result, Japanese beetles (*Popilla japonica*) prefer and consume twice as much foliage from high-CO_2 soybeans (Hamilton and others 2005). Drought stress—something predicted to increase dramatically in western North America—can affect virtually every plant nutrient and may encourage herbivore outbreaks (Mattson and Hauk 1987). Such climate-induced increases in insect damage are expected to negatively impact agricultural production by off-setting potential gains in plant productivity due to the fertilizer effect (DeLucia and others 2008). However, the implications for biocontrol, though potentially far reaching, are unknown.

Climate change can also significantly impact plant nutritional value by altering chemical defenses against herbivores. Plant defensive chemistry can have important consequences for plant fitness and populations (Baldwin 1998) and can drive cycles in herbivore populations (Underwood 1999). Elevated CO_2, temperature, ozone (O_3), and ultra-violet (UV) light are each reported to affect levels of plant secondary chemicals (Bidart-Bouzat and Imeh-Nathaniel 2008). However, available information is limited and dependent on the plant and insect species involved as well as the class of chemicals examined (e.g., C-based versus N-based defenses). For example, elevated CO_2, temperature, O_3, and UV light can each either increase, decrease, or have no effect on plant defensive chemistry (Bidart-Bouzat and Imeh-Nathaniel 2008). These conflicting studies have hindered attempts to develop general predictions about how climate change will affect plant defensive chemistry and point to the involvement of a host of interacting factors. However, climate-induced changes in chemical defenses can have important consequences for plants and herbivores. For example, quaking aspen trees (*Populus tremuloides*) grown in elevated CO_2 and O_3, singly and in combination, had altered physical and chemical leaf defenses that led to increased populations of herbivores and pathogens (Percy and others 2002). It was recently discovered that elevated CO_2 can disrupt herbivore-induced plant defenses, specifically the production of proteinase inhibitors that interfere with insect digestion, resulting in poorly defended leaves and increased growth and development of herbivores (Zavala and others 2008). Moreover, the reduction of proteinase inhibitors can further reduce plant fitness by increasing herbivore attack on younger leaves, which contributes disproportionately to plant growth (Zavala and others 2009).

The production and release of volatiles—airborne chemical compounds emitted by plants—is another important hallmark of plant-herbivore interactions that is expected to be affected by climate change (Yuan and others 2009). These airborne chemicals can significantly impact the fitness of plants and insects by serving as foraging cues for organisms that are beneficial to plants, such as predators and parasites of herbivores (De Moraes and others 1998) or by directly repelling herbivores (De Moraes and others 2001). Volatiles can also convey information about a plant's identity and location to harmful organisms (or beneficial organisms in the case of biocontrol insects) such as herbivores (De Moraes and others 2001; Runyon and others 2006). Climate change can alter the biological functions of plant volatiles with largely unknown consequences (Yuan and others 2009). For example, drought and elevated CO_2 can increase emission of volatile terpenoids, which could increase plant apparency to herbivores or perturb attraction of herbivore natural enemies (Mattson and Hauk 1987; Himanen and others 2009). Increases in CO_2 have been shown to increase volatile production by soybean plants, which seemingly act as a super stimulus that may elicit an exaggerated feeding response in herbivores (O'Neill and others 2010). Conversely, O_3 can react with and rapidly degrade certain volatiles in the atmosphere (Pinto and others 2007). Elevated temperature has long been known to increase plant volatile emission rates (Guenther and others 1993), indicating a general increase in plant volatiles under a warmer climate with unknown but likely profound impacts on ecological interactions between plants and insects (Yuan and others 2009). It is unlikely these changes could lead biocontrol insects to shift to non-target plant species; biocontrol insects are highly host-specific and rely on species-specific chemical cues (e.g., the presence/absence of compounds) to locate and feed. However, our poor current state of knowledge about such potential climate change impacts does not allow us to rule this possibility out.

In summary, we know alarmingly little about how climate change will impact the relationship between plants and insects, despite the profound implications for agriculture and biocontrol. The limited knowledge available indicates that responses are highly variable and dependent on the species involved. Many herbivores will alter how much they eat in response to climate-induced changes in plant nutrition and plant defensive chemistry; yet, we know next to nothing about what this might mean ecologically or economically. If biocontrol is to keep pace with and remain effective in a changing climate, increased funding is needed to:

- Determine how climate change will affect the nutrient content of invasive plants and what impact these changes will have on biocontrol agents.
- Evaluate effects of climate change on the defensive chemistry of invasive plants and determine how these changes impact biocontrol agents.
- Develop a conceptual framework to understand and predict how climate-induced changes will alter broader population- and landscape-level outcomes of biocontrol.
- Develop effective tools and techniques to best use and adapt biocontrol to manage invasive plants in a changing environment.

This is an opportunity to advance our basic understanding of the ecology of plant-insect interactions and the conditions under which herbivory translates into meaningful changes in plant populations—fundamental ecological questions that hold great promise for managing invasive plants in present and future environments. Moreover, because climate-induced changes in western North America—much of which is dominated by grasslands, shrublands, and deserts—have generally outpaced change elsewhere (Overpeck and Udall 2010), biocontrol is likely to be affected first and most severely there. As such, the GSD Ecosystems Program is well positioned to take on the research needed to adapt and respond to future environmental changes.

Climate Change Effects on Wildlife Disease

Disease is a natural process in wildlife communities that, under normal circumstances, acts to regulate communities and interactions. However, when disease dynamics are altered by wildlife manipulations (translocations, hunting, and commercial trade) and lead to new pathogen-host interactions, disease often becomes a destructive force. In general, invasive species, and in particular, vectors and pathogens, can destabilize natural communities and irrevocably change ecosystem structure and function with severe economic and environmental consequences (Crowl and others 2008). Wildlife managers and conservation biologists have become increasingly concerned with the rise in emergence of many serious diseases, including plague (*Yersinia pestis*) encephalitis, canine distemper, and West Nile virus (Daszak and others 2001; Deem and others 2000; Gubler and others 2001).

Disease introductions in wildlife populations usually occur at domestic-wildlife interfaces or are related to translocation efforts. Wildlife disease outbreaks are commonly associated with increased proximity to humans and domestic animals (Deem and others 2000). Multispecies land use, such as occurs in buffer zones where domestic and wildlife share grazing lands, is thought to facilitate disease spread (Daszak and others 2001; Deem and others 2000). However, the primary mechanism for disease spread is translocation (Deem and others 2000). Translocations have multiple consequences for disease management, including an increased risk of exposure of wildlife to new diseases present in new location or unintentional introductions of disease vectors or carrier species (Deem and others 2000). Recent translocations of the white-tailed deer (*Odocoileus virginanus*) resulted in the spread of the lungworm *Parelaphostronglyus tenuis* to Wassa Island, Georgia (Davidson and others 1996). Similarly, reintroduction of a confiscated desert tortoise (*Gopherus agassizii*) infected with mycoplasmosis in Las Vegas Valley led to the spread of that disease in native populations (Jacobson and others 1995), and the transport of infected carcasses was associated with the spread of canine distemper in the Southwest (Davidson and others 1992; Deem and others 2000). The zebra mussel (*Dreissena polymorpha*) is an invasive species whose impact has been amplified through its status as a carrier of the roundworm parasite, *Bucephalus polymorphus*, which can also infect many freshwater cyprinid fish (Crowl and others 2008). Among the invasive diseases currently known to occur in the Interior West, plague, canine distemper, brucellosis (*Brucella* spp.), chronic wasting disease, bovine tuberculosis (*Mycobacterium bovis*), whirling disease (*Myxobolus cerebalis*), and West Nile virus have considerable negative impacts on wildlife population (Bengis and others 2002; Clinton and others 2010; Githecko and others 2000; Longstreth and Wiseman 1989; Mason 2008).

Global warming will impact many wildlife disease patterns, particularly vector-borne diseases (Daszak and others 2001; Harvell and others 2002; Patz and others 2000; Keesing and others 2006; Rosenthal 2009). Local climatic conditions are thought to play an important role in determining disease emergence (Githeko and others 2000; Harvell and others 2002; Hofmeister and others 2010; Lafferty 2009), and global warming is predicted to lead to range expansions of many vector species and increase the frequency of vector borne disease outbreaks (Epstein 2001; Harvell and others 2002). Issues associated with wildlife translocations and their roles in disease emergence are also expected to increase under future climate scenarios (Deem and others 2000). Among other effects, increases in temperature are expected to positively influence the spread of disease by decreasing overwinter mortality of many arthropod vectors and parasites (Harvell and others 2002) and increasing vector and pathogen developmental rates (Wilcox and Gubler 2005). Within the Interior West, the spread of diseases such as West Nile virus and Lyme disease may be encouraged by increases in mean temperature and humidity, which will open up new zones for their mosquito and tick vectors (Deem and others 2000). In higher elevations, warmer temperatures may contribute to the spread of chytrid fungus (*Batrachochytirum dendrobatidis*) among amphibians (Pounds and others 2006; Rohr and Raffel 2010). Furthermore, amphibian host susceptibility may increase as heat stress and high UV-B affect immune response (Harvell and others 2002; Martin and others 2010). Rising water temperatures are likely to exacerbate ongoing issues with the introduced agent of whirling disease, *Myxobolus cerebalis* (Mason 2008; Longstreth and Wiseman 1989). Increases in host breeding season may contribute to the spread of *Ophryosystis elektroscirrha* (protozoal infection) in monarch butterflies (Harvell and others 2002). Of the exotic diseases present in the Interior West, plague and West Nile virus are the most susceptible to climate-related changes in distribution and incidence. Disease distribution and incidence may also increase if wildlife is translocated as part of assisted migration projects being developed to lessen negative climate change impacts (McDonald-Madden and others 2011).

Changes to precipitation regimes will influence the availability of favorable habitat for vectors that rely on water bodies and, in turn, influence the establishment of disease in new areas (Gubler and others 2001; Patz and others 2000). Reduced precipitation might limit breeding sites for many mosquito vectors but could also lead to conditions, such as overcrowding at limited water holes, increased water temperatures, and more organic matter, that are conducive to disease spread, particularly for water-borne diseases such as avian cholera and pox (Friend and Franson 1999). Precipitation also affects intermediate and reservoir hosts by influencing important food resources (Dazak and others 2001). Changes in the overlap of species due to phenological effects of changing temperature and precipitation regimes have consequences for host, reservoir, and vector populations and may lead to new disease issues (Harvell and others 2002; Hofmeister and others 2010; Patz and others 2000). Changes to the timing of host migrations may also influence the risk of disease exposure for some wildlife populations and lead to novel host-pathogen interactions.

However, climate change may not always lead to an expansion of disease and could, in fact, decrease some disease threats. Increased temperatures can reduce adult survivorship of vectors (Harvell and others 2002) and limit transmission of certain diseases such as plague that have upper critical temperature thresholds (Githeko and others 2000). Entomophatogenic fungi in insects (some biocontrol agents), coldwater disease in salmon, and avian cholera in waterbirds (*Pasteurella multocida*) may decline as temperatures rise (Harvell and others 2002). Warming may limit the spread of chytrid and iridoviruses, which rely on cool, moist conditions, in amphibian populations in warmer climates. Hot, dry conditions may impede fungal development and enhance insect immune response (Martin and others 2010). Perhaps to the benefit of some biocontrol efforts, warmer temperatures are expected to reduce the cold-induced mortality of the nuclear polyhedrosis virus *Lymantria dispar* on gypsy moth egg cases (Harvell and others 2002). However, the direction of disease response depends on local conditions and the inherent limitations of the disease agents (Githeko and others 2000). Commonly, pathogens limited by winter mortality show predicted range contractions in the south and corresponding expansions to northern areas (Haile 1989). Ultimately, many diseases may shift rather than experience an absolute change in their area (Lafferty 2009). Identifying if and how climate change will impact specific ecosystems, populations, and pathogens is a critical step toward informing management agency actions with respect to disease emergence.

Wildlife disease becomes a Forest Service issue when it affects threatened and endangered species and human use of Forest Service lands and when management of forest lands can mitigate the introduction or expansion of invasive disease. We need to implement research and build expertise to address invasive disease issues and facilitate actions that allow us to manage rangelands for biological diversity, health, and sustained and enhanced use by our stakeholders. Research needs to focus on mitigating the potential effects of invasive disease on threatened and endangered species to prevent further population declines, identify populations at risk due to inherent susceptibilities or increased exposure (migrating species, species in buffer zones), and identify the important interactions (climate, species interactions, and land use practices) that affect ecosystem integrity and invasibility. In addition, wildlife disease has socioeconomic effects when it relates to human use of land and to human health issues (e.g., zoonotic diseases such as plague, hanta virus, Lyme disease, and West Nile virus).

Specific research needs that address the strategic goals of the Forest Service mission are:

- Identify disease threats to threatened and endangered species.
- Identify disease risk for critical habitats, particularly breeding and migratory stopover sites. Analyze risk factors for species and management units and for translocation or assisted migrations.
- Assess economic and socioeconomic issues related to emergent wildlife disease.
- Identify and monitor susceptible/at risk populations.
- Determine how current and proposed management (e.g., restoration) activities affect disease invasibility of ecosystems or basic health parameters of wildlife populations.
- Determine if certain practices are more or less likely to favor the spread of disease.
- Evaluate the effects of management actions for mitigating disease impacts.

Many diseases affect species present or dependent upon grassland habitats and new diseases will further threaten these populations. Many species, such as the desert tortoise and sagebrush grouse, are already endangered and attention must focus on preventing further population decline. The GSD Ecosystems Program is able to address many relevant research questions with expertise in human resources, disease, soil and invasive species. The diversity of sites and ecosystems available in the GSD region puts scientists in this program in a unique position to address some if not all of these issues and to be able to satisfy recent calls for regional-level monitoring (see Crowl and others 2008) and analysis of disease emergence and spread. If applied successfully, these efforts might also be used effectively in other systems and ranger stations. Current activities with the black footed ferret (*Mustela nigripes*) (Rapid City Lab), which are highly susceptible to plague and canine distemper, are one way the GSD Program can develop a more aggressive and comprehensive disease-oriented research. Furthermore, many activities related to current RMRS research, particularly as they pertain to grazing; human-domestic, animal-wildlife interfaces; and restoration activities are also highly relevant to disease prevention and management issues.

In addition to building upon its own expertise and initiating new research, researchers in the GSD Program need to engage opportunities to work with other programs and agencies with ongoing research relevant to species of interest to the Forest Service (e.g., USGS/BLM SAGEMAP project for the greater sage-grouse, which is threatened by West Nile virus). The recent spread of white-nose syndrome illustrates the devastating impact of introduced disease and points to the critical importance to establish networks and cooperation in anticipation of disease emergence. The recent finding of white-nose syndrome in the cave bat (*Myotis velifer*) in Oklahoma is a troubling predictor that this western bat species could soon bring white-nose syndrome to the western United States. As this disease potentially impacts over half the species endemic to United States, the inevitable spread of this disease is an impending crisis requiring immediate action. Forest Service researchers should have a role in identifying research needs and intervention strategies managing white-nose syndrome.

Literature Cited

Allen, J. A., C. S. Brown and T. J. Stohlgren. 2009. Non-native plant invasions of United States national parks. Biological Invasions 11: 2195-2207.

Andrew, N. R. and L. Hughes. 2005. Diversity and assemblage structure of phytophagous Hemiptera along a latitudinal gradient: predicting the potential impacts of climate change. Global Ecology and Biogeography 14: 249-262.

Andrew, N. R. and L. Hughes. 2007. Potential host colonization by insect herbivores in a warmer climate: a transplant experiment. Global Change Biology 13: 1539-1549.

Baldwin, I. T. 1998. Jasmonate-induced responses are costly but benefit plants under attack in native populations. Proceedings of the National Academy of Sciences USA 95: 8113-8118.

Bale, J. S., G. J. Masters, I. D. Hodkinson, C. Awmack and others. 2002. Herbivory in global change research: direct effects of rising temperature on insect herbivores. Global Change Biology 8: 1-16.

Barnes, T. G. 2007. Using herbicides to rehabilitate native grasslands. Natural Areas Journal 27: 56-65.

Baruch, Z. and G. Goldstein. 1999. Leaf construction cost, nutrient concentration, and net CO_2 assimilation of native and invasive species in Hawaii. Oecologia 121: 183-192.

Bazzaz, F. and K. D. M. McConnaughay. 1992. Plant-plant interactions in elevated CO_2 environments. Australian Journal of Botany 40: 547-563.

Bengis, R. G., R. A. Kock and J. Fischer. 2002. Infectious animal diseases: the wildlife/livestock interface. Revue Scientifique et Technique 21: 53-65.

Bidart-Bouzat, M. G. and A. Imeh-Nathaniel. 2008. Global change effects on plant chemical defenses against insect herbivores. Journal of Integrative Plant Biology 50: 1339-1354.

Blumenthal, D., R. A. Chimner, J. M. Welker and J. A. Morgan. 2008. Increased snow facilitates plant invasion in mixedgrass prairie. New Phytologist 179: 440-448.

Bradley, B. A. 2009. Regional analysis of the impacts of climate change on cheatgrass invasion shows potential risk and opportunity. Global Change Biology 15: 196-208.

Bradley, B. A, D. M. Blumenthal, D. S. Wilcove and L. H. Ziska. 2010. Predicting plant invasions in an era of global change. Trends in Ecology and Evolution 25: 310-318.

Bradley, B. A., M. Oppenheimer and D. S. Wilcove. 2009. Climate change and plant invasions: Restoration opportunities ahead? Global Climate Change Biology 15: 1511-1521.

Brooks M. L., C. M. D'Antonio, D. M. Richardson, J. B. Grace and others. 2004. Effects of invasive alien plants on fire regimes. BioScience 54: 677-688.

Chambers, J. C. and M. Pellant. 2008. Climate change impacts on northwestern and intermountain United States rangelands. Rangelands 30: 29-33.

Chambers, J. C., B. A. Roundy, R. R. Blank, S. E. Meyer and A. Whittaker. 2007. What makes Great Basin sagebrush ecosystems invasible by *Bromus tectorum*? Ecological Monographs 77: 117-145.

Clinton, R. M., H. Carabin and S. E. Little. 2010. Emerging zoonoses in the southern United States: Toxocarieasis, bovine tuberculosis and southern tick-associated rash illness. The American Journal of the Medical Sciences 340: 187-193.

Cobbold, C. A. and J. A. Powell. 2011. Evolution stabilizes the synchronizing dynamics of poikilotherm life cycles. Bulletin of Mathematical Biology 73: 1052-1081.

Coviella, C. E. and J. T. Trumble. 1999. Effects of elevated atmospheric carbon dioxide on insect-plant interactions. Conservation Biology 13: 700-712.

Crowl, T. A., T. O. Crist, R. R. Parmenter, G. Belovsky and A. E. Lugo. 2008. The spread of invasive species and infectious disease as drivers of ecosystem change. Frontiers in Ecology and the Environment 6: 238-246.

D'Antonio, C. M., E. L. Berlow and K. L. Hausensak. 2004. Invasive exotic plant species in Sierra Nevada ecosystems. Gen. Tech. Rep. PSW-GTR-193. Albany, CA: U.S. Department of Agriculture, Forest Service, Pacific Southwest Research Station: 175-184.

Dangles, O., C. Carpio, A. R. Barragan, J.-L. Zeddam and J.-F. Silvain. 2008. Temperature as a key driver of ecological sorting among invasive pest species in the tropical Andes. Ecological Applications 18: 1795-1809.

Daszak, P., A. A. Cunningham and A. D. Hyatt. 2001. Anthropogenic environmental change and the emergence of infectious disease in wildlife. Acta Tropica 78: 103-116.

Davidson, W. R., M. J. Appel, G. L. Doster, O. E. Baker and J. F. Brown. 1992. Disease and parasites of red foxes, gray foxes and coyotes from commercial sources selling to fox chasing enclosure. Journal of Wildlife Disease 28: 581-589.

Davidson, W. R., G. L. Doster and R. C. Freeman. 1996. *Parelaphosptronglyus tenuis* on Wassaw Island, Georgia: a result of translocation white-tailed deer. Journal of Wildlife Disease 32: 701-703.

Davidson, W. R. and V. F. Nettles. 1992. Relocation of wildlife: identifying and evaluating disease risks. Transactions of the North American Wildlife and Natural Resources Conference 57: 466-473.

Davis, A. J., J. H. Lawton, B. Shorrocks and L. S. Jenkinson. 1998. Individualistic species responses invalidate simplistic physiological models of community dynamics under global environmental change. Journal of Animal Ecology 67: 600-612.

Deem, S. L., W. B. Karesh and W. Weisman. 2000. Putting theory into practice: wildlife health in conservation. Conservation Biology 15: 224-1233.

DeLucia, E. H., C. L. Casteel, P. D. Nabity and B. F. O'Neill. 2008. Insects take a bigger bite out of plants in a warmer, higher carbon dioxide world. Proceedings of the National Academy of Sciences USA 105: 1781-1782.

De Moraes, C. M., W. J. Lewis, P. W. Pare, H. T. Alborn and J. H. Tumlinson. 1998. Herbivore-infested plants selectively attract parasitoids. Nature 393: 570-573.

De Moraes, C. M., M. C. Mescher and J. H. Tumlinson. 2001. Caterpillar-induced nocturnal plant volatiles repel conspecific females. Nature 410: 577-80.

Dermody, O., B. F. O'Neill, A. R. Zangerl, M. R. Berenbaum and E. H. DeLucia. 2008. Effects of elevated CO_2 and O_3 on leaf damage and insect abundance in a soybean agroecosystem. Arthropod-Plant Interactions 2: 125-135.

Dijkstra, F. A., D. Blumenthal, J. A. Morgan, D. LeCain and R. F. Follett. 2010a. Elevated CO_2 effects on semi-arid grassland plants in relation to water availability and competition. Functional Ecology 24: 1152-1161.

Dijkstra, F. A., D. Blumenthal, J. A. Morgan, E. Pendall, Y. Carrillo and R. F. Follett. 2010b. Contrasting effects of elevated CO_2 and warming on N cycling in a semiarid grassland. New Phytologist 187: 426-437.

Dijkstra, F. A., E. Pendall, A. R. Mosier, J. Y. King, D. G. Milchunas and J. A. Morgan. 2008. Long-term enhancement of N availability and plant growth under elevated CO_2 in a semi-arid grassland. Functional Ecology 22: 975-982.

Dillon, M. E., G. Wang and R. B. Huey. 2010. Global metabolic impacts of recent climate warming. Nature 147: 704-706.

Dukes, J. S. 2000. Will the increasing atmospheric CO_2 concentration affect the success of invasive species. In: Mooney, H. and R. J. Hobbs, eds. Invasive Species and a Changing World. Washington, DC: Island Press: 95-113.

Dukes, J. S. and H. A. Mooney. 1999. Does global change increase the success of biological invaders? Trends in Ecology and Evolution 14: 135-139.

Durand, L. Z. and G. Goldstein. 2001. Photosynthesis, photoinhibition, and N use efficiency in native and invasive tree ferns in Hawaii. Oecologia 126: 354-354.

Epstein, P. R. 2001. Climate change and emerging infectious diseases. Microbes and Infection 3: 747-754.

Fabina, N. S., K. C. Abbott and R. T. Gilman. 2010. Sensitivity of plant-pollinator-herbivore communities to changes in phenology. Ecological Modeling 221: 453-458.

Fox, L. R., S. P. Ribeiro, V. K. Brown, G. J. Masters and I. P. Clarke. 1999. Direct and indirect effects of climate change on St. John's wort, *Hypericum perforatum* L. (Hypericaceae). Oecologia 120: 113-122.

Friend, M. and J. C. Franson, eds. 1999. Field manual of wildlife diseases, general field procedures and disease of birds/Biological Resources Division. Information and Technology Report 1999-001. U.S. Department of Interior, United States Geological Sciences: 75-92 163-170.

Gaston, K. J. 2009. Geographic range limits: achieving synthesis. Proceedings of the Royal Society B 276: 1395-1406.

Gillooly, J. F., J. H. Brown, G. B. West, V. M. Savage and E. L. Charnov. 2001. Effects of size and temperature on metabolic rate. Science 293: 2248-2251.

Githeko, A. K., S. W. Lindsay, U. E. Confalonieri and J. A. Patz. 2000. Climate change and vector-borne diseases: A regional analysis. Bulletin of the World Health Organization 78: 113611-47.

Gubler, D. J., P. Reiter, K. L. Ebi, W. Yap, R. Nasci and J. A. Patz. 2001. Climate change and variability in the United States: potential impact on vector- and rodent-borne diseases. Environmental Health Perspectives 109: 223-233.

Guenther, A. B., P. R. Zimmerman, P. C. Harley, R. K. Monson and R. Fall. 1993. Isoprene and monoterpene emission rate variability—model evaluations and sensitivity analysis. Journal of Geophysical Analysis—Atmospheres 98: 12609-12617.

Gutierrez, A. P., L. Ponti, T. d'Oultremont and C. K. Ellis. 2008. Climate change effects on poikilotherm tritrophic interactions. Climate Change 87 (Suppl. 1): S167-S192.

Haile, D. G. 1989. Computer simulation of the effects of changes in weather patterns on vector-borne disease transmission. In: Smith, J. B. and D. A. Tirpak, eds. The potential effects of global climate change in the United States. Doc no 230-05-89-057, Appendix G. Washington, DC: U.S. Environmental Protection Agency.

Hamilton, J. G., O. Dermody, M. Aldea, A. R. Zangerl and others. 2005. Anthropogenic changes in tropospheric composition increase susceptibility of soybean to insect herbivory. Environmental Entomology 34: 479-485.

Harvell, C. D., C. E. Mitchell, J. R. Ward, S. Altizer and others. 2002. Climate warming and disease risks for terrestrial and marine biota. Science 296: 2158-2162.

Hegland, S. J., A. Nielsen, A. Lazaro, A.-L. Bjerknes and Ø. Totland. 2009. How does climate warming affect plant-pollinator interactions? Ecology Letters 12: 184-195.

Hellmann, J. J., J. E. Byers, B. G. Bierwagen and J. S. Dukes. 2008. Five potential consequences of climate change for invasive species. Conservation Biology 22: 534-543.

Hiebert, R. D. 1997. Prioritizing invasive plants and planning for management. In: Luken, J. O. and J. W. Thieret, eds. Assessment and Management of Plant Invasion. Springer-Verlag, Inc.: New York: 195-212.

Hill, J. K., H. M. Griffiths and C. D. Thomas. 2010. Climate change and evolutionary adaptations at species' range margins. Annual Review of Entomology 56: 143-159.

Himanen, S. J., A. Nerg, A. Nissinen, D. M. Pinto and others. 2009. Effects of elevated carbon dioxide and ozone on volatile terpenoid emissions and multitrophic communication of transgenic insecticidal oilseed rape (*Brassica napus*). New Phytologist 181: 174-186.

Hodkinson, I. D. and J. M. Bird. 1998. Host-specific herbivores as sensors of climate change in arctic and alpine environments. Arctic and Alpine Research 30: 78-83.

Hofmeister, E., G. M. Rogall, K. Wesenberg, R. Abbott and others. 2010. Climate change and wildlife health: direct and indirect effects. U.S. Geological Survey Fact Sheet 2010-3017.

Holt, R. D. 1990. The microevolutionary consequences of climate change. Trends in Ecology and Evolution 5: 311-315.

Holt, R. D. and M. Barfield. 2009. Trophic interactions and range limits: the diverse roles of predation. Proceedings of the Royal Society B 276: 1435-1442.

Hunt, R., D. W. Hand, M. A. Hannah and A. M. Neal. 1991. Responses to CO_2 enrichment in 27 herbaceous species. Functional Ecology 5: 410-421.

Jacobson, E. R., M. B. Brown, I. M. Schumacher, B. R. Collins and others. 1995. Mycoplasmosis and the desert tortoise (*Gopherus agassizii*) in Las Vegas Valley, Nevada. Chelonian Conservation Biology 1: 279-284.

Johnson, S. N. and J. W. McNicol. 2010. Elevated CO_2 and aboveground-belowground herbivory by the clover root weevil. Oecologia 162: 209-216.

Lafferty, K. D. 2009. The ecology of climate change and infectious diseases. Ecology 90: 888-900.

Leger, E. A., E. K. Espeland, K. R. Merrill and S. E. Meyer. 2009. Genetic variation and local adaptation at a cheatgrass invasion edge in western Nevada. Molecular Ecology 18: 4366-4379.

Longstreth, J. D. and J. Wiseman. 1989. The potential impact of climate change on patterns of infectious disease in the United States: Appendix G Health. In: Smith, J. B. and D. A. Tirpak, eds. The potential effects of global climate change in the United States. Doc no 230-05-89-057. Washington, DC: U.S. Environmental Protection Agency.

Mack, M. C. and C. D'Antonio. 1998. Impacts of biological invasions on disturbance regimes. Trends in Ecology and Evolution 13: 195-198.

Maron, J. L. and E. Crone. 2006. Herbivory: effects on plant abundance, distribution and population growth. Proceedings of the Royal Society of London B 273: 2575-2584.

Martin, L. B., W. A. Hopkins, L. D. Mydlarz and J. R. Rohr. 2010. The effects of anthropogenic global changes on immune functions and disease resistance. Annual of the New York Academy of Sciences 1195: 129-148.

Mason, R. 2008. Great Basin wildlife disease concerns. Gen. Tech. Rep. RMRS-GTR-204. Fort Collins, CO: U.S. Department of Agriculture, Forest Service, Rocky Mountain Research Station: 42-44.

Mattson, W. J. and R. A. Haack. 1987. The role of drought in outbreaks of plant-eating insects. Bioscience 37: 110-118.

McDonald-Madden, E., M. C. Runge, H. P. Possingham and T. G. Martin. 2011. Optimal timing for managed relocation of species faced with climate change. Nature Climate Change 1: 261-265.

Merrill, K. R., S. E. Meyer and C. Coleman. 2012. Population genetic analysis of *Bromus tectorum* (Poaceae) indicates recent range expansion facilitated by specialist genotypes. American Journal of Botany 99: 529-537.

Milchunas, D. G. and W. K. Lauenroth. 1995. Inertia in plant community structure: state changes after cessation of nutrient-enrichment stress. Ecological Applications 5: 452-458.

Morgan, J. A., A. R. Mosier, D. G. Milchunas, D. R. LeCain and others. 2004. CO_2 enhances productivity, alters species composition, and reduces digestibility of shortgrass steppe vegetation. Ecological Applications 14: 208-219.

Morse, L. E., J. T. Kartesz and L. S. Kutner. 1995. Native vascular plants. In: LaRoe, E. T., G. S. Farris, C. E. Puckett, P. D. Doran and M. J. Mac, eds. Our living resources: a report to the nation on the distribution, abundance, and health of u.s. plants, animals, and ecosystems. Washington, DC: U.S. Department of the Interior, National Biological Service: 205-209.

O'Neill, B. F., A. R. Zangerl, E. H. DeLucia and M. R. Berenbaum. 2010. Olfactory preferences of *Popillia japonica*, *Vanessa cardui*, *Aphis glycines* for *Glycine max* grown under elevated CO_2 Environmental Entomology 39: 1291-1301.

Overpeck, J. and B. Udall. 2010. Dry times ahead. Science 328: 1642-1643.

Patterson, D. T. 1995. Weeds in a changing climate. Weed Science 43: 685-701.

Pattison, R. R., G. Goldstein and A. Ares. 1998. Growth, biomass allocation and photosynthesis of invasive and native Hawaiian rainforest species. Oecologia 117: 449-459.

Patz, J. A., T. K. Graczyk, N. Geller and A. Y. Vittor. 2000. Effects of environmental change on emerging parasitic diseases. International Journal for Parasitology 30: 1395-1405.

Pearson, D. and Y. Ortega. 2009. Managing invasive plants in natural areas: moving beyond weed control. In: Kingley, R.V., ed. Weeds: Management, Economic Impacts and Biology. Hauppauge, NY: Nova Science Publishers, Inc.: 1-21.

Percy, K. E., C. S. Awmack, R. L. Lindroth, M. E. Kubiske and others. 2002. Altered performance of forest pests under atmospheres enriched by CO_2 and O_3. Nature 420: 403-407.

Pimentel, D., L. Liach, R. Zuniga and D. Morrison. 2000. Environmental and economic costs of non-indigenous species in the United States. Bioscience 50: 53-65.

Pinto, D. M., J. D. Blande, R. Nykanen, W. X. Dong and others. 2007. Ozone degrades common herbivore-induce plant volatiles: does this effect herbivore prey location by predators and parasitoids? Journal of Chemical Ecology 33: 683-694.

Pounds, J. A., M. R. Bustamante, L. A. Coloma, J. A. Consuegra and others. 2006. Widespread amphibian extinctions from epidemic disease driven by global warming. Nature 439: 161-167.

Ramakrishnan, A., S. E. Meyer, C. Coleman and D. J. Fairbanks. 2006. Ecological significance of microsatellite variation in western North American populations of *Bromus tectorum*. Plant Species Biology 21: 61-73.

Ramakrishnan A. P., S. E. Meyer, J. Waters, C. Coleman, M. Stevens and D. J. Fairbanks. 2004. Correlation between molecular genetic markers and adaptively significant variation in *Bromus tectorum* (Poaceae), an inbreeding annual grass. American Journal of Botany 91: 797-803.

Reich, P. B. 2009. Elevated CO_2 reduces losses of plant diversity caused by nitrogen deposition. Science 426: 1399-1402.

Richardson, D. M., P. Pyšek, M. Rejmánek, M. G. Barbour, F. D. Panetta and C. J. West. 2000. Naturalization and invasion of alien plants: concepts and definitions. Diversity and Distributions 6: 93-107.

Rohr, J. R. and T. R. Raffel. 2010. Linking global climate and temperature variability to widespread amphibian declines putatively caused by disease. Proceedings of the National Academy of Sciences USA 107: 8269-8274.

Rosenthal, J. 2009. Climate change and the geographic distribution of infectious diseases. EcoHealth 6: 489-495.

Runyon, J. B., M. C. Mescher and C. M. De Moraes. 2006. Volatile chemical cues guide host location and host selection by parasitic plants. Science 313: 1964-1967.

Sasek, T. W. and B. R. Strain. 1991. Effects of CO_2 enrichment on the growth and morphology of a native and an introduced honeysuckle vine. American Journal of Botany 78: 69-75.

Scheiner, S. M. 2009. The intersection of the sciences of biogeography and infectious disease ecology. EcoHealth 6: 483-488.

Schrag, S. J. and P. Wiener. 1995. Emerging infectious disease: what are the relative roles of ecology and evolution? Trends in Ecology and Evolution 10: 319-324.

Scott, J. W., S. E. Meyer, K. R. Merrill and V. J. Anderson. 2010. Local population differentiation in *Bromus tectorum* L. in relation to habitat specific selection regimes. Evolutionary Ecology 24: 1061-1080.

Sims-Chilton, N. M., M. P. Zalucki and Y. M. Buckley. 2010. Long term climate effects are confounded with the biological control programme against the invasive weed *Baccharis halimifolia* in Australia. Biological Invasions 12: 3145-3155.

Skinner, K., L. Smith and P. Rice. 2000. Using noxious weeds to prioritize targets for developing weed management strategies. Weed Science 48: 640-644.

Smith, S. D., T. E. Huxman, S. F. Zitzer, T. N. Charlet and others. 2000. Elevated CO_2 increases productivity and invasive species success in an arid ecosystem. Nature 408: 79-82.

Smith, S. D., B. R. Strain and T. D. Sharkey. 1987. Effects of CO2 enrichment on four Great Basin grasses. Functional Ecology 1: 139-143.

Song, L., J. Wu, C. Li, F. Li, S. Peng and B. Chen. 2009. Different responses of invasive and native plants to elevated CO_2 concentration. Acta Oecologica 35: 128-135.

Stein, B. A. and S. R. Flack, eds. 1996. America's Least Wanted: Alien Species Invasions of U.S. Ecosystems. The Nature Conservancy: Arlington, Virginia.

Stein, B. A. and S. R. Flack. 1997. 1997 Species Report Card: The State of U.S. Plants and Animals. The Nature Conservancy: Arlington, Virginia.

Steinbach-Elwell, L. C., K. E. Stromberg, E. K. Ryce and J. L. Bartholomew. 2009. Whirling disease in the United Stations: a summary of progress in research and management. Montana Fish, Wildlife, and Parks.

Stohlgren, T. J., D. Binkley, G. W. Chong, M. A. Kalkhan and others. 1999. Exotic plant species invade hotspots of native plant diversity. Ecological Monographs 69: 25-46.

Sutherst, R. W. 2000. Climate change and invasive species: a conceptual framework. In: Mooney, H. A. and R. J. Hobbs, eds. Invasive Species and a Changing World. Washington, DC: Island Press: 211-240.

Suttle, K. B., M. A. Thomsen and M. E. Power. 2007. Species interactions reverse grassland responses to changing climate. Science 315: 640-642.

Thomas, J. A., R. J. Rose, R. T. Clarke, C. D. Thomas and N. R. Webb. 1999. Intraspecific variation in habitat availability among ectothermic animals near their climatic limits and centres of range. Functional Ecology 13: 55-64.

Tilman, D. 1987. Secondary succession and the pattern of plant dominance along experimental nitrogen gradients. Ecological Monographs 57: 189-214.

Underwood, N. 1999. The influence of plant and herbivore characteristics on the interaction between induced resistance and herbivore population dynamics. American Naturalist 153: 282-294.

van Asch, M., P. H. van Tienderen, L. J. M. Holleman and M. E. Visser. 2007. Predicting adaptation of phenology in response to climate change, and insect herbivore example. Global Change Biology 13: 1596-1604.

Verstraete, M. M., R. J. Scholes and M. S. Smith. 2009. Climate and desertification: looking at an old problem through new lenses. Frontiers in Ecology and the Environment 7: 421-428.

Vitousek, P. M. 1994. Beyond global warming: ecology and global change. Ecology 75: 1861-1876.

Walther, G.-R., A. Roques, P. E. Hulme, M. T. Sykes and others. 2009. Alien species in a warmer world: risks and opportunities. Trends in Ecology and Evolution 24: 686-693.

Watt, M. S., D. J. Kriticos, K. J. B. Potter, L. K. Manning, N. Tallent-Halsell and G. W. Bourdôt. 2010. Using species niche models to inform strategic management of weeds in a changing climate. Biological Invasions 12: 3711-3725.

Wilcox, B. A. and D. J. Gubler. 2005. Disease ecology and the global emergence of zoonotic pathogens. Environmental Health and Preventative Medicine 10: 263-272.

Yuan, J. S., S. J. Himanen, J. K. Holopainen, F. Chen and C. N. Stewart, Jr. 2009. Smelling global climate change: mitigation of function for plant volatile organic compounds. Trends in Ecology and Evolution 24: 323-331.

Zavala, J. A., C. L. Casteel, E. H. DeLucia and M. R. Berenbaum. 2008. Anthropogenic increase in carbon dioxide compromises plant defense against invasive insects. Proceedings of the National Academy of Sciences USA 105: 5129-5133.

Zavala, J. A., C. J. Casteel, P. D. Nabity, M. R. Berenbaum and E. H. DeLucia. 2009. Role of cysteine proteinase inhibitors in preference of Japanese beetles (*Popillia japonica*) for soybean (*Glycine max*) leaves of different ages and grown under elevated CO_2. Oecologia 161: 35-41.

Ziska, L. H. 2003. Evaluation of the growth response of six invasive species to past, present and future atmospheric carbon dioxide. Journal of Experimental Botany 54: 395-404.

Chapter 8

Decision Support: Vulnerability, Conservation, and Restoration

Megan M. Friggens[1], Jeremiah R. Pinto[2], R. Kasten Dumroese[2], and Nancy L. Shaw[3]

[1] U.S. Forest Service, Rocky Mountain Research Station; Grassland, Shrubland, and Desert Ecosystems Program; Forestry Science Laboratory, Albuquerque, New Mexico

[2] U.S. Forest Service, Rocky Mountain Research Station; Grassland, Shrubland, and Desert Ecosystems Program; Forestry Science Laboratory, Moscow, Idaho

[3] U.S. Forest Service, Rocky Mountain Research Station; Grassland, Shrubland, and Desert Ecosystems Program; Aquatic Sciences Laboratory, Boise, Idaho

Executive Summary

Current predictive tools, management options, restoration paradigms, and conservation programs are insufficient to meet the challenges of climate change in western North America. Scientific and management capabilities and resources will be sapped trying to identify risks to genetic resources and ecosystems and determine new approaches for mitigating and managing changing environments. Developing new tools will require innovative research, improvement and creation of predictive models, continuous evaluation of management outcomes, and integration with social scientists and economists.

Climate change threatens the biodiversity of grasslands, shrublands, and deserts at scales ranging from the gene to complex ecosystems. The rate of climate change may overcome normal ecosystem resilience, disrupting ecosystem functioning and provision of critical services. Guidelines for identifying and conserving at-risk species through a variety of experimental methods are available and being utilized. Nonetheless, these approaches and models for predicting future risks are evolving and not universally accepted or applicable.

Elements used to identify species or systems vulnerable to climate change include effects of exposure to climate change, sensitivity or the level to which the organism or system is altered, and its capacity to adjust to the change. Vulnerability assessments focus on unique variables or combinations of variables for comparison of organisms, natural systems, or human systems and range widely in their objectives; all rely on projections of future conditions. These assessments aid in planning adaptation strategies and prioritizing management. Available assessment tools include: vulnerability indices, process simulations, evaluation of shifts in species or community distribution, and integrated models. Research must focus on improved climate change predictions, species and habitat response models, identification of new community compositions, and management options.

Selection of appropriate plant materials for restoration necessitates an understanding of genetic variation and structure across the landscape. Species-specific seed zones are available for commercial trees but only for a few other species. A number of bioclimatic tools are used to delineate provisional seed zones, and broadly adapted seed sources are being developed for selected species and zones. Although western plant communities have constantly reassembled over time in response to changing climatic conditions, rapid climate change will increase fragmentation and cause appropriate habitat to appear in new locations. Assisted migration of native plants, a form of ex situ conservation, involves moving pre-adapted genotypes into remaining portions of the species range or moving a species into new but remote habitat. This approach remains controversial from biological and sociological standpoints. There is an urgent need to better understand future climate scenarios and appropriate transfer of genetic material and to provide analysis and discussion of natural and assisted future redistributions of species.

Climate change impacts on grassland, shrubland, and desert species and ecosystems are expected to increase but are difficult to predict for many areas. There is an immediate need for improved tools and approaches for assessing vulnerabilities at all levels, conserving diversity, and developing new techniques for selecting appropriate native plant materials for restoring disturbed areas and for moving genetic materials to new locations as climatic conditions change. Resources needed to accomplish these goals include genecologists, modelers, nursery and plant materials specialists, biologists, social scientists, and economists.

Introduction

Conservationists and land resource managers are gravely concerned about the impact of climate change because it will involve large numbers of species in diverse ecosystems, climate change interactions with ecosystems are wrought with complicated uncertainties, and our response will be limited by available human resources. Managers require effective tools now to manage natural resources under current climatic conditions. Managers will also need new methods and tools to help identify species and ecosystems at greatest risk of harm due to climate change and how to mitigate, or exploit, that change. To focus limited resources in the most effective and efficient manner, these tools should identify potential management intervention points (e.g., identify how systems are likely to be harmed) and address uncertainties in future conditions modeled by climate model projections and species' responses to those future conditions.

This chapter has three main topics:

- First, we discuss the ramification of the interactions of biodiversity and climate change and why conserving biodiversity is paramount.

- Second, we discuss how biodiversity, either from a species or ecosystem standpoint, can be assessed for its vulnerability to climate change. Vulnerable species or systems can then be identified and targeted for restoration.

- Third, we discuss how appropriate genetic material of vulnerable plant species or systems is currently transferred and may need to be transferred in the future to ensure successful restoration.

Climate Change and Biodiversity

Biodiversity affords ecosystems the plasticity to respond to natural disturbances, including naturally changing climate (Risser 1995). Climates are, however, changing at a rate faster than observed historically, thereby compromising these natural biological responses (Hughes 2000; Parmesan and Yohe 2003). It is therefore critical to identify conservation efforts at all scales (genetic, population, species, and ecosystem) in order to maintain plasticity and ecosystem function (Hannah and others 2002).

The general research consensus is that biodiversity (genetic variation, population variation, species richness, and ecosystem complexity) is threatened by climate change (Hannah and others 2002; Midgley and others 2002; Schwartz 1992; Schwartz and others 2006). Climate change has the potential to reduce valuable ecosystem services (such as production of food, pharmaceuticals, timber, and clean water) can contribute to floods and droughts, and can disrupt biogeochemical cycles (Daily 1997; Hughes and others 1997). Climate change may compromise ecosystem resiliency by reducing or eliminating plant and animal species (Thomas and others 2004) through range shifts in plant distributions (Beckage and others 2008; Soja and others 2007; Thomas 2010), increases in invasive species pressure (Smith and others 2000), and associated changes in disturbance regimes (McKenzie and others 2004). Significant habitat loss, disturbance, and increased habitat fragmentation also threaten native species' genetic diversity through inbreeding depression (Holt 1990; Johnson and others 2010; Thomas and others 2004). In grassland, shrubland, and desert ecosystems of the Great Basin, climate change effects have been forecasted and documented (Friggens and others, Chapter 1 this volume) as they relate to rare and vulnerable species (Fleishman 2008) and water resources, agriculture, native ecosystems, biodiversity, and recreation (summarized in Chambers 2008). The direct pressures on grassland, shrubland, and desert ecosystem biodiversity in the West are varied. Higher-elevation ecosystems are expected to shrink or vanish (Ledig and others 2010); ephemeral riparian and wetland systems may vanish (Hurd and others 1999); and highly invasive species may negatively affect native species through competition or altered fire regimes (Ziska and others 2005).

Conversation surrounding the loss of biodiversity due to climate change is contentious. Although we have clear guidelines, both globally (NatureServe) and nationally (Endangered Species Act; ESA), for identifying species at risk of extinction and conserving them (e.g., the black-footed ferret [*Mustela nigripes*], the models and assessments used for predicting future biodiversity losses of species still relatively abundant have yet to gain wide acceptance (Botkin and others 2007; Hannah and others 2002). In addition, the appropriate conservation strategies (i.e., in management areas [in situ], via assisted colonization [ex situ], or via germplasms, botanical gardens, or captive breeding programs [in vitro]) are under scrutiny (Hoegh-Guldberg and others 2008; Ricciardi and Simberloff 2009). Even so, germplasm of plants critically imperiled on a global level are currently being conserved in vitro (cryogenic storage of germplasm) by the Forest Service's National Seed Laboratory and Agricultural Research Service, while land managers work to protect plant and animal species under the ESA. However, efforts may not be adequate or sufficiently proactive to mitigate species and genetic losses due to climate change (Hoegh-Guldberg and others 2008).

To be sufficiently proactive, we need to identify, develop, and use appropriate vulnerability assessment tools to predict climate related increases in the risk of species extinction and population bottlenecking. To preserve biotic diversity, these assessments must provide potential management actions and refine research needs. These tools also must integrate bioclimatic modeling, genecology, and climate interactions with disturbance, invasive species, and species autecology. It is only through the development of these tools that we will be able to accurately assess and identify effective management actions for the preservation or restoration of critical habitats and biodiversity.

Assessing Species Vulnerability to Climate Change

Vulnerability is commonly defined as a function of exposure, sensitivity, and adaptive capacity (IPCC 2007; Stein and others 2011) and how these elements relate to the likelihood that species or systems are affected by climate change, the degree to which they are impacted by change, and their capacity to deal with change. Vulnerability assessments, using models, scoring systems, and comprehensive synthesis of the literature, determine which species or systems are most likely to be affected by climate change. Assessments usually target a unique variable or set of variables that act as the measure of vulnerability. Biodiversity and degree of expected change in microclimate are common measures to compare habitats, whereas vulnerability comparison among species depends on exposure levels and the possession (or lack thereof) of specific characteristics. Assessments may focus narrowly on species in select habitats or be global in perspective, but all evaluate the potential sensitivity, exposure, and adaptive capacity of their targets and all rely on projections of future conditions.

Climate change vulnerability assessments include a broad array of documents and analyses that synthesize many predictions and projections, and may take the form of qualitative evaluation of species traits or ecosystem function or involve statistical analysis of the relative influence of various parameters on population trends. Climate change vulnerability assessments vary in their objectives and can target human systems, natural systems, and processes of both (Füssel and Klein 2005). Vulnerability assessments are often the first step in planning adaptation strategies and management. By providing information on susceptibility to climate change impacts, assessments help identify targets for mitigation, enable managers to prioritize management activities and resources, and assist with implementing adaptive strategies (Füssel and Klein 2005).

Although many types of assessment tools are used, most fall into four broad categories: (1) vulnerability indices; (2) simulated processes; (3) community distribution shifts; and (4) complex, integrated models.

Vulnerability Indices

Several assessments rely on an indicator or index of vulnerability, which is used to compare the relative vulnerability of plant or animal species or systems. For example, the NatureServe Climate Change Vulnerability Index (http://www.natureserve.org/prodServices/climatechange/ccvi.jsp), designed for both plant and animal species, was used in Nevada and Massachusetts (Galbraith and O'Leary 2011; Young and others 2011); and SAVS, a System for Assessing Vulnerability of Species to climate change (Bagne and others 2011), was used to assess terrestrial vertebrate species in New Mexico (Finch and others 2011; Friggens and others, in prep.) and Arizona (Bagne and Finch 2010; Coe and others, in prep.). On a broader scale, the Environmental Protection Agency has a scoring system that has been applied nationally to assess the combined impact of climate change and non-climate related vulnerabilities for threatened and endangered species (Galbraith and Price 2011; U.S. EPA 2009). Other regional assessments incorporate indices and other projection tools (e.g., Czúcz and others 2009; Tremblay-Boyer and Anderson 2010). For example, an analysis of climate effects for the Pacific Northwest includes the use of sensitivity indicators (traits), downscaled climate projections, and dynamic global vegetation models (Case and Lawler 2011; Lawler and others 2009). This approach is commonly used to prioritize intervention or management actions or to identify research needs. It may also serve to identify new management targets when assessments reveal significant impact for targets not currently of concern.

Process Simulation

Assessments that use models that simulate processes, most commonly biogeochemical models or dynamic global vegetation models, can provide important information for management and policy decision. For example, WaterSim (Gober and Kirkwood 2010) estimates water shortages in the Phoenix area under different scenarios of population growth; the MAPSS biogeography model (Hanson and others 2001) projects biome response to climate changes in forests; and Hauer and others (1997) simulated impacts of climate change on freshwater ecosystems in North America's Rocky Mountains. These types of models formed the basis for species distribution analyses used by Glick and Wilson (2011), Lawler and others (2009), and Rehfeldt and others (2006). Assessments based on these methods are strongly influenced by the quality of data used in generating output, including the projections for future conditions.

Shifts in Species or Community Distributions

A number of assessments use estimates of shifts in species or community distributions to infer climate change impacts, which takes the form of an occupancy or niche modeling effort that relates future species distribution to climate or other abiotic conditions based on current environmental conditions. Future conditions are estimated based on climate projections created from downscaled GCMs or future expectations for biogeochemical processes predicted from computational models. Rehfeldt and others (2006) showed that changes in biotic community and individual plant species distributions for the western United States will be great under a number of different climate scenarios (Friggens and others, Chapter 1 this volume). In the western hemisphere, they predicted 90% of nearly 3000 vertebrate species will be lost from certain habitats (Lawler and others 2009), with some species experiencing declining distribution (e.g., fresh water fishes; Eaton and Scheller 1996) and some experiencing expanded distribution (Humphries and others 2002; Meyer and others 1999; Shutter and Post 1990). These efforts are data intensive but are able to provide scenarios for a potential future. They can be used to infer potential loss of habitat suitability for species or communities.

Complex Analyses

The most complex analyses attempt to integrate adaptive strategies with vulnerability assessments to gauge how actions influence relative susceptibility to climate change impacts. One analysis incorporates sensitivity scores with an analytical framework to create output relevant to both management and policy decisions (Luers 2005) whereas others integrate regional assessments, adaption planning frameworks, and a number of climate modeling tools (Enquist and Gori 2008, described in McCarthy and Enquist 2011; NatureServe Vista found at: http://www.natureserve.org/prodServices/vista/overview.jsp).

Current Assessment Tools

We list, albeit not comprehensively, many widely and freely available tools for managers to assess species or ecosystem vulnerability to climate change (table 8-1). Other syntheses of assessment tools can be obtained from the U.S. Forest Service, Pacific Northwest Research Station (http://www.fs.fed.us/nw/corvallis/mdr/mapss) and the Nairobi Work Programme, under the United Nations Framework Convention on Climate Change (http://unfccc.int/adaptation/nairobi_workprogramme/knowledge_resources_and_publications).

Table 8-1. Examples of the types of tools and data commonly used to assess vulnerability to climate change.

Type	Name	Description	Target/Scope	Sources/Websites
Scoring tools		Typically quantify vulnerability through a tally of traits or characteristics associated with increased risk of negative impact		
	1. NatureServe Climate Change Vulnerability Index	Classifies species into six categories: six possible scores are Extremely Vulnerable, Highly Vulnerable, Moderately Vulnerable, Not Vulnerable/Presumed Stable, Not vulnerable/Increase Likely, and Insufficient Evidence	Animal and plant species	www.natureserve.org/prodServices/climatechange/ClimateChange.jsp
	2. System for Assessing Vulnerability of Species SAVS	Uses a questionnaire format create a score indicating relative vulnerability to expected changes in future conditions	Terrestrial vertebrate species	http://www.fs.fed.us/rm/grassland-shrubland-desert/products/species-vulnerability/savs-climate-change-tool/
	3. EPA Framework	See text	T&E Species	EPA/600/R-09/01
	4. Vulnerability Surface	Uses a three-dimensional analytical surface to determine relative vulnerability	Applicable to variety of systems	Luers 2005; Luers and others 2003
Habitat and species distribution (e.g., bioclimatic) models		Use biophysical measures to define climate space of species or communities.	Typically vegetation communities	
	1. Climate surface models for plant species*	Use climate surfaces and observed species-climate relationships to predict species distributions	Plant communities and species	Rehfeldt and others 2006; http://forest.moscowfsl.wsu.edu/climate/customData/index.php
	3. Genetic Algorithm for Rule-Set Prediction (GARP) niche model	Uses spatial data on temperature, rainfall, and elevation with point data on species range to estimate potential range	Native and non-native species	nhm.ku.edu/destopgarp
	4. Maximum entropy (Maxent) Habitat model	Uses set of environmental variables and georeferenced occurrence locations to produce models of species' ranges	Animal or plant species	Philips and others 2006; Elith and others 2011; http://www.cs.princeton.edu/~schapire/maxent/
	5. Random Forest	Classification system that produces robust estimates of species presence. Used in Rehfeldt and others 2006.	Various	Breiman 2001; Cutler and others 2007; http://www.stat.berkeley.edu/~breiman/RandomForests/cc_home.htm
	7. Climate FVS*	Models species climate profiles. Users input species profile and elevation to get projected distributions under a variety of climate scenarios	Forests/tree species	http://www.fs.fed.us/fmsc/fvs/description/climate-fvs.shtml
Biogeochemical models		Model changes in climate parameters, including		

Table 8-1. Continued.

Type Name	Description	Target/Scope	Sources/Websites
	temperature and relative humidity. Often inform parameterization of the above class of tools.		
1. Instantaneous canopy flux model (PnET)	Merge of three computational models that simulate carbon, water, and nitrogen dynamics	Forest ecosystems	Aber and Federer 1992; http://www.pnet.sr.unh.edu /download.html
2. Soil Organic Matter Model (CENTURY)	Simulates nutrient/hydrological flows and includes fire/harvest frequency	Watershed	www.nrel.colostate.edu/proj ect/century5/
6. BIOCLIM (BIOMAP)	Prediction systems that uses mean monthly climate estimates to predict energy and water balances at specified location	Area defined by user	software.infromer.com/getfr ee-bioclim-download- software
3. Mapped Atmosphere- Plant-Soil systems—MAPSS	Equilibrium model that calculates plant available water and temperature thresholds according to climatic zone, life form, and plant type.	Area defined by user	See Bachelet and others 2001; www.fs.fed.us/pnw/corvaliis /mdr/mapss
Coupled models			
Dynamic global vegetation models	Incorporate vegetation projections and general circulation models (GCMs) with the purpose to inform climate dynamics (e.g., albedo and water evaporation rates)		Botkin and others 2007
1. MC1	Combines CENTURY and MAPSS		http//www.fsl.orst.edu/dgvm
Hydrological Models	Model changes in ground water, stream flow, evaporation, etc.		Christensen and others 2008
1. Regional Hydro-Ecologic Simulation System (RHESSys)	GIS based hydro-ecological model simulates water, carbon and nutrient flow	Watershed	fiesta.bren.ucsb.edu/~rhessy s/setup/downloads/downloa ds.html
2.Sea Level Affecting Marshes Model- SLAMM	Models processes dominating wetland conversion and shoreline modification	Coastal areas	Glick and others 2010; http://www.slammview.org
Others			
1. The Terrestrial Observation and Prediction System (TOPS)	Simulation framework—links historical climate data, remotely sensed data, climate projections, and response models		Nemani and others 2009; http://gcmd.nasa.gov/records /NASA_ARC_TOPS.html
2. Program to Assist in Tracking Critical Habitat (PATCH)	Models species vulnerability by linking landscape pattern and species traits	Ideal for habitat specialists	www.epa.gove/wed/pages/ news/03June/schumaker.htm
Statistical decision support	Statistical methods to estimate potential response of targets to risk factors and uncertainty.		Bernliner and others 2000; Prato 2009

Table 8-1. Continued.

Type	Name	Description	Target/ Scope	Sources/Websites
	1. Bayesian Analysis Toolkit	Software package that allows users to compare model predictions to data, test model validity, and extract values of free parameters of models.		http://www.mppmu.mpg.de /bat/
	2. Treeage Pro	Decision support software that uses various methods to distinguish between models and decisions options		www.treeage.com/products. index.html
	3. Delphi Decision Aid site	Data gathering tool for forecasting purposes		armstrong.wharton.upenn.e du/delphi2/
Conceptual models		Qualitative descriptions and diagrams of attributes and processes of concern	Species, habitats or ecosystems	Heemskerk and others 2003; www.fileheap.com/sofware/ conceptual_data_model.html
Data sources				
	1. U.S. Geological Survey's Gap Analysis Program (GAP)	Online tool to aid in analysis and retrieval of species distribution data	Land cover and vertebrate species	http://www.nbii.gov/portal/s erver.pt/community/gap_onl ine_analysis_tool/1851
	2. National Atlas	Provide GIS format data on land cover, land use, hydrography, climate, digital elevation models	Varies	http://www.nationalatlas.go v/atlasftp.html
	3. Multi-Resolution Land Characteristics Consoritum	Landcover databases	Bioregions	http://www.mrlc.gov/mrlc2k _nlcd.asp
	4. Vegetation/Ecosystem modeling and analysis Project—VEMAP	Uses historical and future projected climate data, soils and vegetation maps, and a number of process models (Century, biome-bgc, gtec, lpj, mc1, tem) to project communities across the globe	Vegetation types/biomes	Kittel and others 1995, 1996; http://www.cgd.ucar.edu/ve map/
	5. ClimateWizard	Estimates historical and future temperature and precipitation changes as absolute or percent change	Climate variables	http://www.climatewizard.org/

The selection of an appropriate assessment tool depends upon stakeholder objectives (see Glick and Stein 2011). Each assessment tool described in table 8-1 varies in how it may be applied (spatial and temporal scales) to systems and used for adaptation planning. Assessments meant to inform policy makers need to be focused on a key outcome as influenced by multiple stressors (e.g., outcome-based approach described in Luers 2005), whereas assessments that describe biological-based vulnerabilities or encompass multiple outcome variables are likely to be more informative from an ecological and research perspective.

Tools that rank species or habitats can provide relatively quick methods for assessing climate change vulnerabilities. However, summarizing the complexity of climate change impacts into a single variable may limit the application of these methods (Patt and others 2009). Those that rely on species distribution models allow users to visualize potential future conditions and responses, which can aid in adaptation planning. Such modeling efforts often inform the creation process for indices of sensitivity (Bagne and others 2011; Young and others 2011). Caution must be used when selecting and applying these models because estimates of future distributions can be biased and users should be aware of the limitations of scope of chosen tools (Graham and others 2004). Still, those ecosystems that are projected to incur the greatest change should be most vulnerable to climate change. Similarly, ecosystems or species that persist under high annual variations in climate, which can be estimated from some of these analyses, should be more resilient to climate change. Mechanistic models form the basis of many distribution modeling efforts and are useful for projecting future climate conditions relevant to species presence. These tools, as well as those commonly used to guide decision making processes (e.g., conceptual models and statistical decision trees), are often critical components of the assessment process.

Assessment Work Within the U.S. Forest Service

The following is research by RMRS and cooperators relevant to the assessment of biodiversity and ecosystem function in grassland, shrubland, and desert ecosystems of the western United States:

- The U.S. Forest Service is mandated by the Renewable Resources Planning Act (RPA, 1974) to conduct periodic assessments of forest and rangeland resources; since 1990, this includes a requirement to address climate change. RMRS provides technical assistance and analysis for each RPA assessment. The 2000 RPA assessment focused on climate impacts to forest systems, and the 2010 assessment was expanded to include climate impacts on water and wildlife. To see a complete list of RPA climate change publications or further description of ongoing projects, see http://www.fs.fed.us/rmrs/climate-change/assessments or http:/www.fs.fed.us/rm/landscapes/Research/Climate.shtml.

- RMRS scientists are developing an index to assess potential effects of climate change on biodiversity and wildlife habitat. Contact Linda Joyce (ljoyce@fs.fed.us) or Curt Flather (cflather@fs.fed.us) for more information.

- RMRS developed a scoring tool, System for Assessing Vulnerability of Species (SAVS) to climate change (Bagne and others 2011), to assess vulnerability of terrestrial vertebrates to climate change. Using this system, managers can prioritize actions for species conservation and management. This scoring tool is available at http://www.fs.fed.us/rm/grassland-shrubland-desert/products/species-vulnerability/savs-climate-change-tool/.

- Rehfeldt and others (2006) produced maps (http://forest.moscowfsl.wsu.edu/climate/) of current and future vegetation species and biotic communities for North America.

Research Needs

In order to develop and improve application of vulnerability assessment tools and frameworks to the grasslands, shrublands, and deserts of the western United States, research areas should focus efforts to:

- Continue to refine our capacity to identify new community composition; this work has the highest priority because of its relevance to inform future management needs and best courses of action.
- Improve accuracy of models and methods used to generate climate change predictions and habitat suitability maps. This includes continued development and improvement of habitat response models (both mechanistic and correlative) for animal and plant species. In addition, distribution models for forest and rangeland habitats and species should incorporate dispersal mechanisms.
- Develop and refine systems for assessing plant species vulnerability.
- Develop physiologically based models of species occurrence (see Glick and Stein 2011).
- Identify measures of species adaptive capacity (Czúcz and others 2009).
- Build tools to identify synergistic effects of climate change, species interactions, and other disturbances.
- Integrate management scenarios with scenarios for climate change.
- Identify the appropriate framework for analyzing vulnerability with respect to adaptation strategies, including potential application of existing frameworks (e.g., National Center for Ecological Analysis and Synthesis).
- Identify need to develop new frameworks for creating adaptation strategies that integrate vulnerability with management decision processes.
- Complete cost benefit analyses that incorporate multiple scenarios, including the validity of inaction as an option. Passive restoration techniques may be more cost effective and feasible for many areas (Birch and others 2010) and should be considered among management options.
- Identify and implement methods to make tools more available and useful for decision makers.

Plant Conservation and Restoration

We discuss some of the specific methods and tools used for selecting, collecting, and deploying native plant materials to ensure proper conservation of genetic resources. These activities provide foundation for, and are particularly relevant to, our future capacity under climate change to manage and restore lands with appropriate genetic materials.

Approaches and challenges for selecting native plant material

Historically, restoration activities made use of "off the shelf," agronomically developed, introduced plant materials to fill specific needs (see Monsen and others 2004). This was particularly true in the Intermountain West where semi-arid and arid lands were often especially challenging sites (Monsen and Shaw 2001). These introduced species were developed through selection and breeding programs for improved germination, establishment, reproduction, and quality (e.g., palatability or erosion control)

(Monsen and others 2004). Consequently, native plants that often had complex germination requirements and unique establishment criteria were discriminated against with little research completed on them. The U.S. Forest Service and other Federal agencies are, however, mandated to use genetically diverse, locally adapted native plants to maintain or restore self-sustaining ecosystems to protect the services (e.g., soil stabilization, clean water, and forage) they provide (Johnson and others 2010; USDI and USDA 2002; USDA 2008). With realization of this mandate, emphasis is now being placed on research that identifies functional traits contributing to native plant competitive ability; improves availability of plant materials; reduces plant materials cost; improves techniques for identifying and describing site conditions suitable for native plants; identifies appropriate species or combinations of species for planting; and identifies effective planting strategies (Call and Roundy 1992; James and Svejcar 2010; Johnson and others 2010; Sheley and James 2010).

Paramount for appropriate use of native plants to meet legislative mandates is an understanding of the patterns of genetic (adaptive) variation and structure in the morphology, phenology, and reproduction of native plants across varied landscapes. For commercial tree species, this is relatively well known, but only a paucity of information exists for most other native plants despite a growing need to better manage them (Hufford and Mazer 2003; Johnson and others 2004; Lesica and Allendorf 1999).

When genetic variation and structure are understood, species-specific genetic transfer zones (commonly referred to as "seed zones") can be mapped and transfer guidelines can be developed to describe how far plant materials can be moved from their point of origin and the risks associated with that movement. To properly understand this genetic variation and structure, researchers enlist genecological studies that entail collecting germplasm representing the variety of climatic and environmental conditions present within a large portion or the entire range of the species. These collections are grown in common gardens and evaluated for survival, growth, and reproduction characteristics. The described genetic diversity is correlated to climatic variation among collection sites through regression models and is mapped to provide seed zones. Although seed zones for western conifer species are provided by Rehfeldt (1986), genecological studies and subsequent seed zones for grasses, forbs, and shrubs are more recent and have been achieved for only a handful of native species in the western United States (e.g., Darris and others 2008; Doede 2005; Erickson and others 2004; Horning and others 2010; Johnson and others, submitted; Kitzmiller 2009; Wilson and others 2008). This research is difficult, time consuming, and expensive, so genetic information is lacking for many native plants of interest to land managers.

When genetic information is lacking, however, the current management paradigm is to use plant materials proximal to their point of origin. This "local is best" prescription is supported by a plethora of studies (Johnson and others 2010; Rice and Knapp 2008), but a major disadvantage is defining "local" (McKay and others 2005) and often this paradigm is more conservatively restrictive than needed. Fortunately, a number of climatic and biogeographic tools can be used as surrogates to aid in matching available plant materials to environmental conditions at the planting site. Referred to as provisional seed zones, these estimates of genetic appropriateness do not address the specificity of adaptation that can vary greatly among species. Thus, provisional seed zones are not expected to provide a best fit for all or any species. Their development, based on climate and ecological factors, can, however, provide interim science-based, decision-making support for land managers until empirical knowledge of adaptive variation is obtained and translated into seed zones and transfer guidelines for individual species (Bower and others 2010).

Commonly used surrogates to species-specific seed zones are:

- Ecoregion maps (Bailey 1995, 2009; Omernik 1987) that consider floristic regions, soils, and other parameters. Subdivision level can be selected to provide broad or narrow zones.

- USDA Cold Hardiness Zones are useful for species with distributions limited by minimum temperatures (Cathey 1990).

- Plant adaptation region maps (Vogel and others 2005) that combine ecoregions with USDA Cold Hardiness Zones.

- Climatic models (Bower and others 2010) that combine multiple climatic variables.

- Focal point models that combine biogeoclimatic characteristics of a region and indicate degree of similarity between potential seed collection and planting sites.

- The Data Extraction Tool (Gearrard and others 2006) that permits users to extract information from a number of data layers.

- The Center for Forest Provenance Data, an online database that archives data from long-term provenance tests and seedling genecology tests. The database currently includes only tree data but may eventually be expanded to include other species (St. Clair and others 2010).

- Seed Zones for Native Plants, an online mapping application for provisional and species specific seed zones for plant materials development, gene conservation and native plant restoration (USDA FS WWETAC 2011).

- An online seed transfer decision-support tool (e.g., Seedlot selection tool http://www.fs.fed.us/ccrc/tools/seedlot.shtml) to aid in selecting appropriate seedlots that can be applied to multiple species using multiple climatic variables and various climate change scenarios (B. St. Clair, personal communication).

- Online databases, such as the Web Soil Survey (USDA NRCS 2009), the Ecological Site Information System (USDA NRCS 2010), and climatic databases such as PRISM (Prism climate group 2010), can aid in describing biotic and abiotic characteristics of seed origin and planting sites.

In the Interior West, current genecological-based and provisional seed zone mapping efforts illustrate the climatic complexities associated with western ecosystems; they are much more complex than those found in the eastern half of the United States. Therefore, impacts of climate change and resulting efforts to manage plant communities will be more difficult in the West, particularly the Intermountain West, as boundaries on seed zone maps diverge from the environmental conditions used to create them. Success where underlying conditions are most complex, however, should readily translate to less complicated systems.

Managing Collections of Genetic Materials Within Species-Specific and Provisional Seed Zones

An ecological approach to providing plant materials for use within species-specific or provisional seed zones requires that multiple seed collections of a species be made from diverse locations within the zone, each representing multiple parent plants. Once pooled, the progeny from these collections provide genetically broad-based materials, maximizing the likelihood that some seeds will be pre-adapted to planting site conditions and capable of adapting to future environmental fluctuations, including climate change. This approach also minimizes the potential for inbreeding and outbreeding depression (Johnson and others 2010; McKay and others 2005; Withrow-Robinson and Johnson 2006).

Selecting Native Plant Material Under Future Climate Scenarios

Climate change may also require movement of genetic material to locations where it currently does not exist. Such anthropogenic movement, referred to as assisted colonization, assisted migration, or managed relocation, may be necessary because climate change is occurring more rapidly than species can adapt and/or disperse along environmental gradients (Warren and others 2001), or anthropogenic activities have narrowed or disrupted natural dispersion corridors (Marris 2008; Minteer and Collins 2010).

Assisted Colonization

Assisted colonization can be accomplished at two levels: (1) moving discrete genetic resources of a species into a new area already occupied by that species (e.g., moving seeds of warmer ecotypes into areas currently occupied by colder ecotypes), or (2) moving genetic resources of a species into areas where that species does not currently exist.

The first scenario attempts to augment current genetic diversity. For example, a collection of seeds from a high-elevation seed zone could be augmented with seeds from a lower-elevation seed zone in anticipation that the higher-elevation site will become warmer because of climate change. This approach leverages diverse genetic mixtures from within seed transfer zones by incorporating genetic material from adjacent seed transfer zones; leading to the expression of new desired traits.

The second scenario, introducing species into areas where they currently do not exist in order to facilitate their continued existence in response to climate change, has become a lightning rod among ecologists and conservationists. Opponents of assisted colonization cite potential for unintended and unpredicted consequence on the recipient ecosystem, such as creation of new invasive species, disruption of evolutionary and ecological processes at the reintroduction site, and negative genetic interactions between relocated and native populations (Ricciardi and Simberloff 2009; Seddon and others 2009; Vitt and others 2009). Fazey and Fischer (2009) argued that assisted colonization is a short-term fix that ignores causal reasons for plant extinction, and Sandler (2010) stated that ethical, philosophical, and socioeconomic values may not be a justifiable method for preserving, through assisted colonization, the value of a species. Proponents purport that such harmful consequences are overstated, can be managed (Sax and others 2009; Schlaepfer and others 2009), and exceed the consequences of species extinction. In fact, such movement is obligate under the Endangered Species Act (Shirey and Lamberti 2009). Indeed, many scientists see assisted colonization as one part of a multi-faceted solution to conserve and preserve genetic diversity, and decision-support matrices have been suggested for such implementation (Hoegh-Guldberg and others 2008; Hunter 2007; Richardson and others 2009; Vitt and others 2009).

Assembled Ecosystems

This assisted colonization debate, unfortunately, often fails to recognize the transitory nature, in terms of species composition, of functional ecosystems; current ecosystems have no historic analogs and will, under climate change, probably not persist (Williams and Jackson 2007). Thus, land managers perhaps need not only contemplate moving species to ensure their survival, but contemplate assembling new "ecosystems" representing novel species compositions in order to provide ecosystem function and vital delivery of ecological services (e.g., clean water, fiber supply, and healthy soil) necessary to civilization (Minteer and Collins 2010). In addition, climate change, species introductions, and human activities may cause shifts in land use patterns, thus requiring land managers to conduct adaptive ecosystem management of drastically altered sites (domesticated or severely degraded) back to a naturally sustainable state (Hobbs and others 2006; Hobbs and others 2009; Seastedt and others 2008). Both of these management activities would require a holistic evaluation to maintain a sustainable suite of symbiotic flora, and fauna are present to ensure sustainability.

Genetic Transfer Work Within the Forest Service

The following is ongoing research by RMRS and cooperators in plant materials development and use in grassland, shrubland, and desert ecosystems of the western United States:

- Delineation of provisional seed zones based on biogeoclimatic factors.
- Genecological studies of widespread native grass and forb species.
- Increase of genetically diverse, locally adapted stock seed of native forbs and grasses for provisional and species-specific zones.
- Evaluation of native species existing in long-established stands of exotic species as potential competitive native plant materials (rapid evolution research) (Leger 2008; Mealor and others 2004).
- Identification of selective climatic gradients of importance to big sagebrush distribution and development of climate responsive seed zones for the entire range of big sagebrush.
- Design of a website tool for managers to match big sagebrush seed sources to restoration sites.

Research Needs

The following are research areas for developing genetic transfer guidelines to mitigate climate change impacts in grasslands, shrublands, and desert ecosystems of the western United States:

- Develop risk assessment tools for selecting seeding and planting sites to reduce negative impacts and the incidence of failures.
- Continue development of provisional and species-specific seed zones and seed transfer guidelines.
- Refine tools for identifying and mapping future environments suitable for these species.
- Provide recommendations for developing seed production areas of genetically diverse populations pre-adapted to climatic change and other environmental perturbations.
- Examine autecology and adaptive characteristics of key restoration species and species at risk from climate change and other biotic and abiotic stressors (species that are long-lived, inbreeding, or characterized by small or disjunct populations or species with low genetic variation and rare species).
- Research and develop approaches for managing genetic variation to influence plant response to climate change; enhance and conserve genetic diversity within seed zones; and promote natural migration, gene flow (establish outlier populations) and assisted migration.

- Examine completed research on native species and species specific seed zones for generalizations regarding such areas as specificity in environmental requirements, capacity for in situ adaptation to climate change, and potential rates of migration.

- Provide for *ex situ* and *in situ* conservation.

- Develop a simple, readily accessible tool for nursery managers, seed producers, and land managers to help them move plants across the landscape in a genetically appropriate manner to conserve genetic diversity, facilitate current management decisions, and provide a foundation for reaction to climate change.

- Investigate the intersection of socioeconomic, environmental, and philosophical debate toward a better understanding of the difficult decisions associated with assisted colonization of plants and animals to new locations. A decision support matrix that conceptualizes and quantifies the advantages and disadvantages of assisted colonization is required. Use paleobotanic and paleoclimatic data to further understand and model plant community evolution from the last glaciation to contemporary associations, and how those processes can be leveraged toward ensuring development of new, non-analogous ecosystems under evolving climate conditions.

RMRS Expertise and Partners

The GSD Program includes a cadre of scientists and their collaborators working with wildland restoration from plant selection, to seed increase, nursery stock production, outplanting, monitoring, and management. Multiple partners are essential for progress due to the large number of plant species and variety of landscapes involved as well as the multidisciplinary nature and immense time commitment of the research. Forest geneticists in RMRS and Pacific Northwest Research Station are now providing leadership for non-conifer genecology research and plant response to climate change. Our current sponsors, collaborators, and partners include: U.S. Forest Service National Forest System Regions 1, 2, 3, 4, 6, and 8, Research and Development, and State and Private Forestry; USDA Agricultural Research Service and Natural Resources Conservation Service; USDI Bureau of Land Management, National Park Service, and U.S. Fish and Wildlife Service; Department of Defense; U.S. Geological Survey; universities; state departments of natural resources; state and private crop improvement associations and foundation seed programs; non-profit organizations; and the native plant and seed industries.

Literature Cited

Aber, J. D. and A. C. Federer. 1992. A generalized, lump-parameter model of photosynthesis, evapotranspiration and net primary production in temperate and boreal forest ecosystems. Oecologia 92: 463-474.

Anderson, R. P., D. Lew and A. T. Peterson. 2003. Evaluating predictive models of species' distributions: criteria for selecting optimal models. Ecological Modeling 162: 211-232.

Bachelet, D., R. P. Neilson, J. M. Lenihan and R. J. Drapek. 2001. Climate change effects on vegetation distribution and carbon budget in the United States. Ecosystems 4: 164-185.

Bagne, K. E. and D. M. Finch. 2010. An assessment of vulnerability of threatened, endangered, and at-risk species to climate change at the Barry M. Goldwater Range, Arizona. DoD Legacy Program Report. 185 p.

Bagne, K. E., M. Friggens and D. M. Finch. 2011. A system for assessing vulnerability of species (SAVS) to climate change. Gen. Tech. Rep. RMRS-GTR-257. Fort Collins, CO: U.S. Department of Agriculture, Forest Service. Rocky Mountain Research Station.

Bailey, R. G. 1995. Description of the ecoregions of the United States. 2nd ed. Misc. Publ. 1391. 1:7,500,000. U.S. Department of Agriculture, Forest Service.

Bailey, R. G. 2009. Ecosystem Geography: From Ecoregions to Sites. 2nd ed. New York: Springer-Verlag. 252 p.

Beckage, B., B. Osborne, D. G. Gavin, C. Pucko, T. Siccama and T. Perkins. 2008. A rapid upward shift of a forest ecotone during 40 years of warming in the Green Mountains of Vermont. Proceedings of the National Academy of Sciences of the United States of America 105: 4197-4202.

Berliner, L. M., R. A. Levine and D. J. Shea. 2000. Bayesian climate change assessment. Journal of Climate 13: 3805-3820.

Birch, J. C., A. C. Newton, C. A. Aquino, E. Cantarello and others. 2010. Cost-effectiveness of dryland forest restoration evaluated by spatial analysis of ecosystem services. Proceedings of the National Academy of Sciences of the United States of America 107: 21925-21930.

Botkin, D. B., H. Saxe, M. B. Araujo, R. Betts and others. 2007. Forecasting the effects of global warming on biodiversity. BioScience 57(3): 227-236.

Bower, A., B. St. Clair and V. Erickson. 2010. Provisional seed zones for native plants. Washington, DC: U.S. Department of Agriculture, Forest Service. Available: http://www.fs.fed.us/wildflowers/nativeplantmaterials/rightmaterials.shtml [2010, December 10].

Breiman, L. 2001. Random forests. Machine Learning 45: 5-32.

Call, C. A. and B. A. Roundy. 1992. Perspectives and processes in revegetation of arid and semiarid rangelands. Journal of Range Management 44: 543-549.

Case, M. and J. Lawler. 2011. Case study 7: Pacific Northwest climate change vulnerability assessment. In: Glick, Patty; Stein, Bruce A., eds. Scanning the conservation horizon: a guide to climate change vulnerability assessment. National Wildlife Federation. Washington, DC: 129-134.

Cathey, H. M. 1990. USDA plant hardiness zone map. Misc. Publ. 1475. Washington, DC: U.S. Department of Agriculture, Agricultural Research Service, U.S. National Arboretum. Available: http://www.usna.usda.gov/Hardzone/ushzmap.html [2010, December 10].

Cayan, D. R., T. Das, D. W. Pierce, T. P. Barnett, M. Tyree and A. Gershunov. 2010. Climate change and water in Southwestern North American special feature: future dryness in the Southwest U.S. and the hydrology of the early 21st century drought. Proceedings of the National Academy of Sciences of the United States of America 107: 21271-21276.

Chambers, J. C. 2008. Climate change and the Great Basin. USDA Forest Service Gen. Tech. Rep. RMRS-GTR-204. Fort Collins, CO: U.S. Department of Agriculture, Forest Service, Rocky Mountain Research Station: 29-32.

Christensen, L., C. L. Tague and J. S. Baron. 2008. Spatial patterns of simulated transpiration response to climate variability in a snow dominated mountain ecosystem. Hydrological Processes 22: 3576-3588.

Coe, S., D. M. Finch and M. Friggens. 2012. Applying a decision support tool for assessing vulnerability of wildlife to climate change: a case study on Coronado NF. Washington, DC: U.S. Department of Agriculture, Forest Service.

Crookston, N. L., G. E. Rehfeldt, G. E. Dixon and A. R. Weiskittel. 2010. Addressing climate change in the forest vegetation simulator to assess impacts on landscape forest dynamics. Forest Ecology and Management 260: 1198-1115.

Czúcz, B., G. Kröel-Dulay, G. Torda, Z. Molnár and L. Tõkei. 2009. Regional scale habitat-based vulnerability assessment of the natural ecosystems. Climate change: global risks, challenges and decisions Institue of Physics (IOP) Publishing IOP Conf. Series: Earth and Environmental Science 6; 442006. doi: 10.1088/1755-1307/6/4/442006.

Cutler, D. R., T. C. Edwards, Jr., K. H. Beard, A. Cutler and others. 2007. Random forest for classification in ecology. Ecology 88: 2783-2792.

Daily, G. C. 1997. Nature's Services: Societal Dependence on Natural Ecosystems. Washington, DC: Island Press. 412 p.

Darris, D. C., B. L. Wilson, R. Fiegener, R. Johnson and M. E. Horning. 2008. Polycross populations of the native grass *Festuca roemeri* as pre-varietal germplasm: their derivation, release, increase and use. Native Plants Journal 9: 304-312.

Doede, D. L. 2005. Genetic variation in broadleaf lupine (*Lupinus latifolius*) on the Mt. Hood National Forest and implications for seed collection and deployment. Native Plant Journal 5: 141-148.

Eaton, J. G. and R. M. Scheller. 1996. Effects of climate warming on fish thermal habitat in streams of the United States. Limnology and Oceanography 41: 1109-1115.

Elith, J., S. J. Phillips, T. Hastie, M. Dudik, Y. E. Chee and C. J. Yates. 2011. A statistical explanation of MaxEnt for ecologists. Diversity and Distributions 17: 43-57.

Enquist, C. and D. Gori. 1998. Implication of recent climate change on conservation priorities in New Mexico. Technical Report. The Nature Conservancy and Wildlife Conservation Society. 68 p.

Erickson, V., N. L. Mandel and F. C. Sorensen. 2004. Landscape patterns of phenotypic variation and population structuring in a selfing grass, *Elymus glaucus* (blue wildrye). Canadian Journal of Botany 82: 1776-1789.

Fazey, I. and J. Fischer. 2009. Assisted colonization is a techno-fix. Trends in Ecology and Evolution 24(9): 475.

Finch, D. M., M. Friggens and K. Bagne. 2011. Case study 3. Species vulnerability assessments for the Middle Rio Grande, New Mexico. In: Glick, Patty; Stein, Bruce A., eds. Scanning the conservation horizon: a guide to climate change vulnerability assessment. National Wildlife Federation. Washington, DC: 96-103.

Fleishman, E. 2008. Great Basin rare and vulnerable species. USDA Forest Service Gen. Tech. Rep. RMRS-GTR-204. Fort Collins, CO: U.S. Department of Agriculture, Forest Service, Rocky Mountain Research Station: 61-64.

Ford, J. D. and B. Smit. 2004. A framework for assessing the vulnerability of communities in the Canadian arctic to risks associated with climate change. Arctic 57: 38-400.

Friggens, M., K. Bagne, D. M. Finch, S. Coe and D. Hawksworth. In prep. Vulnerability of species to climate change in the Southwest: terrestrial vertebrates of the Middle Rio Grande. Washington, DC: U.S. Department of Agriculture, Forest Service.

Füssel, H.-M. and R. J. T. Klein. 2005. Climate change vulnerability assessments: an evolution of conceptual thinking. Climatic Change 75: 301-329.

Galbraith, H. and J. O'Leary. 2011. Case study 4. Vulnerability of Massachusetts Fish and Wildlife Habitats to Climate Change. In: Glick, Patty; Stein, Bruce A., eds. Scanning the conservation horizon: a guide to climate change vulnerability assessment. National Wildlife Federation. Washington, DC: 90-95.

Galbraith, H. and J. Price. 2011. Case study 2. US EPA's threatened and endangered (T&E) species vulnerability framework. In: Glick, Patty; Stein, Bruce A., eds. Scanning the conservation horizon: a guide to climate change vulnerability assessment. National Wildlife Federation. Washington, DC: 90-95.

Gearrard, C., C. M. McGinty and R. D. Ramsey. 2006. A web-based extraction tool for the USA. Logan, UT: Utah State University. Available: http://www.gis.usu.edu/awards/present/2006/garrard_foss4g_2006.pdf [2010, December 10].

Glick, P., J. Clough and B. Nunley. 2010. Assessing the vulnerability of Alaska's coastal habitat to accelerating sea-level rise using the SLAMM model: a case study for Cook Inlet. National Wildlife Federation.

Glick, P. and B. A. Stein, eds. 2011. Scanning the conservation horizon: a guide to climate change vulnerability assessment. National Wildlife Federation. Washington, DC. 164 p.

Glick, P. and M. Wilson. 2011. Case study 5. Vulnerability to sea-level rise in the Chesapeake Bay. In: Glick, P. and B. A. Stein, eds. Scanning the conservation horizon: a guide to climate change vulnerability assessment. National Wildlife Federation. Washington, DC: 115-122.

Gober, P. and C. W. Kirkwood. 2010. Vulnerability assessment of climate-induced water shortage in Phoenix. Proceedings of the National Academy of Sciences of the United States of America 107: 21295-21299.

Graham, C. H., S. Ferrier, F. Huettman, C. Moritz and A. T. Peterson. 2004. New developments in museum-based informatics and applications in biodiversity analysis. Trends in Ecology and Evolution 19: 497-503.

Hannah, L., G. F. Midgley and D. Millar. 2002. Climate change-induced conservation strategies. Global Ecology and Biogeography 11: 485-495.

Hansen, A. J., R. P. Neilson, V. H. Dale, C. H. Flather and others. 2001. Global change in forests: responses of species, communities and biomes. Bioscience 51: 765-779.

Hauer, F. R., J. S. Baron, D. H. Campbell, K. D. Fausch and others. 1997. Assessment of climate change and freshwater ecosystems of the Rocky Mountains, USA and Canada. Hydrological Processes 11: 903-924.

Heikkinen, R. K., M. Luoto, M. B. Araújo, R. Virkkala, W. Thuiller and M. T. Sykes. 2006. Methods and uncertainties in bioclimatic envelop modeling under climate change. Progress in Physical Geography 30: 1-27.

Heemskerk, M., K. Wilson and T. Pavao-Zuckerman. 2003. Conceptual models as tools for communication across disciplines. Conservation Ecology 7(3): 8. Available: http://www.consecol.org/vol7/iss3/art8.

Hobbs, R. J., S. Arico, J. Aronson, J. S. Baron and others. 2006. Novel ecosystems: theoretical and management aspects of the new ecological world order. Global Ecology and Biogeography 15: 1-7.

Hobbs, R. J., E. Higgs and J. A. Harris. 2009. Novel ecosystems: implications for conservation and restoration. Trends in Ecology and Evolution 24: 599-605.

Hoegh-Guldberg, O., L. Hughes, S. McIntyre, D. B. Lindenmayer and others. 2008. Assisted colonization and rapid climate change. Science 321: 345-346.

Holt, R. D. 1990. The microevolutionary consequences of climate change. Trends in Ecology and Evolution 5: 311-315.

Horning, M. E., T. R. McGovern, D. C. Darris, N. L. Mandel and R. Johnson. 2010. Genecology of *Holodiscus discolor* (Rosaceae) in the Pacific Northwest. U.S.A. Restoration Ecology 18: 235-243.

Hufford, K. M. and S. J. Mazer. 2003. Plant ecotypes: genetic differentiation in the age of ecological restoration. Trends in Ecology and Evolution 18: 147-155.

Hughes, J. B. 2000. Biological consequences of global warming: is the signal already apparent? Trends in Ecology and Evolution 15: 56-61.

Hughes, J. B., G. C. Daily and P. R. Ehrlich. 1997. Population diversity: its extent and extinction. Science 278: 689-692.

Humphries, M. M., D. W. Thomas and J. R. Speakman. 2002. Climate-mediated energetic constraints on the distribution of hibernating mammals. Nature 418: 313-314.

Hunter, M. L., Jr. 2007. Climate change and moving species: furthering the debate on assisted colonization. Conservation Biology 21(5): 1356-1358.

Hurd, B., N. Leary, R. Jones and J. Smith. 1999. Relative regional vulnerability of water resources to climate change. Journal of the American Water Resources Association 35(6): 1399-1409.

Intergovernmental Panel on Climate Change [IPCC]. 2007. Climate change 2007: impacts, adaptation and vulnerability. Contribution of Working Group II to the Fourth Assessment Report of the Intergovernmental Panel on Climate Change, M. L. Parry, O. F. Canziani, J. P. Palutikof, P. J. van der Linden and C. E. Hanson, eds. Cambridge University Press, Cambridge, UK. 976 p.

James, J. and A. Svejcar. 2010. Limitations to postfire seedling establishment: the role of seeding technology, water availability and invasive plant abundance. Rangeland Ecology and Management 63: 491-495.

Johnson, G. R., F. C. Sorenson, J. B. St. Clair and R. C. Cronn. 2004. Pacific Northwest forest tree seed zones-A template for native plants? Native Plants 5: 131-140.

Johnson, G. R., L. Stritch, P. Olwell, S. Lambert, M. E. Horning and R. Cronn. 2010. What are the best seed sources for ecosystem restoration on BLM and USFS lands? Native Plants Journal 11(2): 117-131.

Johnson, R. C., V. J. Erickson, N. L. Mandel, J. B. St. Clair and K. W. Vance-Borland. In press. Mapping genetic variation and seed zones for *Bromus carinatus* in the Blue Mountains of eastern Oregon, U.S.A. Botany.

Johnson, R. C., B. Hellier and K. W. Vance-Borland. Submitted. Fitting tapertip onion genetic variation with climate in the Great Basin.

Jones, T. A. and T. A. Monaco. 2009. A role for assisted evolution in designing native plant materials for domesticated landscapes. Frontiers in Ecology and the Environment 7(10): 541-547.

Kittel, T. G. F., N. A. Rosenbloom, T. H. Painter, D. S. Schimel and others. 1996. The VEMAP phase I database: an integrated input dataset for ecosystem and vegetation modeling for the conterminous United States. [CDROM and Online]. Available: http://www.cgd.ucar.edu/vemap [2010, December 29].

Kittel, T. G. F., N. A. Rosenbloom, T. H. Painter, D. S. Schimel and VEMAP modeling participants. 1995. The VEMAP integrated database for modeling United States ecosystem/vegetation sensitivity to climate change. Journal of Biogeography 22(4-5): 857-862.

Kitzmiller, J. H. 2009. Regional genetic variation in three native grasses in northern California. Native Plants Journal 10: 263-280.

Lawler, J. J., S. L. Shafer, D. White, P. Kareiva and others. 2009. Projected climate-induced faunal change in the Western Hemisphere. Ecology 90: 588-597.

Ledig, F. T., G. E. Rehfeldt, C. Saenz-Romero and C. Flores-Lopez. 2010. Projections of suitable habitat for rare species under global warming scenarios. American Journal of Botany 97(6): 970-987.

Leger, E. A. 2008. The adaptive value of remnant native plants in invaded communities: An example from the Great Basin. Ecological Applications 18: 1226-35.

Lesica, P. and F. W. Allendorf. 1999. Ecological genetics and the restoration of plant communities: mix or match? Restoration Ecology 7: 42-50.

Luers, A. L. 2005. The surface of vulnerability: an analytical framework for examining environmental change. Global Environmental Change 15: 214-223.

Luers, A. L., D. B. Lobella, L. S. Sklard, C. L. Addamsa and P. M. Matson. 2003. A method for quantifying vulnerability, applied to the agricultural system of the Yaqui Valley, Mexico. Global Environmental Change 13: 255-267.

Marris, E. 2008. Moving on assisted migration. Nature Reports 2: 112-113.

McCarthy, P. and C. Enquist. 2011. Case study 6. An integrated climate change assessment framework, in the four corners region. In: Glick, P. and B. A. Stein, eds. Scanning the conservation horizon: a guide to climate change vulnerability assessment. National Wildlife Federation. Washington, DC: 123-128.

McKay, J. K., C. E. Christian, S. Harrison and K. J. Rice. 2005. How local is local?—a review of practical and conceptual issues in the genetics of restoration. Restoration Ecology 13: 432-440.

McKenzie, D., Z. M. Gedalof, D. L. Peterson and P. Mote. 2004. Climate change, wildfire and conservation. Conservation Biology 18: 890-902.

McLachlan, J. S., J. L. Hellman and M. W. Schwartz. 2007. A framework for debate of assisted migration in an era of climate change. Conservation Biology 21(2): 297-302.

Mealor, B. A., A. L. Hild and N. L. Shaw. 2004. Native plant community composition and genetic diversity associated with long-term weed invasions. Western North American Naturalist 64: 503-513.

Meyer, J. L., M. J. Sale, P. J. Mulholland and L. N. Poff. 1999. Impacts of climate change on aquatic ecosystem functioning and health. Journal of the American Water Resources Association 35: 1373-1386.

Midgley, G. F., L. Hannah, D. Millar, M. C. Rutherford and L. W. Powrie. 2002. Assessing the vulnerability of species richness to anthropogenic climate change in a biodiversity hotspot. Global Ecology and Biogeography 11: 445-451.

Minteer, B. A. and J. P. Collins. 2010. Move it or lose it? The ecological ethics of relocating species under climate change. Ecological Applications 20: 1801-1804.

Monsen, S. B. and N. L. Shaw. 2001. Development and use of plant resources for western wildlands. In: McArthur, E. D. and D. J. Fairbanks, comps. Shrubland ecosystem genetics and biodiversity. Proceedings: June 13-15, 2000; Provo, UT. Proc. RMRS-P-21. Ogden, UT: U.S. Department of Agriculture, Forest Service, Rocky Mountain Research Station: 47-61.

Monsen, S. B., R. Stevens and N. L. Shaw. 2004. Chapter 18. Grasses. In: Monsen, S. B., R. Stevens and N. L. Shaw, comps. Restoring western ranges and wildlands, vol. 2. Gen. Tech. Rep. RMRS-GTR-136-vol-2. Fort Collins, CO: U.S. Department of Agriculture, Forest Service, Rocky Mountain Research Station: 295-424.

Neelin, J. D., A. Bracco, H. Luo, J. C. McWilliams and J. E. Meyerson. 2010. Considerations for parameter optimization and sensitivity in climate models. Proceedings of the National Academy of Sciences of the United States of America 107(50): 21349-21354.

Nemani, R., H. Hashimoto, P. Votava, F. Melton and others. 2009. Monitoring and forecasting ecosystem dynamics using the terrestrial observation and prediction system (TOPS). Remote Sensing of Environment 113: 1497-1509.

Omernik, J. M. 1987. Ecoregions of the coterminous United States. Map scale 1:7,500,000. Annals of the Association of American Geographers 77: 118-125.

Parmesan, C. and G. Yohe. 2003. A globally coherent fingerprint of climate change impacts across natural systems. Nature 421: 37-42.

Parry, M. L., O. F. Canziani, J. P. Palutikof, P. J. van der Linden and C. E. Hanson, eds. 2007. Climate change 2007: impacts, adaptation and vulnerability. Contribution of Working Group II to the Fourth Assessment Report of the Intergovernmental Panel on Climate Change. Cambridge, UK: Cambridge University Press. 976 p.

Patt, A. G., D. Schröter, A. C. Vega-Leinert and R. J. T. Klein. 2009. Vulnerability research and assessment to support adaptation and mitigation: common themes from a diversity of approaches. In: Patt, A. G., D. Schröter, R. J. T. Klein and A. C. Vega-Leinert, eds. Assessing Vulnerability to Global Environmental Change: Making Research Useful for Adaptation Decision Making and Policy. Earthscan, London UK: 1-27.

Pearson, R. G. and T. P. Dawson. 2003. Predicting the impacts of climate change on the distribution of species: are bioclimate envelope models useful? Global Ecology and Biogeography 12(5): 361-371.

Phillips, S. J., R. P. Anderson and R. E. Schapire. 2006. Maximum entropy modeling of species geographic distributions. Ecological Modeling 190: 231-259.

Prato, T. 2009. Evaluating and managing wildlife impacts of climate change under uncertainty. Ecological Modeling 220: 923-930.

PRISM climate group. 2010. Corvallis, OR: Oregon State University. Available: http://www.prism.oregonstate.edu [2010, December 10].

Rehfeldt, G. E. 1986. Adaptive variation in *Pinus ponderosa* from intermountain regions I. Snake and Salmon River basins. Forest Science 32: 79-92.

Rehfeldt, G. E. 1994. Evolutionary genetics, the biological species and the ecology of interior cedar-hemlock-white pine forests: ecology and management. Pullman, WA: Washington State University: 91-100.

Rehfeldt, G. E., N. L. Crookston, M. Warwell and J. S. Evans. 2006. Empirical analyses of plant-climate relationships for the western United States. Journal of Plant Science 167: 1123-1150.

Ricciardi, A. and D. Simberloff. 2009. Assisted colonization is not a viable conservation strategy. Trends in Ecology and Evolution 24(5): 248-253.

Rice, K. J. and E. E. Knapp. 2008. Effects of competition and life history stage on the expression of local adaptation in two native bunchgrasses. Restoration Ecology 16: 12-23.

Richardson, D. M., J. J. Hellmann, J. S. McLachlan, D. V. Sax and others. 2009. Multidimensional evaluation of managed relocation. Proceedings of the National Academy of Sciences of the United States of America 106(24): 9721-9724.

Risser, P. G. 1995. Biodiversity and ecosystem function. Conservation Biology 9(4): 742-746.

Sandler, R. 2010. The value of species and the ethical foundations of assisted colonization. Conservation Biology 24(2): 424-431.

Sax, D. F., K. F. Smith and A. R. Thompson. 2009. Managed relocation: a nuanced evaluation is needed. Trends in Ecology and Evolution 24: 472-473.

Schlaepfer, M. A., W. D. Helenbrook, K. B. Searing and K. T. Shoemaker. 2009. Assisted colonization: evaluating contrasting management actions (and values) in the face of uncertainty. Trends in Ecology and Evolution 24(9): 471-472.

Schröter, D., C. Polsky and A. G. Patt. 2005. Assessing vulnerabilities to the effects of global change: An eight step approach. Mitigation and Adaptation Strategies for Global Change 10: 573-596.

Schwartz, M. W. 1992. Potential effects of global climate change on the biodiversity of plants. Forestry Chronicle 68: 462-471.

Schwartz, M. W., L. R. Iverson, A. M. Prasad, S. N. Matthews and R. J. O'Connor. 2006. Predicting extinctions as a result of climate change. Ecology 87(7): 1611-1615.

Seastedt, T. R., R. J. Hobbs and K. N. Suding. 2008. Frontiers in Ecology and the Environment 6: doi:10.1890/070046.

Seddon, P. J., D. P. Armstrong, P. Soorae, F. Launay and others. 2009. The risks of assisted colonization. Conservation Biology 23: 788-789.

Sheley, R. L. and J. James. 2010. Resistance of native plant functional groups to invasion by medusahead (*Taeniatherum caput-medusae*). Invasive Plant Science and Management 3: 294-300.

Shirey, P. D. and G. A. Lamberti. 2009. Assisted colonization under the U.S. Endangered Species Act. Conservation Letters 3(1): 45-52.

Shutter, B. J. and J. R. Post. 1990. Climate, population viability and the zoogeography of temperate fishes. Transaction of the American Fisheries Society 119: 316-336.

Smith, S. D., T. E. Huzman, S. F. Zitzer, T. N. Charlet and others. 2000. Elevated CO_2 increases productivity and invasive species success in an arid system. Nature 408:79-81.

Soja, A. J., N. M. Tchebakova, N. H. F. French, M. D. Flannigan and others. 2007. Climate-induced boreal forest change: predictions versus current observations. Global and Planetary Change 56: 274-296.

St. Clair, B., G. Howe, J. Wright and D. Cooper. 2010. Center for Forest Provenance Data. Corvallis, OR: Oregon State University. Available: http://cenforgen.forestry. oregonstate.edu/index.php [2010, December 10].

Stein, B. A., P. Glick and J. Hoffman. 2011. Vulnerability assessment basics. In: Glick, P. and B. A. Stein, eds. Scanning the conservation horizon: a guide to climate change vulnerability assessment. National Wildlife Federation. Washington, DC.

Thomas, C. D. 2010. Climate, climate change and range boundaries. Diversity Distributions 16: 488-495.

Thomas, C. D., A. Cameron, R. E. Green, M. Bakkenes and others. 2004. Extinction risk from climate change. Nature 427: 145-148.

Tremblay-Boyer, L. and E. R. Anderson. In review. 2010. A preliminary assessment of ecosystem vulnerability to climate change. McGill University and the Smithsonian Tropical Research Institute, Clayto, Panama. 70 p. Available at: http://revistavirtual. redesma.org/vol5/pdf/lecturas/assessment-ofecosystemvulnaerabilitytoclimatechan ge_Panama.pdf. Related manuscript: Characterizing sensitivity to climate change at the ecosystem scale: a case-study for Panama submitted to Mitigation and Adaptation Strategies for Global Change.

U.S. Environmental Protection Agency [EPA]. 2009. A framework for categorizing the relative vulnerability of threatened and endangered species to climate change. Washington, DC: National Center for Environmental Assessment. EPA/600/R-09/011.

U.S. Department of Agriculture, Forest Service [USDA]. 2008. Vegetation ecology. In: Forest Service Manual. FSM 2000—National Forest Resource Management. Washington, DC: Chapter 2070.

U.S. Department of Agriculture, Forest Service, Western Wildland Environmental Threat Assessment Center [USDA FS WWETAC]. 2011. Seed zone mapper. Prineville, OR: U.S. Department of Agriculture, Forest Service, Western Wildland Environmental Threat Assessment Center. Available: http://www.fs.fed.us/wwetac/threat_map/SeedZones_Intro.html.

U.S. Department of Agriculture, Natural Resource Conservation Service [USDA NRCS]. 2009. Web soil survey. Available: http://websoilsurvey.nrcs.usda.usda.gov/app/HomePage.htm [2010, December 10].

U.S. Department of Agriculture, Natural Resources Conservation Service [USDA NRCS]. 2010. Ecological Site Information System. Available: http://esis.sc.egov.usda.gov/ [2010, December 10].

U.S. Department of the Interior and U.S. Department of Agriculture [USDI & USDA]. 2002. Report to the Congress. Interagency program to supply and manage native plant materials for restoration and rehabilitation on Federal lands. Washington, DC: U.S. Department of the Interior and U.S. Department of Agriculture. 17 p. Available: http://www.nps.gov/plants/npmd/Native%20Plant%20Materials%202002%20Report%20To%20Congress.pdf [2010, December 28].

Vegetation/Ecosystem Modeling and Analysis Project [VEMAP]. 1995. Vegetation/ecosystem modeling and analysis project: comparing biogeography and biogeochemistry models in a continental-scale study of terrestrial ecosystem responses to climate change and CO_2 doubling. Global Biogeochemical Cycles 9: 407-437.

Vitt, P., K. Havens and O. Hoegh-Guldberg. 2009. Assisted migration: part of an integrated conservation strategy. Trends in Ecology and Evolution 24: 473-474.

Vitt, P., K. Havens, K., A. T. Kramer, D. Sollenberger and E. Yates. 2010. Assisted migration of plants: changes in latitudes, changes in attitudes. Biological Conservation 143(1): 18-27.

Vogel, K. P., M. R. Schmer and R. B. Mitchell. 2005. Plant adaptation regions: ecological and climatic classification of plant materials. Rangeland Ecology and Management 58: 315-319.

Warren, M. S., J. K. Hill, J. A. Thomas, J. Asher and others. 2001. Rapid responses of British butterflies to opposing forces of climate and habitat change. Nature 414: 65-69.

Williams, J. W. and S. T. Jackson. 2007. Novel climates, no-analog communities, and ecological surprises. Frontiers in Ecology and the Environment 5: 475-482.

Wilson B. L., D. C. Darris, R. Fiegener, R. Johnson, M. E. Horning and K. Kuykendall. 2008. Seed transfer zones for a native grass Festuca roemeri: genecological evidence. Native Plant Journal 9: 287-303.

Withrow-Robinson, B. and R. Johnson. 2006. Selecting native plant materials for restoration projects: insuring local adaptation and maintaining genetic diversity. EM 8885-E. Corvallis, OR: Oregon State University. 10 p. Available: http://extension.oregonstate.edu/catalog/pdf/em/em8885-e.pdf [2010, December 10].

Woodward, F. I. 1987. Climate and Plant Distribution. New York: Cambridge University Press. 174 p.

Young, B., J. Newmark and K. Szabo. 2011. Case study 1. NatureServe's climate change vulnerability index for species in Nevada. In: Glick, Patty and B. A. Stein, eds. Scanning the conservation horizon: a guide to climate change vulnerability assessment. National Wildlife Federation. Washington, DC: 83-89.

Ziska, L. H., J. B. Reeves, III, and B. Blank. 2005. The impact of recent increases in atmospheric CO_2 on biomass production and vegetative retention of cheatgrass (*Bromus tectorum*): implications for fire disturbance. Global Change Biology 11: 1325-1332.

www.ingramcontent.com/pod-product-compliance
Lightning Source LLC
Chambersburg PA
CBHW081216280526
45787CB00006B/2421